PSYCHOLOGICAL
TESTING AND ASSESSMENT

PSYCHOLOGICAL
TESTING AND ASSESSMENT

DAVID SHUM
JOHN O'GORMAN
BRETT MYORS

OXFORD
UNIVERSITY PRESS
AUSTRALIA & NEW ZEALAND

253 Normanby Road, South Melbourne, Victoria 3205, Australia

Oxford University Press is a department of the University of Oxford.
It furthers the University's objective of excellence in research, scholarship,
and education by publishing worldwide in

Oxford New York

Auckland Cape Town Dar es Salaam Hong Kong Karachi
Kuala Lumpur Madrid Melbourne Mexico City Nairobi
New Delhi Shanghai Taipei Toronto

With offices in

Argentina Austria Brazil Chile Czech Republic France Greece
Guatemala Hungary Italy Japan Poland Portugal Singapore
South Korea Switzerland Thailand Turkey Ukraine Vietnam

OXFORD is a trade mark of Oxford University Press
in the UK and in certain other countries

National Library of Australia
Cataloguing-in-Publication data:

Shum, David H. K.
    Psychological testing and assessment.

    Bibliography
    Includes index.
    For tertiary students.
    ISBN 978 0 19 555094 8.

    ISBN 0 19 555094 3.

    1. Psychological tests. I. O'Gorman, John. II. Myors,
    Brett. III. Title.

150.287

Typeset by Cannon Typesetting, Melbourne
Printed in China by Golden Cup Printing Co. Ltd

Contents

Boxes, Tables and Figures

Boxes

Tables

Figures

Preface

The purpose of this book is to provide users of psychological tests, whether they be students, researchers, or practitioners, with an introduction to the theory, research, and best practice in the field of psychological testing and assessment.

It may surprise you to find another book on psychological testing and assessment. After all, this topic has been treated in many excellent texts and references (eg, Anastasi, 1988; Cronbach, 1990); nevertheless, we consider that we make a positive contribution to this literature in four broad ways. First, although many previous books exist, the field of psychological testing and assessment is a dynamic one, subject to an intense international research and development effort. New tests are coming onto the market every year, and scientists are continually building and refining psychological theories which inevitably lead them to devise new constructs to measure and new ways to measure them. For this reason alone it is important that texts are continually updated. Even where an old test continues to be used, new research often provides additional information or even a fresh perspective on where that particular instrument fits into broader psychological theories.

Second, we hope to provide a more international perspective on psychological testing and assessment. As noted above, the research and development effort in this field is an international one which demands a truly international approach. Globalisation is a fact of life in our current world but globalisation does not mean global homogeneity. Rather, successful globalisation of any product or service requires careful tailoring to the local context. Psychological testing and assessment is no exception. Indeed, as we shall see, psychological tests are often precise enough to identify differences among groups of people that may go unnoticed to the more casual observer. Thus, a text for a globalised world should be sensitive to local differences between countries and make suggestions as to how these can be factored into the psychological testing and assessment process. For example, many of the tests routinely used in our own country had their origin in North America, and although their migration across the Pacific has been largely successful, there are nevertheless unique social, legal, and cultural issues that arise in carrying out testing in Australia.

Third, we hope that this book can serve as a useful introductory and intermediate text for teaching students the theory and practice of psychological testing and assessment in colleges and universities. We have tried to write using non-technical language so that non-psychologists who may have a need to understand the principles of psychological testing and assessment, such as managers or lawyers, can readily develop their understanding by working their way through the material presented. To this end, we provide a thorough grounding in the basic psychometric theory underlying contemporary test development and highlight a number of specialist fields of psychology in which psychological testing and assessment is used extensively. We seek to encourage readers to think about issues, solve problems, and become informed users and consumers of information about psychological tests. The later chapters of the book survey the various specialisations that psychologists may find themselves working in and we have sought to provide best practice examples of psychological assessment to anyone working in one of these fields.

Fourth, besides being a useful learning tool, we hope that this book will succeed as an important reference for practitioners and others who may have already completed training in psychological testing and assessment, but who need an up-to-date guide to the latest findings in this area. We hope that our organisation of the later chapters into specialist areas will facilitate this.

We should also mention what this book is not. This book is not a text in axiomatic measurement theory. The field of psychological measurement has proven fertile ground for refining and elaborating just what is meant by the concept of measurement (Krantz, Luce, Suppes, & Tverskey, 1972; Michell, 1990) and psychological measurement theorists have contributed greatly to the philosophy of science that underpins the physical sciences as well. Although highly rigorous, an axiomatic measurement theoretical approach has not been widely adopted among psychological researchers or practitioners (Cliff, 1992). One reason for this is that where it works (and there are many examples of axiom failure which lead to non specification of the measurement scale), the results are often highly correlated with the results of classical methods. We maintain our commitment to classical test theory because we believe that it continues to provide easier access for understanding the basic concepts behind psychological testing and assessment. Further, the classical approach permits greater appreciation of what the fundamental measurement theorists were trying to achieve.

In addition, this book does not teach students or practitioners skills in the administration, scoring, and interpreting of psychological tests. In Australia, training in such skills is usually included in professional postgraduate programs such as clinical and organisational psychology. However, the knowledge and materials covered in this book form an important basis for learning skills in testing.

We thank Debra James of Oxford University Press for her interest and support of our project. We also thank Greg Alford and Tim Campbell for their editorial input and support. We acknowledge the feedback by the reviewers of our book proposal and drafts, and the feedback by our colleagues Analise O'Donovan, Cliff Leong, and Mark Kebbell on individual chapters. Finally, thanks go to Kerryn Neulinger, Rebecca Kearney, Elissa Waterson, Bronwyn Watson, and Heather Ward who ably assisted us in researching, editing, and referencing this book and to Rebecca Kearney for helping with the illustrations of the brain in Chapter 9.

part one

The Context of
Psychological Testing
and Assessment

chapter one

Psychological Tests: What Are They and Why Do We Need Them?

1

> ▶ The Chairperson of Air New Zealand was reported as insisting members of his board were to undergo psychological testing as part of the selection process. (*New Zealand Herald*, 22 January 2002)
>
> ▶ In Victoria, Australia, lobbyists proposed that: (1) new drivers be given psychological tests to weed out road rage and (2) people with road offences be given personality tests before renewing their licences. (The *Sunday Herald Sun*, 9 June 2002)
>
> ▶ Based on the results of psychological tests and other tests (eg, medical and academic), a young man was accepted into the Australian Defence Force Academy to complete a Science Degree. (The *Herald Sun*, 22 January 2002)
>
> ▶ Staff in Australian Football League (AFL) clubs used results of neuropsychological tests to determine when players who had suffered concussion should play for the team again. (The *Herald Sun*, 22 July 2003)

INTRODUCTION

The development and application of psychological tests is considered one of the major achievements of psychologists in the last century (Zimbardo, 2004). The news items above illustrate some of the ways psychological tests have been applied in our societies. For the most part, tests are used to assist in making decisions or promoting self-understanding by providing more accurate information about human behaviour than is available without them. Psychological tests are also important tools for conducting psychological research. In this book our focus will be on the former rather than the latter application.

The ability to select, administer, score, and interpret psychological tests is considered a core skill for professional psychologists (Australian Psychological Society, 2000). Thus, the teaching of this ability is usually included as one or more courses for undergraduate and postgraduate psychology programs in Australia and other countries. Who developed the first psychological test and how has psychological testing progressed through time? What are the advantages in using psychological tests to promote understanding and to assist decision-making processes about people in our society? What are psychological tests and what are their defining characteristics? What are the advantages and limitations of psychological tests? These are the topics of the first chapter of this book.

A BRIEF HISTORY OF PSYCHOLOGICAL TESTING

The history of psychological testing has been well documented by DuBois (1970). O'Neil (1987), Keats and Keats (1988), and Ord (1977) have provided accounts of relevant developments in Australia. The following section draws freely on these sources (Box 1.1 highlights some of these historical developments).

BOX 1.1

Timeline of major developments in the modern history of psychological testing
1890   The term 'mental test' is first used by James McKeen Cattell
1905   Binet and Simon devise the first test of intelligence for use with children
1916   Lewis Terman publishes the Stanford-Binet test, based on the pioneering work of Binet and Simon
1917   Robert Yerkes leads the development of the Army Alpha and Beta tests for selection for military service in the USA
1917   Robert Woodworth devises the first self-report test of personality
1921   Hermann Rorschach publishes *Psychodiagnostics* on the use of inkblots in evaluating personality
1927   The first version of the Strong Vocational Interest Blank is published
1939   David Wechsler reports an individual test of adult intelligence
1942   The Minnesota Multiphasic Personality Inventory is published to assist the differential diagnosis of psychiatric disorder
1948   Henry Murray and colleagues publish *Assessment of Men* and the term 'assessment' comes to replace mental testing as a description of work with psychological tests
1957   Cattell publishes on performance tests of motivation
1962   Computer interpretation of the MMPI introduced
1968   Walter Mischel publishes his widely cited critique of personality assessment
1970   Computers used for testing clients and computerised adaptive testing follows
1971   The Federal Court in the USA challenges testing for personnel selection
1988   Ziskin and Faust challenge the use of psychological test results in court

Note: Based on a more extensive timeline in Sundberg (1977)

The origins of psychological testing can be found in the public service examinations used by the Chinese dynasties to select those who would work for them. These were large-scale exercises, involving many applicants and several days testing, and from the era of the Han dynasty involved written examinations (Bowman, 1989). Programs of testing were run from about 2000 BC up to the early years of the twentieth century when they were discontinued, at about the time the modern era of psychological testing was introduced in the USA. A major impetus to this modern development of testing was the need to select men for military service when America entered World War I without a standing army. There were, however, a number of precursors to this development, the most significant being the work of Alfred Binet and his colleagues in France in the late nineteenth and early twentieth centuries.

Binet was asked by the Office of Public Instruction in Paris to provide a method for objectively determining which children would benefit from special education. In responding to this request, Binet devised the first of the modern intelligence tests, using problems not unlike those covered in a normal schooling program. In the process, he proposed a method for quantifying intelligence in terms of the concept of mental age, that is, the child's standing among children of different chronological ages in terms of his or her cognitive capacity. For example, a child whose knowledge and problem solving ability was similar to that of the average 10 year old was described as having a mental age of 10 years. The child's chronological age may be in advance or behind that. Binet showed how a test of intelligence might be validated by comparing the test performance of older with younger children or the performance of those considered bright by their teachers with those considered dull. Given our understanding of ability, older children should do better on a test purporting to be a test of intelligence than younger children and bright children should perform better than dull children. Determining the appropriate content, finding a unit of measurement, and specifying methods for validating tests of this sort were all significant achievements, with the result that Binet is often thought of as the originator of psychological testing. Binet himself may not have been entirely pleased with this honour, because he was more concerned with remediation of difficulties than with the classification process that has preoccupied many who adopted his procedures.

The assumption implicit in Binet's work, that performance on a range of apparently different problems can be aggregated to yield an overall estimate of, in his terms, mental age, was examined by Charles Spearman in the UK in a series of investigations that yielded the first theory of intelligence. This theory proposed that there was something common to all tests of cognitive abilities, *g* in Spearman's terms. This proposal was to be sharply criticised by a number of American researchers, chief among them Thurstone.

The theoretical arguments did not deter a number of researchers from adapting Binet's test to the cultural milieu in which they worked. Henry Goddard in the USA, Cyril Burt in the UK, and Gilbert Phillips in Australia all developed versions of Binet's test, but it was Lewis Terman at Stanford University who published the most ambitious version for use with English speakers. His test was appropriate for children aged from 3 years to 16 years. It was Terman's version, which he termed the

Stanford-Binet, that was to dominate as a test of intelligence for individuals, until David Wechsler published a test for the individual assessment of adult intelligence in 1948.

Binet's test and the adaptations of it depended heavily on tapping skills that were taught in school, which importantly included verbal skills. A number of researchers saw the need for practical or performance tests of ability that did not depend on verbal skills or exposure to mainstream formal schooling. One of the earliest of these researchers was Stanley Porteus, who in 1915 reported the use of mazes for assessing comprehension and foresight. Porteus was born and educated in Australia but spent most of his working life in the USA, first at the Vineland Institute in New Jersey and then at the University of Hawaii. He returned to Australia from time to time to study the abilities of Aboriginal Australians. His test required the test taker to trace with a pencil increasingly complex mazes while avoiding dead ends and not lifting the pencil from the paper. The test is still used by neuropsychologists in assessing executive functions. Porteus's work was the forerunner of the development in Australia of a number of tests of ability that are not dependent on access to English for their administration, the most notable of which was the Queensland Test of D W McElwain and G E Kearney. In New Zealand, tests of cognitive ability of Maori children were undertaken by St George (see Ord, 1977).

Binet's test and its adaptations and the early performance tests were individual tests of ability in that they required administration to one person at a time. An individual test of intelligence was of little use when thousands of individuals had to be tested in a short space of time, the situation in World War I. A S Otis in the USA and Cyril Burt in England trialled a variety of group tests of intelligence, but the most convincing demonstration of their usefulness was to come with Yoakum and Yerkes and their colleagues, who developed two group tests of general mental ability for use with recruits to the American armed services during World War I. The Army Alpha test was developed for assessing the ability levels of those who could read and write, and the Army Beta test for those who were not literate. Although there is some dispute about how valuable the Army Alpha and Beta tests were to the war effort, they gave considerable impetus to psychological testing in the post-War period and their basic structure was relied on subsequently by Wechsler in developing Verbal and Performance subscales for his test of adult intelligence.

Wechsler developed his test for use in an adult inpatient psychiatric setting as an aid in differential diagnosis. A patient in this setting might present with symptoms of schizophrenia, alcoholism, or be of low general intelligence. Wechsler sought a test that would provide not just an overall assessment of intellectual level, but would assist in identifying which possible diagnosis was the more likely. The success of the test for this purpose has been criticised, but it is clear that, as an individual test of general ability for adults, Wechsler's test was superior to the Stanford-Binet. Not only was the content more age appropriate but the method of scoring performance replaced the idea of mental age with that of the Deviation IQ, based on earlier work by Godfrey and his team in Edinburgh (Vernon, 1979). The Deviation IQ related the performance of the individual to that of his or her age peers, by dividing the difference between the individual's score and the mean for the peer group by the standard deviation of scores for the peer group. The idea was used in a subsequent revision of the Stanford–Binet (the LM revision) and continues to this day in both the Wechsler and the Binet tests.

During World War I, Woodworth developed the first self-report personality test. It was a screening test for psychological adjustment to the military situation and comprised short questions identified from textbooks of psychiatry and other expert sources. It was used as a screening test, in that endorsement of a certain number of items in a direction suggestive of psychopathology led to further evaluation by a military psychiatrist. It was the forerunner of a number of self-report tests, the most notable being the Minnesota Multiphasic Personality Inventory (MMPI) developed by Hathaway and McKinley at Minnesota in 1942. The test was designed to discriminate between those without symptoms of mental illness ('normals') and patient groups with particular diagnoses. Items were sought that would yield two clear patterns of response, one characteristic of normals and the other characteristic of a particular patient group (eg, patients diagnosed with schizophrenia). The same strategy ('empirical keying' as it came to be called) had been used by Strong in his development of a test of vocational interest in 1928, which provided a basis for occupational and vocational guidance. The MMPI was long (566 items), heterogeneous in content, and sophisticated to the extent that it included four scales for the purpose of identifying various forms of responding by the test taker that could invalidate inferences drawn from the content scales.

These various tests of cognitive and personality functioning provided a modest but important adjunct to clinical judgment, the principal method of evaluation practised until that time. Just as physical medicine relied on various tests of physiological functioning (eg, the X-ray) to aid the process of judgment, so too the mental test became a supplement to the unaided diagnostic ability of the doctor or psychiatrist.

The various tests mentioned to this point are sometimes described as objective, in that the method of scoring is sufficiently straightforward for two or more scorers of the same test performance to agree closely on the final score. There is another category of tests (or techniques as advocates prefer to call them) that involve a good deal of judgment in their scoring. These 'projective techniques' had their genesis in psychodynamic theorising. Freud's fundamental assumption of psychic determinism, that all mental events have a cause, was taken to mean that no behaviour is accidental, that it betrays the operation of unconscious motivational effects. With such a premise, Hermann Rorschach, a Swiss psychiatrist and follower of Jung's theory, developed a test that purported to identify the psychological types that Jung postulated. The test involved a series of blots created by pouring ink on a page and folding the page in half. Such a random process gave rise to meaningless designs that the patient was asked to make sense of. In so doing, as Henry Murray was later to formulate in the projective hypothesis, the test taker draws on their own psychic resources and thus demonstrates something of the workings of their mind. Expertise was essential for interpretation and required careful study of the interpretative strategies of psychodynamic theory.

With the acceptance of the projective techniques, the task of testing was raised from a technical routine activity to one requiring the exercise of considerable judgment. A new title was required for this, and Henry Murray provided it. Working at the Psychological Clinic at Harvard University in the 1930s, he and his colleagues set about an intensive study of forty-nine undergraduate students. The project ran for several years and gave rise to Murray's theory of personality and to a number of techniques and procedures for studying personality. One was a projective test called the Thematic Apperception Test (TAT), which he developed with Christiana Morgan, and which became the second-most widely used projective technique after the Rorschach. The other was the diagnostic council, a case conference at which all staff involved with a particular participant in the project would provide information and interpretation. From discussion, a consensus view would emerge about the personality structure and dynamics of the individual. When the USA entered World War II, Murray with a number of other psychologists joined the war effort. In Murray's case it was in the Office of Strategic Services, the forerunner of the CIA, charged with the task of selecting and preparing volunteers for espionage activities. Murray used many of the techniques from his Harvard days and added situational tests to them and relied on a form of the diagnostic council. This work was one of the forerunners of the Assessment Centre to be used successfully by AT&T after the war for the selection and promotion of senior executives and is used widely today in organisational psychology. Murray reported this wartime work in a book titled *Assessment of Men*. 'Assessment' was the term required for the high-level reasoning process involved in the application of psychological procedures to the individual case and henceforth almost completely replaced the term 'mental testing'.

The late 1940s and 1950s were the heyday of psychological testing and assessment, particularly in the USA. One estimate by Goslin in 1963 was that by that date more than 200 million tests of intelligence alone were being administered annually in the USA (Vernon, 1979). A public reaction to this was brewing, however, and hard questions were being asked about the evidence base of the projective techniques, with the theorising of Freud and other psychodynamic theorists being questioned. In the public arena, there were several challenges to psychological testing. One was that it involved a serious invasion of privacy, as for example with the questions asked on self-report tests of personality. A second was a concern about the homogenising effects on the workforce of using psychological tests for selection, with only a limited set of personality characteristics and abilities being acceptable to the organisation. Most damaging to the testing enterprise was the charge that psychological tests are discriminatory. Because black and Hispanic Americans were found to score, on average, lower on ability tests than white Americans and because test score was used for selection in a number of workplace and academic settings, psychological tests of this sort were considered to be denying access to many members of minority groups. The criticisms began in magazine articles and popular books but were given forceful expression in the State and federal courts and legislatures. The criticism and legal intervention were more muted outside the USA but the critique was by no means limited to that country.

One of the benefits of this critique of psychological testing and assessment was the recognition that psychological testing may be a value-neutral technology in itself but its application is always in a social context in which outcomes are valued differently by different observers. The most dramatic demonstration of this was the use of testing to impose immigration policies that most of us today would recognise as manifestly unfair and unjust (see Box 1.2 for an example in the Australian context). The moral of the story is clear: test users need to appreciate the social context in which tests are used.

BOX 1.2

Testing in the service of ideology

Immigration to the USA was restricted in the first part of the twentieth century by procedures aimed at preventing the entry of 'feebleminded' individuals from European countries who, it was thought, might adversely affect the gene pool or become a burden on the State (Richardson, 2003). Psychological testing formed a part of this process, which was supported by a social consensus on the dangers of unrestricted migration. In Australia, a similar social ideology prevailed but psychological tests as such were not used in its service. Instead a dictation test was used to prevent entry by anyone judged to be undesirable, a judgment aided considerably by knowledge of the person's racial background (Commonwealth of Australia, 2000). The *Immigration Restriction Act* 1901, known popularly as the White Australia policy, sought to maintain racial purity by preventing non-European migration and was part of Australia's culture for the first 50 years or more of the twentieth century.

The dictation test of some 50 words could be administered in any 'prescribed language' but in practice was in a European language and commonly in English. The text was read to the migrant in the prescribed language and the migrant had to write the text in the same language. An example of the content is: 'Very many considerations lead to the conclusion that life began on sea, first as single cells, then as groups of cells held together by a secretion of mucilage, then as filaments and tissues' (Australian Broadcasting Commission, 2003). The test could be applied many times and the likelihood of success when it was administered was low. In 1903, for example, 153 people were tested and only 3 passed. Although its use was directed principally to non-Europeans, it could be used with felons, prostitutes, and those with 'a loathsome or dangerous character'. A German migrant, who had served a prison sentence, was reported to have been given the dictation test in Greek although he could speak German, English, and French.

Applied psychology had not begun in Australia when the dictation test was introduced and many members of the profession would hope that if it had been established, the profession would have been a vociferous critic of such unfair testing procedures.

By the 1950s the major forms of psychological test had been developed for measurement of behavioural differences and researchers such as Eysenck and Cattell had begun work on developing performance measures of the personality and motivation domains similar to those developed in the cognitive domain. There were new tests published after that date but they were refinements of the basic methods developed in the first half of the twentieth century. From the 1960s on, however, there were important developments in the use of computer technology to assist in psychological testing and assessment. The earliest use was to reduce the labour and the likelihood of error in manually scoring tests. The computer was at first an aid to other technology for machine reading answer-forms but with the desktop computer it soon became a method of administering and scoring the test in its own right, and storing large amounts of data on test performance. It was a short step from here to computer interpretation of test results, with programs being written to provide a textual description of characteristics of individuals with scores within various score ranges on the scale or scales making up the test. Not all psychologists (eg, Matarazzo, 1986) considered this was a positive development because of the danger of invalid interpretation in the hands of the novice.

The real power of the computer for psychological testing awaited developments in the theory of tests, and in particular the formulation of item-response theory (see Hulin, Drasgow & Parsons, 1983). Test developers had recognised from the earliest stages that single items were poor candidates for capturing psychologically interesting constructs, because variation among individuals in responding to them could be determined by a host of factors aside from the one of interest. By aggregating over items, however, the noise associated with individual items could be submerged in the signal that each of them provided. Test theory developed to show why this was so and the implications of it. One implication was that a large number of items was usually required to determine any particular psychological characteristic. This implication was challenged by item-response theory that showed how, by specifying in advance a particular statistical model for the test, more precise estimates could be obtained, and when this was linked with the calculating speed of the computer much shorter tests could result. Computerised adaptive testing (Weiss, 1983), as it came to be called, provided not only a considerable saving in time and effort for the test administrator but, importantly, for the client as well.

As a practical example of the value of this development, consider the case of a young person who decides to join the armed services in the 1950s. After completing the necessary paperwork they would need to wait until a group testing session for recruit selection was held, often a matter of months, and then set aside 2 to 3 hours to complete the tests and then wait to determine if they had been successful. By the 1980s, with the advent of computerised adaptive testing, the potential recruit could attend the recruiting centre, complete the necessary paperwork, take the computer-based test on the spot or at a time of their choosing, and within half an hour or less, have the answer on whether or not they were suitable. Rather than have to answer questions numbering in the hundreds, a dozen to twenty questions were now sufficient to give as reliable an estimate of their abilities.

A further extension of the role of computing in psychological testing was ushered in by the arrival of the Internet, as it became possible to administer tests to individuals at sites remote from the psychologist or test administrator. Although now a relatively simple procedure to implement, the technology raises salient issues for the security of test content and test results, and opens testing procedures to fraud in a way that had not existed previously with individual or group tests. No doubt these problems will be overcome in time, and information technology in all its forms, including its capacity to simulate environments, will push the technology of psychological testing in interesting and useful directions.

The controversies and legal battles of the 1960s and 1970s over psychological testing taught the testing community how to accommodate many of the constraints placed on them, not always for the most sensible of reasons. The 1980s and 1990s brought fresh challenges for which these earlier accommodations were of no particular value. One challenge was the drive for cost containment in both the private and public sectors, exemplified, for example, in managed care in the USA, but seen in most Western countries. In the health sector, the drive for cost containment led to a questioning of the time taken to administer and interpret psychological tests and their value for the cost involved. Psychologists had to begin to justify their procedures not in terms of their judgments or the judgments of other professionals as to their value but in terms of their dollar value. Although there were attempts to do this in the organisational context by showing the dollar savings entailed in good selection practices using psychological tests (eg, Schmidt, Hunter, McKenzie & Muldrow, 1979), the task was far more difficult in the health care context, and the response here was to stop using tests that took considerable time or to substitute short forms of the tests of lesser validity.

The second challenge came with the increasing use of psychological assessments in determining personal injury and compensation cases in the courts. Psychological assessments and those who prepared them became caught up in the adversarial system that characterises courts that derive from the English legal tradition. Within this system, expert witnesses can expect to have to justify their conclusions quite precisely and to have their opinions attacked by the other side. With outcomes involving large amounts of money, there is considerable incentive to find fault with testimony based on psychological assessment. Ziskin and Faust (1988) reviewed many of the procedures being used by psychologists and challenged the evidence that supported them. The response in this case was for psychologists to undertake more research to justify the procedures they used or to discontinue a procedure where evidence was lacking for its value at the now quite high level of expert testimony required.

The twentieth century saw a remarkable flowering of psychological tests. A period of sustained enthusiasm in the first half of the century was tempered by waves of public criticism of testing in the second half, but the enterprise was left on a very firm foundation.

PSYCHOLOGICAL TESTS: WHY DO WE NEED THEM?

In the last section, we briefly reviewed the history of psychological testing. However, we have not directly explained why psychologists think that psychological tests are better than other methods in assisting individuals in our societies to make decisions or in promoting better understanding of human behaviour. The need to make decisions about people is not a new challenge for the human race. Every day somewhere people in our societies are faced with the task of making decisions that are important and have long-term implications for individuals. Similarly, human beings have always been fascinated by their own and others' behaviours. Traditionally, we have relied on a number of methods (eg, tradition, supernatural forces, laws, logic) to assist us in these processes. For example, in ancient China, astrology and numerology were used to evaluate the compatibility between potential brides and grooms.

For the profession of psychology, personal judgment and clinical intuition have been used for a long time to assist psychologists to arrive at a decision or to understand behaviour. For example, psychologists who work in business organisations have made decisions about hiring individuals based on interviewing them. Similarly, clinicians have used interviews to decide if someone is suffering from mental illness or brain injury. It has been shown repeatedly, however, that human judgment is subjective and fallible (Dahlstrom, 1993; Zimbardo, 2004). Some of the factors that can influence the outcomes of human judgment include stereotyping, personal bias, positive and negative halo effect, and errors of central tendency. Given that most decisions relating to professional psychology have significant implications for the person involved or the person who made the decision, an error in making the decision can be costly, devastating, and may not be reversible. For example, an erroneous judgment about the mental competency of a person can lead to the rights of the person being wrongfully removed. As another example, a lot of time and money could be wasted if the wrong person was hired for a job. Psychologists consider psychological tests better than personal judgment in informing decision making in many situations because of the nature and defining characteristics of these tests (Dahlstrom, 1993).

PSYCHOLOGICAL TESTS: DEFINITIONS, ADVANTAGES, AND LIMITATIONS

What is a psychological test? This seems to be a difficult question to answer when one examines the plethora of published tests in the market and finds that they can differ in so many respects. While some psychological tests take only a few minutes to complete, others can take up to hours to administer. For some psychological tests, a respondent is required to provide only a simple yes/no answer; other tests expect a person to solve a multi-step auditory or visual problem. Some psychological tests can be administered to a large group of people at one time and scored and interpreted by a computer, but other tests require face-to-face administration and individual scoring and interpretation that require years of training and experience.

Despite the above wide-ranging differences, all psychological tests are considered to have one thing in common: that is, they are tools that psychologists use to collect data about people (Maloney & Ward, 1976). More specifically, a psychological test is an objective procedure for sampling and quantifying human behaviour to make inference about a particular psychological construct using standardised stimuli and methods of administration and scoring. In addition, to demonstrate its usefulness, a psychological test requires appropriate norms and evidence (viz, psychometric properties). To elaborate, the defining characteristics of psychological tests and their associated advantages are discussed below.

First, a psychological test is a sample of behaviour that is used to make inferences about the individual in a significant social context. The behaviour sample may be considered complete in itself or, as is more often the case, as a sign of an underlying disposition that mediates behaviour. Take, for example, a psychological test that is used to decide whether an individual will be able to understand instructional material to be used in job training. The test for this purpose may consist of sample passages from the daily newspaper. The test taker's task is to read each of them and report their meanings. If comprehension of most of the passages is accurate, the test taker can be judged to read well enough for the purposes of the job. As long as the difficulty level of the passages approximates that of the instructional material, the test provides a basis for inferring adequate performance in training.

In a clinical setting, a test may provide a sample of the behaviour that the client finds disturbing. For example, a client may suffer an irrational fear of an object that is not actually dangerous, such as harmless spiders. As a result of the fear, the client cannot enter a darkened room or clean out cupboards because of the likelihood of confronting a spider. To assess the magnitude of the irrational fear, the tester may ask the client to approach a harmless spider being held in a glass case. The distance from the spider that induces a report of anxiety is taken as an indication of the severity of the client's avoidance behaviour. This can be used to judge the effectiveness of any planned intervention to reduce the problem. After treatment the client should be able to approach the spider more closely than before.

In both of these cases, the sample of behaviour is complete in itself, in that it assesses directly what the tester wants to know, comprehending common passages of English text or avoiding an object of a phobia. The samples could be used, however, as the basis for indirect inferences, by arguing that each in its own way reflects an underlying disposition that is responsible for the individual's behaviour. Thus, the comprehension test might be used to infer the individual's level of general mental ability or intelligence and the avoidance test may be used to infer the individual's level of neuroticism, that is, the likelihood that they will suffer an anxiety disorder. In these cases, the content of the particular sample is incidental and can be replaced by a different sample that is thought also to reflect the disposition. Thus, a sample of mathematical problem solving could be substituted for the test of verbal comprehension as a sign of general mental ability, or a set of questions about episodes of anxiety and depression may be substituted for the avoidance test as a sign of the individual's level of neuroticism. Such substitution would make no sense if the test were being used as a sample rather than a sign.

The distinction between tests as samples of behaviour or as signs of an underlying disposition rests on theoretical differences about the causes of human behaviour. Important as these theoretical differences are, they are outside the scope of the present book. We draw attention to the distinction here for two reasons. First, it is important for the tester to be aware whether any particular test is being used principally as a sample of behaviour or as a sign of an underlying disposition. We say 'principally', because the distinction when probed is not hard and fast.

The other reason for making the distinction is that tests used in these two ways are interpreted differently. Where the test is a sample, interpretation of test performance is usually in terms of what has been called 'criterion referencing'; where the test is used as a sign, what is termed a 'norm referencing' strategy is usually adopted. In the case of the former, what is effective behaviour in the situation in question can be specified reasonably objectively and the individual's performance is judged against this standard or criterion. Thus, a person might be expected to understand most, if not all, of what they read in a newspaper if they are to deal with instructional manuals on the job. A person free of a spider phobia can be expected to come close to a harmless spider, but perhaps not touch it. In the case of norm referencing, on the other hand, the performance of the individual is related to the performance of a group of individuals similar to the test taker in important respects (eg, age, cultural background). How well or badly a person has performed is thus assessed against what the average person can do, or what the norm is. Many psychological tests are thought of as signs of underlying dispositions and as such are norm referenced. The distinction is encountered again in Chapter 2.

The second characteristic of a psychological test, similar to other scientific measurement instruments, is that it is an objective procedure. It uses the same standardised materials, administration instructions, and scoring procedures for all test takers. This ensures that there is no bias, unintended or otherwise, in collecting the information and that meaningful comparisons can be made between individuals who are administered the same psychological test. Unless two people are treated in the same way (eg, same instructions, same order of questions), it is not possible to attribute any differences in their performance to differences between them. The difference in performance could just as well be due to the difference in the ways they were tested. To ensure uniformity of test stimuli and procedures, the manual that accompanies a psychological test usually includes detailed and clear instructions to administer the test so that the same or similar score will be obtained even though the test is administered by different testers. The objective nature of psychological tests is one of the main advantages they have over other methods for assisting us to understand human behaviour and make decisions about it, not the least because it minimises error of judgment relating to personal bias or subjectivity (Dahlstrom, 1993).

Third, unlike subjective human judgment, the result of a psychological test is summarised quantitatively in terms of a score or scores. Again this characteristic is similar to that of other scientific measurement instruments that use numbers to represent the extent of variables such as weight, temperature, and velocity. The quantification of psychological test results allows human behaviour to be described more precisely and to be communicated more clearly.

Fourth, a psychological test provides an objective reference point for evaluating the behaviour it measures. In the case of a criterion-referenced test, a standard of performance is determined in advance by some empirical method and the test taker's performance is compared with this standard in determining whether they pass or fail. It may be, for example, the judgment of experts that determines the standard, but it is open to all to see what the standard is that is being set. It is not the personal viewpoint of the person collecting the information. In the same way, in a norm-referenced test, the performance of a representative group of people on the test is used in preparing the test norms and these are used in scoring the test. The individual's performance is thus referred to that of the norming group, a reference point that is not an individual's judgment.

Fifth, and possibly the most important defining characteristics of a psychological test is that it must meet a number of criteria to be a useful information-gathering device. The criteria relate to its quality as a measuring device; for example, how accurate and reproducible are the scores obtained with it. These psychometric properties are evaluated in the course of its construction and again subsequently and are reported on to test users. This is in fact a process of quality control to ensure that the test is operating in the way the authors claim it does. By showing that the psychometric properties of a psychological test have reached a required standard, we can have confidence in using the results obtained by this test.

Although it is important to know that psychological tests have a number of advantages, it is also necessary to be aware of the limitations of tests. Not knowing these limitations can lead to an over-reliance on or misunderstanding of psychological test results obtained.

The first of these limitations, as mentioned earlier, is that psychological tests are only tools. As such, they do not and cannot make decisions for test users. Decision making is the responsibility of the person who commissioned use of the test and to whom the test results are made available. The person may be the psychologist who administered the test, but the two roles should not be confused. The test provides a way of gathering information and if well chosen will provide accurate and pertinent information, but the use of the information, including a bad decision, is the decision maker's. Not being aware of this limitation can lead the test user and the person involved to be dependent on the test results and accept them passively. Instead, psychological test results should be used as a source of data to assist the test user or the individual to arrive at or make an informed decision.

Second, psychological tests are often used in an attempt to capture the effects of hypothetical constructs. As in other scientific disciplines, psychology employs constructs that are not directly expressed in behaviour. Rather their effects can only be inferred. As such, we need to be aware that sometimes a gap exists between what the psychologist intends to measure using a psychological test and what a test actually measures. For example, although IQ tests were developed to measure intelligence, one needs to be aware that how good these tests are in telling us about a person's intelligence depends very much on our understanding of the construct of intelligence and the type(s) of behaviours included in any particular test. Not being aware of this issue can lead to the development of unwarranted faith in psychological tests and total acceptance of the test results without being aware of their limitations.

Third, because of continual development or refinement of psychological theories, development of technology, and passage of time, psychological tests can become obsolete. They may no longer be suitable for use because the theory that their construction was based on has been shown to be wrong or because the content of the item is no longer appropriate because of social change. In the early part of the twentieth century, for example, church attendance in Western countries was very much higher than it is now and a reasonable level of Bible knowledge could be assumed. A test item might draw on this fact. Although useful then, it might now be far too esoteric to be of any use. According to the Australian Psychological Society and the American Psychological Association, tests should be revised or updated and data for the new population should be collected.

Finally, although it may not be the intention of a test developer, sometimes a psychological test can disadvantage a subgroup of test takers because of their cultural experience or language background. A vocabulary test that usefully discriminates levels of verbal ability among children from white, English-speaking, middle class homes may be of no use for this purpose with those with a different subcultural experience or for whom their first language was not English. Tests are not universally applicable and to treat them as such may do an injustice to some.

CONCLUDING REMARKS

In the first chapter of this book, we have provided a brief introduction to the history of psychological testing. In addition, we have defined what a psychological test is and discussed its characteristics, advantages, and limitations. In doing so, we trust you will start to appreciate why psychological tests were developed and how they can be used to assist individuals in our societies to promote better understanding of human behaviour and to make decisions.

Questions for consideration

1   From the section on the history of psychological testing, select three developments in psychological testing and discuss why you think they have made a significant impact on our lives.
2   Select an Australian psychologist mentioned in the 'A Brief History of Testing' section and (a) write a short biography of this person and (b) discuss his contribution to the field of psychological testing/psychological assessment.
3   What are some of the ways that psychological tests have been used to assist individuals in promoting understanding and making decisions?
4   What are the five defining characteristics of a psychological test?
5   The advantages of a psychological test outweigh its limitations. Discuss.
6   Some questionnaires (eg, Am I a moody individual?; How is your marital relationship?) in popular magazines look like but are not psychological tests. Why are they not?

Further reading

Dahlstrom, W G (1993). Tests: Small samples, large consequences. *American Psychologist, 48,* 393–9.

Keats, D M, & Keats, J A (1988). Human assessment in Australia. In S H Irvine, & J W Berry (Eds), *Human abilities in cultural context.* Cambridge, UK: Cambridge University Press.

Weiner, I B (2003). Assessment psychology. In D K Freedheim (Ed), *Handbook of Psychology: Vol. 1 History of Psychology* (pp 279–302). Hoboken, NJ: John Wiley & Sons.

chapter two

Psychological Testing and Assessment: Processes, Best Practice, and Ethics

- A member of the general public telephoned a psychologist because she wanted to take a psychological test to find out her IQ. After discussing her request, the psychologist suggested that she needed psychological assessment as well as psychological testing.

- A student who graduated with an undergraduate degree majoring in psychology wanted to purchase a personality test from a publisher. Her request was refused because she did not meet the user qualification requirement for that particular test.

- A State Licensing (Registration) Board for Psychologists received a complaint from a client of a psychologist who claimed that the psychologist had not provided him with a written copy of a psychological testing report.

- The psychological test librarian of a university department received a request from a member of the general public who wanted to borrow some psychological tests. The reason for the request was to prepare for a job interview.

- A psychologist received a request from the personnel officer of a company. The officer wanted to obtain a copy of a psychological test report for a former client of the psychologist to assist with decision making.

INTRODUCTION

Administering psychological tests and conducting psychological assessments are core skills of psychologists. Interestingly, these are one of the most common areas of complaint against psychologists lodged with psychologists registration boards in

Australia and overseas. To improve the standard of practice in psychological testing and assessment, there is a need for better education about the nature of psychological tests and the processes of psychological assessment. In addition, psychologists need to be aware of the ethical principles and professional guidelines relating to best practice in this area.

Is psychological testing the same as psychological assessment? What are some of the main areas in professional psychology where psychological testing and assessment have been applied? What are some of the ethical issues to which psychologists have to pay attention when conducting psychological testing and assessment? What are the processes and best practices in psychological testing? These questions are some that we aim to answer in this chapter.

PSYCHOLOGICAL TESTING VERSUS PSYCHOLOGICAL ASSESSMENT

A distinction is sometimes made between psychological testing and psychological assessment (Groth-Marnat, 2003; Maloney & Ward, 1976; Matarazzo, 1990). When we talk of psychological testing we are referring to the process of administering a psychological test and obtaining and interpreting the test scores. On the other hand, when we talk of psychological assessment we are referring to a process that is broader in scope. Whereas psychological testing is commonly undertaken to answer relatively straightforward questions such as 'What is the IQ of a child?', psychological assessment is usually required to deal with more complex problems such as 'Why is a child experiencing study problems at school?'

Maloney and Ward (1976) defined psychological assessment as 'a process of solving problems (answering questions) in which psychological tests are often used as *one* of the methods of collecting relevant data' (p 5). Thus, to answer the referral problem/question 'Why is a child experiencing study problems at school?', a psychologist will usually administer an intelligence test such as the Stanford–Binet Intelligence Scale – fifth edition (Roid, 2003) or the Wechsler Scale of Intelligence for Children – fourth edition (WISC–IV; Wechsler, 2003). However, the psychologist will also use other data-collection techniques (eg, interviewing the child's parents and teachers, observing the child in class) to obtain other relevant information such as medical, family, developmental, and educational history to help answer the question. The importance of this distinction is that it emphasises that psychological testing forms only a part of psychological assessment and that best practice assessment must take into account other sources of information (see Figure 2.1). In a properly conducted assessment, conclusions drawn by the psychologist are based on data obtained from all these sources. In the hands of a good psychologist, scores on psychological tests are not seen as some immutable quantity possessed by the person tested, but as data bearing on hypotheses that need to be tested before being (provisionally) accepted. Of course, in many cases these various sources of information all point in the same direction, for example, that the person in question has some type of mental impairment, or that they are eminently suited for a particular job.

FIGURE 2.1 Relationship between psychological assessment and psychological testing

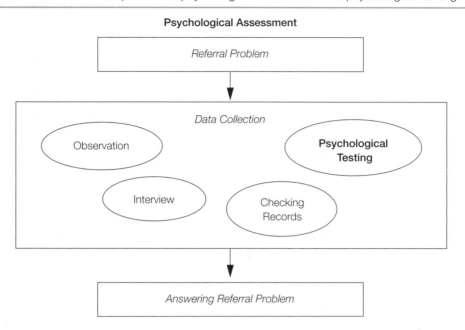

AREAS OF APPLICATION

The discipline of psychology comprises both research and applied areas (Gazzaniga & Heatherton, 2003). Although psychological tests are used by research psychologists in their studies, most individuals in the general community encounter these tests through the practice of professional psychologists. In Australia and in other parts of the world, psychological testing and assessment are most commonly applied in the following branches of psychology: Clinical, Counselling, Industrial and Organisational, Forensic, Clinical Neuropsychology, Developmental and Educational. (Readers who are interested in a more in-depth description of these different branches of applied psychology can visit the following web site of the Australian Psychological Society: www.psychology.org.au/psych/special_areas/default.asp)

Clinical psychologists specialise in the assessment, diagnosis, treatment, and prevention of psychological and mental health problems. Counselling psychologists typically assist otherwise normal people who are experiencing problems in their everyday lives. Industrial and organisational psychologists are specialists in the areas of work, human resource management, and organisational training and development. The provision of assessment, intervention, and counselling services to children and adults with learning and developmental needs are the domains of educational and developmental psychologists. Forensic psychologists are concerned with the legal and criminal justice areas and provide services for perpetrators or victims of crime and personnel of the courts and correctional systems. Clinical neuropsychologists are concerned with the effects of brain injury on human behaviour and provide diagnosis, assessment, counselling, and intervention for these individuals. In the second part of this book, a chapter is devoted to each of these areas of professional psychology, with a discussion of the psychological tests and assessment procedures commonly used in each.

TYPES OF PSYCHOLOGICAL TESTS

As mentioned in the last chapter, although all psychological tests share some common characteristics, published tests on the market differ in a number of ways. First, they differ in terms of the type of responses required from the test taker. The most common distinction is between self-report and performance. For example, the MMPI (Hathaway & McKinley, 1951) simply requires a test taker to indicate, by marking a box, whether or not each written statement in the inventory is an appropriate description of their behaviour or experience. The Wechsler Adult Intelligence Scale (WAIS, Wechsler, 1955), on the other hand, requires the test taker to answer questions or solve problems, in some cases by manipulating test materials provided. Self-report tests have practical advantages in that they usually take less time to complete and can be given to numbers of people at the one time. Performance tests are usually limited to individual administration but indicate what the person can actually do as distinct from what they say they do. In practice, the two formats are used in assessing different psychological constructs. Self-report tests are most common when the interest is in typical behaviour, what the person frequently does, as in the case of personality and attitude. Performance tests, on the other hand, are used in assessing the limits of what a person can do, such as in assessing their aptitudes or abilities.

Second, psychological tests differ in terms of the number of individuals who can be administered the tests. The distinction is between individual versus group administration. For example, the WAIS is a test of intelligence that can only be administered to one person face-to-face, whereas the advanced intelligence tests developed by the Australian Council for Educational Research (viz, the AL–AQ; ACER, 1982) were designed to be administered to groups of individuals. There are, however, some tests (eg, the Beck Depression Inventory; Beck & Steer, 1987b) that can be administered to one or to a group of people. Although the group-administered tests are usually more economical to administer and score, the individually administered tests allow psychologists to observe the performance of the person tested and to clarify her answers if needed.

Third, with the development of the personal computer, tests can differ in terms of whether or not a computer is used in administration, scoring, and interpretation. The distinction is between human- versus computer-assisted psychological testing. The National Adult Reading Test (NART; Nelson & Willison, 1991), for example, was designed to be administered, scored, and interpreted by a person experienced in the use of the test. Other tests have been designed or redesigned to take advantage of computer assistance with one or more of these processes. For example, computer programs have been developed to score and interpret the performance of a person on the Wechsler Memory Scale – third edition (WMS – III; Wechsler, 1997b). The development, practice, and advantages/limitations of computer-assisted psychological testing are discussed in detail in Chapter 12.

Finally, psychological tests can differ in terms of the frame of reference for comparing the performance of an individual on the test. This distinction is commonly called norm versus criterion (or domain) referenced testing. As mentioned in Chapter 1, while the former compares an individual's performance on a test with the average performance of a group of individuals called the norming or standardisation sample, the latter compares the individual's performance with a set of a priori criteria of adequate or good performance. For example, the score of a person on the Symbol Digit Modality Test (Smith, 1982), a test of attention, is interpreted by comparing it with the average score of a group of individuals (previously tested) who are similar in age and educational level. The group provides an appropriate norm for describing whether the person's score is above or below average. In contrast, the performance of the same individual on the Bader Reading and Language Inventory (Bader, 1998) is interpreted based on a set of objectively specified criteria (eg, graded word list, graded reading passages). Most of the psychological tests developed and available commercially are norm-referenced tests. Criterion-referenced tests are more likely to be found in education in assessing learning outcomes.

PROCESSES AND BEST PRACTICES IN PSYCHOLOGICAL TESTING

Determining whether psychological testing is needed for a client

Although psychologists who conduct psychological assessment usually use psychological tests as one of the assessment techniques, this is not necessary or possible for every client. For example, a client who is referred to a psychologist might have already been tested by other professionals or by another psychologist recently. Consequently, it is not necessary to repeat the testing process. As another example, some clients may refuse to undertake a psychological test because they are concerned about the potential negative impact of the test results. In addition, it should be reiterated that psychological tests are only one of the techniques of psychological assessment and the use of these tests may not be necessary for every client who needs assessment. According to Kendall, Jenkinson, de Lemos, and Clancy (1997), the skill to determine whether a client needs psychological testing is one of the characteristics of a proficient user of psychological tests. To develop this competence, a psychologist needs to be familiar with the major psychological constructs commonly assessed (eg, psychopathology, intelligence, personality, memory, stress) and be aware of the advantages and limitations of using psychological tests.

Selection of appropriate and technically sound psychological tests

After deciding that psychological testing is necessary for a client and settling on the particular construct or constructs to be assessed, a psychologist needs to select the most appropriate and psychometrically sound tests from the large number of instruments available in the literature and from test suppliers (Groth-Marnat, 2003). Psychometrics, as the name implies, is concerned with psychological measurement and the theory that underpins it. Part 2 of this book (Chapters 3 to 6) is meant to introduce students to the principles of psychometrics commonly employed in testing and assessment. Selecting psychometrically sound tests is a very important step because the quality and soundness of the results and findings of a psychological assessment depend very much on this selection. Careful consideration during this step also enables the psychologist to explain, justify, and defend their choice of tests subsequently. The skills to select appropriate instruments are also considered by Kendall et al (1997) as essential in being a competent user of psychological tests.

There are a number of resources available to a psychologist to assist with test selection. First, to find out what tests have been published, psychologists can peruse the catalogue of major publishers of psychological tests and references such as *Tests in Print* (Murphy, Plake, Impara, and Spies, 2002), and *Tests* (Maddox, 1997). Table 2.1 shows a list of major publishers of psychological tests in Australia and overseas and their corresponding addresses and web sites. These catalogues provide psychologists with information about what tests are available for use with which constructs, the purpose, content, length, price of a test, and other pertinent information. In Australia and overseas, test publishers, such as those listed in Table 2.1, usually require test purchasers to register before they are allowed to buy tests. The purpose of registration is to ensure that confidential test materials are supplied to professionals who are appropriately trained and qualified. For example, Table 2.2 shows the different user levels developed by the Psychological Corporation to restrict and regulate the supply of test materials. In the test catalogue supplied by the Psychological Corporation, the test user level is clearly specified for each test listed so that potential test buyers can determine if they meet the requirement for purchasing that test.

TABLE 2.1 Name, address, and web site of major test suppliers

Test Supplier	Address	Web site
Australian Council for Educational Research	19 Prospect Hill Road, Camberwell, Melbourne, Victoria, Australia 3124	www.acer.edu.au
	347 Camberwell Road, Camberwell, Melbourne, Victoria, Australia 3124	
	1/140 Bourke Road, Alexandria, Sydney, NSW, Australia 2015	
Australian Psychologists Press	142–4 Leicester Street, Carlton South, Melbourne, Victoria, Australia 3053	www.austpsychpress.com.au
CPP, Inc. (known formerly as the Consulting Psychologists Press)	1055 Joaquin Road, Suite 200 Mountain View, CA 94043 USA	www.cpp.com
nfer-Nelson	The Chiswick Centre 414 Chiswick High Rd London W4 5TF UK	www.nfer-nelson.co.uk
PRO-ED, Inc.	8700 Shoal Creek Boulevard Austin, TX 78757-6897 USA	www.proedinc.com

TABLE 2.1 (cont.)

Test Supplier	Address	Web site
Psychological Assessment Resources, Inc.	16204 N. Florida Ave, Lutz, FL 33549 USA	www.parinc.com
Psychological Assessments Australia	Suite 2, 96–100 Railway Parade, Jannali, Sydney NSW, Australia 2226	www.psychassessments.com.au
Saville Holdsworth Ltd	Level 14/77 Pacific Highway North Sydney NSW, Australia 2060	www.shl.com.au
Harcourt Assessment The Psychological Corporation (Australia and New Zealand)	30–52 Smidmore Street Marrickville, Sydney, NSW, Australia 2204	www.psychcorp.com.au
Western Psychological Services	12031 Wilshire Blvd. Los Angeles, CA 90025-1251 USA	www.wpspublish.com

*Addresses and web sites accurate at time of publication.

TABLE 2.2 User levels developed and used by the Psychological Corporation in supplying test materials

User Level	Qualifications Required
A	No specialist qualifications required
B	Requires relevant specialist professional qualifications or postgraduate studies which involve studies in testing and statistics (eg, Speech Pathology, Occupational Therapy, Physiotherapy, and Special Education)
T	Requires qualifications in teaching or early childhood/preschool teaching
M	Requires relevant professional qualifications in a medical field (eg, psychiatrists, specialist paediatricians, or GPs who specialise in treatment of depression or other psychological problems)
HR	Requires postgraduate level studies in Human Resource Management, Psychology or Statistics with technical knowledge of psychological test use
D	Requires training or professional experience in alcohol and drug counselling
C	Requires conditional or full registration with the relevant registration board or full membership of the Australian or New Zealand Psychological Societies

Other resources such as *Tests in Print* and *Tests* are bibliographic encyclopaedias that summarise all the commercially published tests in terms of test title, intended population, publication date, acronyms, author(s) publishers, administration time, cost, foreign adaptations, and references. However, it should be noted that most of the test publishers do not include critical reviews of psychological tests in their catalogues. This is because the test catalogues are designed to promote and sell tests rather than evaluate them according to scientific principles.

To obtain information about the strengths and weakness of psychological tests, a psychologist needs to turn to other sources. These include the manuals of the test under consideration, specialised test review volumes (eg, the *Mental Measurements Yearbook*, *Test Critiques*), journals (eg, *Psychological Assessment*, *Journal of Personality Assessment*, *Journal of Psychoeducational Assessment*, *Journal of Educational Measurement*, *Assessment*, *Educational and Psychological Measurement*), and colleagues/supervisors who are experienced in assessment in that particular area.

A psychologist can locate most of the technical information (eg, reliability, validity, standardisation sample, norms) about a psychological test in its manual. More and more test developers have also included this information on web sites (eg, the Depression, Anxiety and Stress Scale; Lovibond & Lovibond, 1995a; www.psy.unsw.edu.au/dass/). Although professional societies have developed guidelines (eg, *Standards for educational and psychological testing*, published by the American Educational Research Association (AERA), the American Psychological Association (APA), and the National Council on Measurement in Education (NCME), 1999) regarding the kind of technical information to be included in a test manual, test developers do not always follow these guidelines and users of psychological tests need to be wary, particularly if only a small amount of technical information can be found in the manual of a test.

Compendiums of specialist test reviews, such as the *Mental Measurements Yearbook* (see Box 2.1), provide comprehensive reviews of psychological tests. Because the reviews are written independently of the test authors and publishers and are evaluated using a set format and carefully developed criteria, they are generally objective and critical. Technical information about psychological tests can also be found in journals that specialise in this area (eg, *Psychological Assessment*). Compared to the specialist volumes, journal articles are less systematic in format and length, but often more up to date. Finally, colleagues can also be a source of advice about what tests to use for a particular client.

BOX 2.1

The *Mental Measurements Yearbook (MMY)*

The *MMY* is one of the oldest and most authoritative sources for test reviews and it is published by the Buros Institute of Mental Measurements in Lincoln, Nebraska, USA. The first edition was published in 1938 and was edited by Oscar Buros. The latest edition, the sixteenth, was published in 2005 and edited by Robert Spies and Barbara Plake. To be included in the *MMY*, a psychological test needs to be new or revised since the publication of the previous edition of the *MMY*. In addition, the publisher of the test needs to be willing to provide documentation that supports the technical properties of the test. For each of the tests included, one or more reviews are provided by qualified psychologists. Each review comprises the following five sections:

- Description (purpose and intended use of the test; target populations; information on administration, scoring, and scores)
- Development (theoretical base, assumption, and construct of the test; details on item development, evaluation, and selection)
- Technical (standardisation sample and norms, reliability, and validity)

- Commentary (strengths and weaknesses of the test; adequacy of the theory, assumption and construct of the test)
- Summary (conclusions and recommendations)

In recent years, the Buros Institute of Mental Measurements has introduced a web-based service called Test Review Online (www.unl.edu/buros). Basically, this web site contains all current test reviews that have been published in the *MMY* since its ninth edition. For a fee (US$15.00), users can download individual reviews for any of over 2000 psychological tests.

Below is an example of a test review from the 15th MMY (2003):

Learning Style Inventory, Version 3

Purpose: Designed to describe the ways an individual learns and deals with day-to-day situations.

Population: Ages 18–60.

Publication Dates: 1976–2000.

Acronym: LSI3.

Scores: 4 scores: Concrete Experience, Active Experimentation, Reflective Observation, Abstract Conceptualization; 4 learning styles: Accommodating, Diverging, Converging, Assimilating.

Administration: Group or individual.

Price Data, 2001: $79 per 10 self-scoring booklets; $50 per facilitator's guide to learning (2000, 81 pages); $38 per 15 transparencies; also available online at $15 per person.

Foreign Language Editions: French and Spanish versions available.

Time: (20–30) minutes.

Author: David A Kolb.

Publisher: Hay Group.

Cross References: See T5:1469 (13 references) and T4:1438 (12 references); for a review of an earlier edition, see 10:173 (17 references); see also 9:607 (7 references).

Review of the Learning Style Inventory, Version 3 by DAVID SHUM, Senior Lecturer of Psychology, Griffith University, Brisbane, Australia:

Description
The Learning Style Inventory, Version 3 (LSI3) is a self-report 12-item test developed by David A. Kolb to help people describe how they learn and to identify their learning style. The test describes a person's learning mode according to two polar dimensions: Concrete Experience (CE) vs Abstract Conceptualization (AC) and Active Experimentation (AE) vs Reflective Observation (RO). Based on these descriptions, the person's

learning style is classified into one of four basic types: Diverging, Assimilating, Converging, and Accommodating.

The LSI3 is suitable for people between 18 and 60 years old with a seventh grade reading level or above. No special requirements for the administration, scoring, and interpretation of the test are specified. According to Kolb, the main applications of the LSI3 are self-exploration, self-understanding, and self-development.

The LSI3 was designed in such a way that it can be administered, scored, and interpreted by the test taker. One is required to complete 12 sentences that describe learning by ranking 4 endings (from 4 to 1 for best description to worst description) that correspond to the four learning modes (viz, CE, AC, AE, RO). The 12 sentences are written in easily understood language and printed on a two-part (answer and score) form. The instructions for the test are well organized and clearly written. The scores for the four learning modes can range from 12 to 48. Given the way the sentences are answered and scored, these scores are ipsative in nature.

To find one's preferred learning mode, a diagram called The Cycle of Learning is used to transform the four raw scores into percentile scores based on a normative group of 1446 adults. Two combined scores are also obtained by calculating the differences, AC – CE and AE – RO. Finally, one's preferred learning style type is determined by plotting the two difference scores on a Learning Style Type Grid.

Development

Kolb originally developed the LSI in 1971 based on Experiential Learning Theory, which in turn is based on the Jungian concept of styles or types. The LSI3 is the latest revision of the inventory and there are four main changes. First, in LSI2, the endings that represent the four learning modes were organized in the same order for all 12 sentences to facilitate scoring. To control for possible response bias, the order of the endings is randomized in the LSI3. Second, Kolb modified the wordings of the learning style type in the LSI3 (eg, Converger to Converging) to address the concern that the old terms might give an impression that learning styles do not change. Third, the response sheet for the LSI3 was changed to a 2-part color-coded form and it is produced in such a way that answers written on the first page are automatically transferred to the second page. Fourth, a number of experiential activities and information on career development have been added to a 19-page test booklet. An 81-page *Facilitator's Guide to Learning* was published in 2000 to accompany the test.

Technical

The technical specifications of the LSI3 are included as a six-page section in the *Facilitator's Guide to Learning*. The normative group for the LSI3 comprised 1446 adults aged between 18 and 60 years old. According to the guide, there were 638 males and 801 females, which for reasons not explained do not total 1446. Kolb states that this group was ethnically diverse, represented a wide range of career fields, and had an average education of two years of college. However, detailed description and breakdown of these demographic variables are not available. The percentile scores for all test takers are based on the average performance of this group. Separate norms for different age and gender groups are not provided. This is a concern because there seem to be age and gender differences on some of the scores (see p. 10 and p. 68 of the guide).

Evidence for the internal consistency and test-retest reliability of the LSI scores is based on the data (initial sample $N = 711$, replication sample $N = 1052$) collected by Veres, Sims, and Locklear (1991) using a version with randomized sentence endings. Mean coefficient alphas for the four learning modes scores ranged from 0.53 to 0.71 in the initial sample and from 0.58 to 0.74 in the replication sample. These indices are lower than expected and they are lower than those obtained for the LSI2 (from 0.82 to 0.85). The test-retest (8-week interval) reliabilities of the four learning modes scores ranged from 0.92 to 0.97 in the initial sample and from 0.97 to 0.99 in the replication sample. Similar statistics obtained for the LSI2 were much lower and ranged from 0.25 to 0.56. Kappa coefficients were also calculated to examine classification stability for the four learning style types and were generally high, ranging from 0.71 to 0.86 for the initial sample and 0.86 to 0.93 for the replication sample.

The Facilitator's Guide to Learning contains a section that discusses the validity of the LSI3 but it is only 10 lines long. In that section, Kolb directs readers to a bibliography that includes studies that tested the validity and applicability of the LSI. In other parts of the guide, Kolb refers to the validity of the LSI3. For example, on page 41, he states that 'research on the LSI has tested the relationship between individual learning styles and the careers people choose, and found a strong correspondence between the two'. On p 12, he mentions a number of studies that examined the relationships between performance on the LSI and other instruments (eg, Myers-Briggs Type Indicator, Learning Style Questionnaire) that measure similar constructs. Nevertheless, these points are not elaborated and the studies are not referenced.

Commentary

The strength of the LSI3 lies in its brevity and its simplicity. It can be administered, scored, and interpreted by most people in a relatively short time. The content and instructions of the test are clearly written, and are easy to follow and understand. The color-coded scoring format facilitates scoring and the extensive use of graphics and diagrams in the test booklet and the guide enhances the test taker's understanding of the theory of learning and its associated constructs.

There is a concern regarding the appropriateness of the norms. According to Kolb, the comparison group used for the LSI3 is the same as the one used in the LSI2. This might not be appropriate given that the formats of the two versions are different. The order of the sentence ending for the four learning modes is the same for the 12 sentences of the LSI2, but the order of the ending of the LSI3 is randomized. Given that this change in format has led to changes in internal consistency and test-retest reliability (Veres et al, 1991) and that the equivalence of the two versions has not been demonstrated, the use of the LSI2 normative comparison group for the LSI3 might not be appropriate.

Changing the order of the sentence ending from fixed to random allows for a more accurate estimation of the internal consistency and test-retest reliability of the LSI. The internal consistency of the latest version is found to be lower than that of the previous version, and lower than expected. The test-retest reliability of the test is found to be better than that of the previous version.

Given that validity was the main concern raised in a review of the LSI2 (Gregg, 1989), it is disappointing to see that very little effort was devoted to addressing the validity of LSI3. Rather than summarizing and discussing data and evidence that provide support for the various types of validity, Kolb simply refers readers to a bibliography and makes general statements about the validity of the LSI3. This lack of effort is also surprising given that interesting issues have emerged in the literature regarding the psychometric properties of the LSI3, such as whether it is appropriate to use ipsative test scores in a factor analysis to evaluate the construct validity of the LSI (Geiger, Boyle & Pinto, 1993; Loo, 1999). It is also disappointing to see that Kolb does not clarify in the validity section whether new data have been collected specifically to examine the validity of the LSI3 and whether evidence that supports the validity of earlier versions of the LSI can be used to support the LSI3. Given that the equivalence of the various versions of the LSI has not been demonstrated and that the correlations between these versions are not included in the validity section, it is difficult to evaluate the validity of this latest revision of the LSI.

Summary

The LSI3 is the latest revision of a self-report instrument for describing and identifying one's learning mode and learning style. Although the author has provided evidence to support the reliability of the instrument, he has not provided adequate and suitable evidence to support the validity of this latest version of the instrument. This is disappointing given that the LSI seems to be a popular and promising instrument in the educational and organizational literature.

References

Geiger, M A, Boyle, E J & Pinto, J K (1993). An examination of ipsative and normative versions of Kolb's Revised Learning Style Inventory. *Educational and Psychological Measurement*, *53*, 717–26.

Gregg, N (1989). Review of the Learning Style Inventory. In J C Conoley and J J Kramer (Eds), *The tenth mental measurements yearbook* (pp. 441–2). Lincoln, NE: The Buros Institute of Mental Measurements.

Loo, R (1999). Confirmatory factor analyses of Kolb's Learning Style Inventory (LSI-1985). *British Journal of Educational Psychology*, *69*, 213–19.

Veres, J G, Sims, R R, & Locklear, T S (1991). Improving the reliability of Kolb's Learning Style Inventory. *Educational and Psychological Measurement*, *51*, 143–50.

Administering psychological tests

After selecting a psychological test for a client, the following needs to be considered before administering the test:

(a) Ensure that the test is appropriate for use with the particular client in terms of age, educational level, ethnic background.

(b) Ensure a suitable venue is selected and booked for administration of the test.
(c) Check that all test materials are present and intact.
(d) Ensure adequate time is spent becoming familiar with the test so that standardised instructions and procedures are used. (Kendall et al, 1997)

Failure to ensure that the test chosen is appropriate for the client's age, gender, educational level, and ethnic background can have serious implications for the client. For example, erroneous conclusions may be drawn and wrong decisions made based on a low aptitude test score for a client who was born overseas. Despite having aptitude in the area, the client may not have the required language skills to complete the test.

To obtain reliable and valid results for a client on a test, the venue for testing must have enough space, suitable furniture, adequate lighting and ventilation, and minimal distraction. For example, in conducting a group testing session for 20 clients, it is important to select and reserve a room that is big enough and has enough tables and chairs for everyone. Also, flat, stable, and sizeable surfaces are needed for conducting tests that require writing on test booklets. In testing younger clients, children's furniture is needed to ensure that the child is seated comfortably and at the appropriate height. Finally, a room that is too hot or too cold will definitely affect the comfort and test performance of a client.

Before administering a test, a check needs to be made to ensure that all the materials required for a test session are in the test kit and that the test materials are intact (eg, test apparatus is not broken and test booklets or record forms are not torn or are not marked intentionally or unintentionally by the previous test user). Although this point applies particularly to where test materials are shared, it is good practice for any test users to spend time checking the test kit before the assessment session.

For the novice test user or for users who have not administered a particular test for some time, it is essential that time be set aside to review the details of administration (viz, instructions, starting and ending rules, time limit, number of subtests that need to be administered). Failure to do so can lead to embarrassment during the testing session, wasting of testing time, and collection of incorrect test responses and results.

As pointed out in Chapter 1, one of the important characteristics of a psychological test is the use of standardised materials, instructions, and procedures for assessing a construct. This ensures that the results obtained for a client are comparable to the normative group and to other individuals who are administered the same test.

Scoring psychological tests

Despite the fact that clear instructions for scoring are provided in most psychological test manuals, errors can still occur among both novice and experienced test users. Some of the most common errors include miscalculations, incorrectly reading tables, and incorrectly transferring scores on test forms. For example, Simons,

Goddard, and Patton (2002) found significant and serious error rates in a sample of 1452 test results collected by a national Australian private sector employment agency on a number of psychological tests that included the Vocational Interest Survey for Australia, Rothwell Miller Interest Blank, Beck Depression Inventory – second edition, Myers Briggs Typology Indicator – Form M, Competing Values Managerial Skills Instrument, the ACER Higher Test ML–MQ, and the Multifactor Leadership Questionnaire – 5 X Revised. As another example, Charter, Walden, and Padilla (2000) found that many different types of clerical errors (viz, in addition, in using conversion tables, and in plotting scores) were found for 325 test performance of the Rey-Osterreith Complex Figure Test administered by a psychologist and two test technicians who were well trained and experienced.

Interpreting results of psychological tests

The ability to interpret the results of psychological tests for a client is an essential requirement for competent test use, although this is one of the more difficult skills to teach and acquire (Groth-Marnat, 2003). To interpret test results properly and meaningfully, it must be recognised that, compared to measurement in the physical sciences, measurement in psychology is less precise and more prone to error. It follows that the final score obtained cannot be taken as absolute. Rather, there is a margin of error for the score obtained and allowance for this fact must be made during interpretation (see discussion of the standard error of measurement in Chapter 4). Moreover, there are frequently interpretative guidelines provided in the test manual or established interpretative procedures for the test published in the research literature and these need to be followed in test interpretation. Finally, test results of a client cannot be interpreted in isolation. Rather, they should be interpreted within the context of all the other relevant background information collected (eg, educational background, developmental and medical history). It is also the case that extraneous factors such as anxiety, depression, medication, and lack of sleep can influence test performance and these need to be ruled out as alternative explanations before drawing conclusions based on the test results.

Communicating the findings of psychological testing

To be useful, the results of psychological testing should be communicated to the client or the referral agent in a clear and timely manner. This is usually done in the form of a written report, often supported by an oral explanation. There is an accepted format for a psychological report and agreement about what information should be included (more discussion of psychological report writing is included in Chapter 7). To be understandable, a report needs to be written in language that is free from jargon and conforms with accepted standards of spelling, grammar, and usage. Most importantly, a psychological report should directly and adequately answer the referral questions and include suggestions or recommendations that are based on the results obtained, logical and implementable.

Keeping case records

One of the aspects of psychological testing and assessment that is not usually emphasised or sometimes not even discussed is the importance of maintaining a clearly labelled and well-organised file of cases that have been seen (Vandecreek & Knapp, 1997). A good system facilitates the filing of information for clients and speedy retrieval of records when they are required for retesting, legal consultation, or other purposes. In this regard, there are usually legal requirements in keeping records which may differ across countries and states and which ethical practice dictates need to be observed.

ETHICS

No discussion of psychological testing and assessment would be complete without consideration of some of the ethical issues involved in assessment. Indeed the most extensive set of ethical guidelines issued by the Australian Psychological Society (APS) is concerned with psychological testing and assessment. Clearly the topic of assessment is a very salient one to psychology as a profession. Copies of the APS Code of Ethics and supplementary ethical guidelines are available at its web site: http://www.psychology.org.au/aps/ethics/default.asp.

Consideration of ethical behaviour can be traced through the millennia, from the writings of ancient Greek philosophers such as Pythagoras, Plato, and Aristotle, through medieval religious scholars to modern philosophers such as Hobbes, Locke, Mill, Kant, and Rousseau. Contemporary professional ethics is more concerned with standards of daily practice within the domain of a profession than with the development of a complete ethical system, although many of the principles underlying appropriate professional behaviour can be found in philosophical and religious writings. Indeed, it can be said that one of the defining features of a profession is adherence to a code of ethics and most professional bodies, such as legal, medical, or psychological societies, are concerned with developing such codes.

Ethics can be defined simply as the formulation of principles to guide behaviour, in this case *professional* behaviour, with respect to clients, colleagues, and the general public. Codes of ethics are an attempt at self-regulation by a group of professionals. Self-regulation and a sense of propriety and ethics are one of the defining features of any profession. It has been said that more careers have been damaged by lack of ethical knowledge than by lack of technical knowledge or of subject matter (Francis, 1999) so knowledge of a code of ethics and a sense of ethical behaviour is vital for any professional. Indeed, professional practice relies heavily on professional reputation, and reputation can be easily ruined by unethical conduct. The good news is that virtually all ethical problems are preventable and arise more through carelessness than through malice.

Sometimes students new to studying ethical issues ask: What if I don't belong to a professional society, does that mean I am exempt from their code? A better question might be to ask yourself: Do you really think you can sidestep broadly held standards of behaviour within your profession and get away with it? Irrespective of your professional membership, is anyone going to take you seriously after that? Like it or not you will be held accountable to the standards of your profession and any psychologist registered in Australia is automatically bound by the code of ethics formulated by their registration board within their state or the APS. As such, it behoves all students of psychology to remain vigilant to potential ethical problems— society at large certainly will (see Box 2.2)—and study of a code of ethics is a step in that direction. One advantage of employing a psychologist for conducting testing and assessment is that they are bound by a code of professional ethics.

BOX 2.2

Lessons from Chelmsford

Between 1963 and 1980, a psychiatrist working at a private clinic in outer metropolitan Sydney developed his own unique method of treating mental illness (Slattery, 1989a, p 47). Having the legal authority to prescribe medication, he massively sedated patients and confined them to bed. So called 'deep sleep therapy' (DST) was based on the idea that patients could literally sleep off their mental illness and wake up well. Patients were kept unconscious, sometimes for weeks on end, during which time they were also subjected to daily bouts of electroconvulsive shock. It certainly made for an easily managed psychiatric ward, described by some as 'quiet as a tomb' (Slattery, 1989b, p 32). There were no patients wandering around in a confused state or shouting meaninglessly into the air. The only problem was that some of them started to die. Psychiatric treatments are not supposed to be fatal and eventually people began to take notice.

Under pressure from several media exposés into the hospital, the New South Wales state government eventually set up a Royal Commission into the affair in 1988. The Royal Commission into Deep Sleep Therapy, chaired by Justice John Slattery, tabled its final report in 1989, totalling 14 volumes of evidence and discussion. Royal Commissioner Slattery concluded that at least 24 deaths between the years 1964 and 1977 could be directly attributed to DST (Slattery, 1989b, p 25) with at least two cases of brain damage caused by the treatment (Slattery, 1989b, p 1). Ironically, the psychiatrist checked himself in for DST in 1978 and committed suicide seven years later in the lead-up to the Royal Commission.

What has this awful tragedy got to do with psychological assessment? Well, one of the main sources of evidence used by the psychiatrist to support his continued use of DST was psychological assessment reports provided by a Sydney-based psychologist which purported to show an improvement in patient symptoms and functioning as a result of the treatment. As such, the terms of the Royal Commission were expanded to include psychological testing in 1989 and two volumes of the final report directly relate to these matters. There is little doubt that the psychiatrist truly believed DST was helping his patients and he sought what he believed to be quality scientific evidence to back up his procedures.

Although there was no strong correlation between the assessment reports and patients being given DST (Slattery, 1989c, p 70), the final decision to use DST being purely the province of the psychiatrist, the psychologist's assessments were used to support DST in a number of ways. First, they were used to help explain to patients their particular condition and why they needed DST. Second, they were used to show that there appeared to be no adverse effects associated with DST, and indeed that DST was in fact beneficial.

An expert panel of psychologists comprising local academics and experienced practitioners was formed at the behest of the Royal Commission to independently evaluate the assessment reports. The panel criticised the assessments on several grounds (Slattery, 1989c, p 68). First, some of the tests used lacked reliability. Second, their validity had not been established in some cases, certainly not for the use to which they were put, ie, diagnosing improvements in psychiatric conditions. Third, some of them had inappropriate norms; and fourth, the psychologist in question was 'idiosyncratic' in his application and use of the tests. That is, he scored them differently on different occasions, sometimes combining scores in undocumented ways. No doubt readers are aware that all of these shortcomings are in areas directly covered by this text. We have chapters on reliability, validity, and the use of norms. The criticism of idiosyncratic use clearly indicates a lack of standardised administration and scoring procedures. Such processes are undocumented and unable to be replicated and therefore cannot claim to have any scientific basis.

The psychologist in question claimed to have an 'eclectic approach to testing' and justified his idiosyncratic use of the tests on the grounds that it was a legitimate application of his clinical judgment and experience (Slattery, 1989c, p 70). A number of other psychologists making submissions to the Royal Commission concurred with these views. Psychological assessment, they claimed, was broader than the mechanical administration of tests and inevitably required the amalgamation of a diverse set of information even to the extent of coming up with one's own set of unique composite scoring rules.

It has been said, paraphrasing Newton's third law of motion, that for every expert there is an equal and opposite expert and nowhere is this more true than in psychology. The two volumes dedicated to psychological testing by the Royal Commission contain argument and counter argument by respected psychologists on the use of psychological tests and sometimes it is difficult to determine who is right. This is the hallmark of an ethical dilemma. There is also the suggestion that the psychologist may have unwittingly used his clinical judgment to exaggerate patients' symptoms prior to treatment which were subsequently found to be reduced after DST during post-test (Slattery, 1989c, p 70). We can only reiterate that psychological testing emphasises standardisation of procedures for good reason and that the objective information provided by mechanical procedures is probably the only safeguard against wishful thinking clouding one's clinical or subjective judgment.

In the end the Royal Commissioner concluded that it was not possible to determine which conclusions were based on the results of the tests and which were based on the psychologist's subjective clinical opinion, but nevertheless implicated the tests in contributing to the continued use of DST (Slattery, 1989d).

What conclusions can be drawn from this sorry tale? Looking at the code of ethics in Box 2.3, we can see the relevance of paragraphs 1, 2, 4, and especially 5. It is probably no coincidence that registration of psychologists was introduced into New South Wales in 1990 just after the completion of the Royal Commission, almost 20 years after registration occurred in other parts of Australia. Without a register of psychologists it was impossible for authorities to impose any disciplinary action other than legal proceedings and these, as we have seen, only pertain to minimal standards of behaviour. With a code of ethics and a register, you can be struck off and all states and territories in Australia now have registration boards.

Some commentators have claimed that ethics is something that can't be taught, or learnt from a book, or captured in a code; it can only be acquired through experience. Indeed, Kohlberg's famous psychological theory of moral reasoning puts ethical understanding at the most advanced stage of development and it is certainly possible that some individuals may never advance to that level (Kohlberg, 1981). Conversely, it must be conceded that no one is born with a sense of ethical behaviour. There is no such thing as an ethics gene so each of us must develop an ethical mindset through experience and conscious consideration of ethical issues. Learning and reading about ethical issues can take you a long way towards developing an ethical mindset.

How does ethics differ from related issues like morality or the law? Considerations of morality, law, or virtue are usually more general than an ethical code. Morality pertains to a pervasive set of values to live by whereas ethics focuses on principles to guide behaviour in certain situations. Conversely, the law seeks to define minimum standards of acceptable behaviour, and many people are satisfied with behaving just within those minimum standards. Ethics on the other hand seeks to define the highest standards of behaviour. As such the law is slow to change, whereas codes of ethics are readily amended. For example, the APS code has been updated several times since its introduction in 1968. It is important to realise that you can be considered to have acted unethically even though you may have done nothing illegal.

CODE OF ETHICS OF THE AUSTRALIAN PSYCHOLOGICAL SOCIETY

The Code of Ethics of the Australian Psychological Society (2003) is based on three broad principles. These are Responsibility, Competence, and Propriety. The basic principle of Responsibility states that psychologists remain responsible for their decisions and actions. Psychologists should endeavour to provide high standards of service and not to act in a way that may bring the profession into disrepute. Competence requires psychologists to understand the scope and limit of their expertise and not to practise outside these limits. Further, there is a responsibility to remain up to date within one's chosen area of expertise.

This can be achieved through further education or professional development activities such as regular attendance at relevant conferences and seminars. Finally, the principle of propriety requires psychologists to put the welfare of the public and the profession before their own self-interest, and this includes maintaining appropriate levels of confidentiality. Psychological information is by definition very personal and should not be disclosed to outside parties who do not have a need to know. As a rule, personal information should never be passed on without the person's consent.

After the statement of these general principles, the APS Code of Ethics is broken down into eight specific sections. Section A addresses psychological assessment procedures and is the focus here (see Box 2.3), section B is concerned with

BOX 2.3

Section A of the Australian Psychological Society's Code of Ethics: Psychological Assessment Procedures

1   Members must ensure that assessment procedures are chosen, administered, and interpreted appropriately and accurately.

2   Members must supply clients with explanations of the nature and purpose of the procedures used and results of the assessment, in language the recipient can understand and with appropriate accompanying contextual information, unless an explicit exception to this right has been agreed upon in advance.

3   Members responsible for the development and standardisation of psychological tests and other assessment techniques must use established scientific procedures and observe relevant psychometric standards. They must specify the purposes and uses of the assessment techniques and clearly indicate the limits of their applicability.

4   Members must not endorse, or otherwise lend credence to, inappropriate use or interpretation of assessment results.

5   Members offering scoring and interpretation services must have appropriate evidence for the validity of the programs and procedures used in arriving at interpretations.

6   Members must not compromise the effective use of psychological tests, nor render them open to misuse, by publishing or otherwise disclosing their contents to persons unauthorised or unqualified to receive such information.

7   Assessment data obtained on an individual for one purpose, may subsequently be used for another purpose only with the informed written consent of that individual. This does not apply to the subsequent use of such data in research provided that the anonymity of the individual is preserved and the interests of the client initiating the assessment are safeguarded.

8   Members must not use or otherwise facilitate the use of obsolete assessment data.

9   Members must not permit, encourage or promote the use of psychological assessment techniques by inappropriately trained or otherwise unqualified persons through teaching, sponsorship, supervision, or employment.

relationships with clients, section C addresses the teaching of psychology, section D applies to supervision and training, section E concerns research, section F addresses reporting and publication of research results, section G discusses public statements and advertising, and section H considers psychologists' relationships with other professionals.

Finally, acting ethically means more than memorising a list of do's and don'ts even though this is what most codes of ethics appear to be. Ethical principles extend beyond circumstances specifically mentioned in any code and learning to behave ethically is more about understanding the principles that underlie the code than being able to recite it point for point.

CONCLUDING REMARKS

In this chapter we have explained the difference between psychological testing and assessment. The latter is a broader process that aims to answer referral questions. Psychological testing is one of the tools that are commonly used in psychological assessment. Other tools include observation, interview, and record checking. We have also provided some examples to illustrate the different types of psychological tests. Finally, we have introduced and described some of the best practices and ethical principles relating to psychological testing and assessment. These guidelines and principles are important for ensuring the quality of assessment services provided by psychologists.

Questions for consideration

1   Is psychological testing the same as psychological assessment? Discuss.
2   What are some of the major areas of professional psychology and what are their specialities?
3   What are some of the major differences between psychological tests?
4   What is ethics and why are ethical principles needed?
5   Why do we need ethical principles to guide the practice of psychological testing and assessment?
6   When one wants to purchase a new psychological test where can one go to find information to guide the purchase?
7   Go to the ACER website and find out about its system for supplying tests to users. How is this system different from that used by the Psychological Corporation?
8   A psychologist wants to use the WISC–IV to test the IQ of a 5 year old boy. Find out who supplies this test and how much it costs. Do you think it is a suitable instrument for this purpose?

Further reading

Adams, H E, & Luscher, K A (2003). Ethical considerations in psychological assessment. In W T O'Donohue & K E Ferguson (Eds), *Handbook of professional ethics for psychologists: Issues, questions and controversies* (pp 275–83). Thousand Oaks, CA: Sage.

Francis, R D (1999). *Ethics for psychologists: A handbook*. Melbourne: ACER Press.

Kendall, I, Jenkinson, J, de Lemos, M, & Clancy, D (1997). *Supplement to guidelines for the use of psychological tests*. Melbourne: Australian Psychological Society.

Matarazzo, J D (1990). Psychological assessment versus psychological testing: Validation from Binet to the school, clinic and courtroom. *American Psychologist, 45,* 999–1017.

part two

2

Methodological and Technical Principles of Psychological Testing

chapter three

Test Scores
and Norms

▶ High school students in different Australian states complete different forms of final examination and yet compete on the same terms for places in Australian universities. How is this done?

▶ The average IQ is 100. Why is this so?

▶ A high school student obtains scores on tests in five different subjects (English, Mathematics, History, Science, French). Can we combine those scores into an overall aggregate mark indicating school performance?

▶ Can we use the performance of samples of American citizens on intelligence tests to evaluate the performance of, say, New Zealanders?

INTRODUCTION

Scores on psychological tests do not have direct meaning but must be interpreted. The commonest form of interpretation of a score on a psychological test is to refer it to the scores similar individuals obtain on the test. Essentially the question asked is how likely this score is for individuals similar in important respects to the person tested. To the extent that the score is unlikely, it attracts our interest. To interpret a test score then we need data on how samples of individuals score on the test (technically, a set of norms) and a way of expressing the test score so that the likelihood of obtaining it becomes apparent. The present chapter is concerned with common ways of expressing test scores and with the construction of adequate norms for interpreting them. We consider: the two major means for transforming scores on tests to allow their interpretation, their strengths and limitations, and the relationships between them; and the major considerations that need to be borne in mind in developing norms for psychological tests and examples of these as applied to some of the major tests in use.

INTERPRETING TEST SCORES

A psychological test is made up of a number of questions or tasks that the person taking the test must answer or complete. The term 'item' is used to refer generically to the questions or tasks that make up a test. A raw score on a psychological test is the score obtained by aggregating over the item scores on the test. Consider, for example, a test of ability that comprises 50 general knowledge questions (eg, What is the capital of New Guinea?). Each question or item can be scored in terms of whether the respondent provided the correct or the incorrect answer. In the simplest case, an item is scored 1 for correct and 0 for incorrect, although it is possible to formulate rules for allowing partial credit for items. The term 'raw score' is then the score across all the items on the test and in the example would be a number between 0 and 50.

Raw scores on psychological tests typically are of little use by themselves and require some way of giving them meaning. To know that Person X obtains a score of, say, 35, on the general knowledge test, of itself, tells us very little, because there are many more questions that could have been included in the test. Even if it is assumed that the set of items included is a good sample of the population of general knowledge items, we need to interpret the score of 35 in some way. We might say that a raw score of 35 constitutes 70 per cent of the total that could be obtained, and because, conventionally, 50 per cent is the 'Pass Mark' on a test, this represents a reasonably good result. The 50 per cent mark is a useful convention in some circumstances; it indicates that the person knows as much as they don't know and is thus at a threshold point of achievement. In other circumstances, for example, assessing the competence of a brain surgeon, one might want a greater grasp of what is to be known.

When it is possible to specify what is to be known with some precision, the raw score can have meaning in itself. Driving a motor vehicle involves a set of skills, such as engaging the engine, steering into a lane of traffic, stopping, turning, and the like. For a person to be judged a competent driver, they need to be able to show mastery of this skill set. To know, for example, how to start the car but not how to stop it, or to go straight but not how to turn would be considered insufficient. The nature of the task determines the items on the test and gives a score on the test its meaning. The term criterion referencing (see Chapter 1, p 14) is sometimes used to describe this situation; the task itself is the yardstick (criterion) to which performance is referred (Allen & Yen, 1979).

Not many variables in psychology allow this form of interpretation, because the potential item pool for a test often cannot be determined with precision. What, for example, is the possible set of behaviours that lead to a person being described as hostile or depressed or intelligent? It is possible to list a number of these but the list is far more open-ended than it is in the case of skills such as driving a motor vehicle. Thus, for most psychological variables, the raw score on a test cannot be directly interpreted.

To give a raw score meaning in these circumstances, test developers have resorted to 'norm' rather than criterion referencing. That is, they have sought to relate the raw score to the average score (or norm) of a representative group of people similar to the person being tested. A simple example of norm referencing occurs when a parent attempts to give meaning to their child's result in a spelling test by asking how other children in the class performed on the test. A score of, say, 55 per cent takes on very different meaning if most children obtained scores of less than 30 per cent than if most obtained scores of better than 70 per cent.

The idea of norm referencing is simple, although the way it is put into practice requires some understanding of statistics. The idea is to express the raw score in terms of its position in a distribution of raw scores for a sample of individuals with whom it is sensible to compare the individual being tested. The meaning of the raw score is thus given by where it lies in the distribution of scores: if it is toward the top end of the distribution the person's performance is better than most; if it is toward the bottom end, performance is poorer than most. The use of this approach to interpretation has, it must be acknowledged, proved controversial in some circles, because the comparison process is thought to be demeaning or as having adverse motivational consequences. The approach seems to be saying to some critics that the individual only has importance when considered in the context of other individuals. Alternatively, to be told that one's score is low relative to the scores of one's peers may lead to feelings of failure and possibly less effort in future. Without wishing to minimise the importance of these issues, suffice it to say that these concerns arise with respect to the way tests are used and are not intrinsic to the tests themselves.

TRANSFORMING SCORES FOR NORM REFERENCING

To refer a raw score to an appropriate reference group, the raw score has to be changed or transformed to a score which has normative information. Two basic forms of transformation are typically employed: linear and nonlinear. The term linear means that there is a straight-line relationship between two variables, in this case between the raw and the transformed scores. That is, if one were to plot the transformed score against the raw score the plot would be a straight line.

A simple linear transformation is the addition of a constant to all raw scores. Consider the following scores for five students on an achievement test that has a maximum score of 40: 35, 20, 17, 11, 5. A constant value, say 100, is added to each of the raw scores, and a new set of scores results but one closely related to the first: 135, 120, 117, 111, 105. Note that plotting the transformed scores against the raw scores results in a straight line, as in Figure 3.1. The transformation is linear. An essential feature of this type of transformation is that the differences between raw scores are maintained in the transformed scores, although their magnitude has changed. Thus 17 minus 11 in the raw score set is equivalent to 11 minus 5, and this equivalence is maintained among the transformed scores ($17 - 11 = 11 - 5 = 117 - 111 = 111 - 105$).

The same effect would be produced if instead of adding a constant we subtracted (or divided or multiplied) each number by a constant. In case of division by a constant, say 5, the set of numbers that results is 7, 4, 3.4, 2.2, 1. A plot of transformed scores against original again results in a straight line and the equivalence

FIGURE 3.1 Plotting the raw scores in our example with the transformed scores

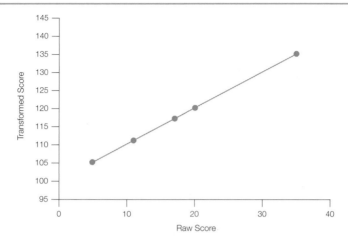

of differences in the original set (eg, $17 - 11 = 11 - 5$) remains in the transformed set ($3.4 - 2.2 = 2.2 - 1$). In this case, the scale of the differences has changed (the absolute differences in the two sets are not equal as they were with the addition of a constant) but this is easily dealt with, if we want to, by simply multiplying the differences by the constant that was used for division in the first place: $17 - 11 = 11 - 5 = 5(3.4 - 2.2) = 5(2.2 - 1)$. It is worth noting that the linear transformation is not limited to one operation as long as the straight-line relationship is preserved. For example, we could both divide through by 5 and add 100 to all numbers. You might want to satisfy yourself that the transformation is linear. In general, a linear transformation is one in which the transformed scores are related to the raw scores in terms of a straight-line function, and this means that the equivalence of distances between points on the raw score distribution is maintained in the transformed distribution.

A linear transformation is not the only form of transformation possible, and there are many forms of nonlinear transformation that are used for different purposes. In the case of psychological tests we sometimes find that numbers in the raw score distribution are bunched in the middle of the range of scores, affording little discrimination in that region. A test developer might want to draw out the differences in the middle of the range while leaving the values in the tails of the distribution unchanged. This means a nonlinear transformation of the raw scores because in these circumstances the plot of transformed and raw scores will not produce a straight line. Nonlinear transformations are as legitimate as linear ones, but one needs to bear in mind that the equivalence of differences only holds with linear transformations. We will say more about the nonlinear transformation when we encounter one.

The straight line is fundamental to the distinction being made here between linear and nonlinear transformations. In geometry, the straight line has an equation that is useful in transforming test scores. The equation is:

$$Y = mX + c$$

It can be read for present purposes as meaning that the value of a linearly transformed score (Y) is equal to a weighting factor (m) times the raw score (X) plus a constant (c). In terms of the linear transformations considered to this point, the equation can be written as follows.

For addition of a constant 100, the constant is 100 and the weighting factor is 1:

$$Y = 1 \times X + 100$$

For division by 5, the weighting factor is 1/5 and the constant is 0:

$$Y = \frac{1}{5} \times X + 0$$

For division by 5 and addition of 100:

$$Y = \frac{1}{5} \times X + 100$$

The same basic equation characterises all of these transformations because they are all linear. (Note that if Y were a function of some power of X, say $Y = X^a$, the relationship would not be linear.)

In transforming psychological test scores to give them normative meaning, linear and nonlinear transformations are used. The most common form of linear transformation is the z score and the most common form of nonlinear transformation is the percentile. Percentiles have been widely used in education and for some users are more intuitively understandable than z scorers. For that reason percentile equivalents are sometimes given even when the basic transformed score being used is the z score. It is necessary to understand both and the relationship between them that holds when the distribution of scores being transformed is normal or nearly so. In what follows we use the term percentile, although the term centile is also used in the testing literature. The two have exactly the same meaning.

STANDARD SCORES AND TRANSFORMED SCORES BASED ON THEM

Students first encounter standard scores in discussions of the normal curve, a statistical distribution that has a characteristic bell shape and many interesting properties. A normal distribution is symmetrical about the mean with half the scores below the mean and half above. When scores are specified in terms of their distance from the mean, the mean is 0 and the standard deviation is 1. The standard score is a way of specifying where in a normal distribution a score lies with reference to its mean. The procedure is simple: subtract the mean from the score and divide the result by the standard deviation:

$$z = \frac{(X - M)}{SD}$$

If the number is positive, the score must be larger than the mean, that is, it lies in the distribution above the mean; if negative, the score is less than the mean and it lies below it in the distribution. The magnitude of the z score can be read as a proportion: how far the score is from the mean as a proportion of a standard deviation. Consider again the scores on the achievement test discussed earlier. Each can be converted to a z score as follows:

TABLE 3.1 Calculating z scores from raw scores

	Raw score	$X - M$	$\dfrac{(X - M)}{SD}$
	35	17.4	1.54
	20	2.4	0.21
	17	−0.6	−0.05
	11	−6.6	−0.58
	5	−12.6	−1.11
Mean	17.6		
SD	11.3		

The first score, 35, is equivalent to a z score of 1.54. This means that it lies just over one and a half standard deviations (1.54) above (positive) the mean, whereas the score of 11 is just over half a standard deviation (0.58) below (negative) the mean. The z score thus locates the individual score in relation to the mean of the distribution of scores, which is what we want for norm referencing purposes (where the individual's score lies with respect to those of others).

The z score transformation is linear, because we can write it in terms of the equation for a straight line:

$$Y = mX + c$$

$$Y = \left(\frac{1}{SD}\right) \times X + \left(\frac{-M}{SD}\right)$$

The weighting factor is $\dfrac{1}{SD}$ and the constant is minus the mean divided by the SD.

The z transformation is a useful one because if we can assume a distribution of scores is normal or nearly so, the properties of the normal curve can be invoked in interpreting a z score. (We can always calculate z scores from a raw score distribution but their interpretation depends on being able to make a reasonable guess about the distribution from which they come.) One of these properties is that there is a fixed relationship between the height of the normal curve at any point (y) and the distance along the X axis (x). Figure 3.2 shows this for a z value of + 1. There are 84 per cent of cases below this value.

This relationship is expressed in the equation of the normal curve, which is rather forbidding when first encountered and is not given here but can be found in a statistics text. The equation can be solved for various values of x (or y) and these are summarised in tables of the normal curve which are more useful for practical purposes than the equation of the normal curve. Table 3.2 is a table of the normal

FIGURE 3.2 Percentage of cases below z of +1 in a normal distribution

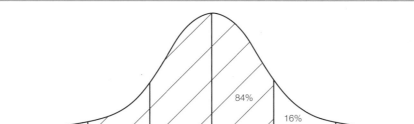

curve and does not include all the possible values but will suffice for illustration. The table is set up in three columns. The first lists values of z; the second the proportion of cases in the distribution that lie between the mean and the value of z for that row; the third provides the proportion of cases that lie beyond that value of z. The tabled values are all positive but because the normal curve is symmetrical about the mean the values for negative zs are the same. Note that the values in Columns 2 and 3 sum to 0.5 in all cases because half the scores in a normal distribution lie above and half below the mean. Not included in this table but included in some versions of the tables of the normal curve is the height of the curve corresponding to the z score.

The tables can be used for many purposes but for interpretation of the z score the tables can be used to determine how many cases there are in the distribution up to a particular z score. Take the z score of 0.21 corresponding to the raw score of 20 in the achievement score distribution. Column 2 indicates that there are 0.0832 of the cases in a normal distribution between the mean and a z of 0.21. Half the cases lie below the mean. Therefore, there are 0.5 + 0.0832 or 0.58 of the cases up to a z score of 0.21. In our example with only five cases this is not very informative but if our five cases were a sample from a distribution of scores we assumed were normal, the usual case in test construction, it would be. The score of 20 is one we would expect to exceed 58 per cent of cases in the population. What of the z score of −0.58? Because this is negative it lies below the mean and Column 3 is therefore the relevant table (scores are approaching the mean in this case). Up to a z score of −0.58 there are 0.2810 of the cases (from Column 3).

If the assumption that scores on the psychological test of interest are distributed normally or this is a reasonably good approximation to the underlying distribution, the calculation of a z score conveys a good deal of information for use in norm referencing, in giving meaning to a raw score. The assumption of normality is a necessary one, otherwise incorrect inferences can be drawn. For example, if a distribution is badly skewed (ie, scores are bunched toward the top or bottom end of the distribution), the actual proportion of cases derived from the normal curve tables will not apply. This becomes even more of a problem if two scores are being compared that are drawn from distributions skewed in different directions. Many psychological variables come from distributions that are sufficiently close approximations to normal, however, to make this necessary assumption less limiting than it might first appear.

TABLE 3.2 Area under the standard normal distribution

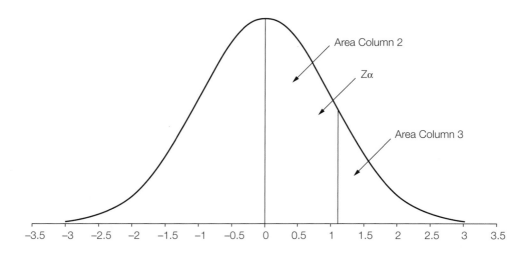

z_α	Area between zero and z_α	Area beyond z_α	z_α	Area between zero and z_α	Area beyond z_α
0.00	0.0000	0.5000	0.27	0.1064	0.3936
0.01	0.0040	0.4960	0.28	0.1103	0.3897
0.02	0.0080	0.4920	0.29	0.1141	0.3859
0.03	0.0120	0.4880	0.30	0.1179	0.3821
0.04	0.0160	0.4840	0.31	0.1217	0.3783
0.05	0.0199	0.4801	0.32	0.1255	0.3745
0.06	0.0239	0.4761	0.33	0.1293	0.3707
0.07	0.0279	0.4721	0.34	0.1331	0.3669
0.08	0.0319	0.4681	0.35	0.1368	0.3632
0.09	0.0359	0.4641	0.36	0.1406	0.3594
0.10	0.0398	0.4602	0.37	0.1443	0.3557
0.11	0.0438	0.4562	0.38	0.1480	0.3520
0.12	0.0478	0.4522	0.39	0.1517	0.3483
0.13	0.0517	0.4483	0.40	0.1554	0.3446
0.14	0.0557	0.4443	0.41	0.1591	0.3409
0.15	0.0596	0.4404	0.42	0.1628	0.3372
0.16	0.0636	0.4364	0.43	0.1664	0.3336
0.17	0.0675	0.4325	0.44	0.1700	0.3300
0.18	0.0714	0.4286	0.45	0.1736	0.3264
0.19	0.0753	0.4247	0.46	0.1772	0.3228
0.20	0.0793	0.4207	0.47	0.1808	0.3192
0.21	0.0832	0.4168	0.48	0.1844	0.3156
0.22	0.0871	0.4129	0.49	0.1879	0.3121
0.23	0.0910	0.4090	0.50	0.1915	0.3085
0.24	0.0948	0.4052	0.51	0.1950	0.3050
0.25	0.0987	0.4013	0.52	0.1985	0.3015
0.26	0.1026	0.3974	0.53	0.2019	0.2981

TABLE 3.2 (cont.)

z_α	Area between zero and z_α	Area beyond z_α	z_α	Area between zero and z_α	Area beyond z_α
0.54	0.2054	0.2946	1.01	0.3438	0.1562
0.55	0.2088	0.2912	1.02	0.3461	0.1539
0.56	0.2123	0.2877	1.03	0.3485	0.1515
0.57	0.2157	0.2843	1.04	0.3508	0.1492
0.58	0.2190	0.2810	1.05	0.3531	0.1469
0.59	0.2224	0.2776	1.06	0.3554	0.1446
0.60	0.2257	0.2743	1.07	0.3577	0.1423
0.61	0.2291	0.2709	1.08	0.3599	0.1401
0.62	0.2324	0.2676	1.09	0.3621	0.1379
0.63	0.2357	0.2643	1.10	0.3643	0.1357
0.64	0.2389	0.2611	1.11	0.3665	0.1335
0.65	0.2422	0.2578	1.12	0.3686	0.1314
0.66	0.2454	0.2546	1.13	0.3708	0.1292
0.67	0.2486	0.2514	1.14	0.3729	0.1271
0.68	0.2517	0.2483	1.15	0.3749	0.1251
0.69	0.2549	0.2451	1.16	0.3770	0.1230
0.70	0.2580	0.2420	1.17	0.3790	0.1210
0.71	0.2611	0.2389	1.18	0.3810	0.1190
0.72	0.2642	0.2358	1.19	0.3830	0.1170
0.73	0.2673	0.2327	1.20	0.3849	0.1151
0.74	0.2704	0.2296	1.21	0.3869	0.1131
0.75	0.2734	0.2266	1.22	0.3888	0.1112
0.76	0.2764	0.2236	1.23	0.3907	0.1093
0.77	0.2794	0.2206	1.24	0.3925	0.1075
0.78	0.2823	0.2177	1.25	0.3944	0.1056
0.79	0.2852	0.2148	1.26	0.3962	0.1038
0.80	0.2881	0.2119	1.27	0.3980	0.1020
0.81	0.2910	0.2090	1.28	0.3997	0.1003
0.82	0.2939	0.2061	1.29	0.4015	0.0985
0.83	0.2967	0.2033	1.30	0.4032	0.0968
0.84	0.2995	0.2005	1.31	0.4049	0.0951
0.85	0.3023	0.1977	1.32	0.4066	0.0934
0.86	0.3051	0.1949	1.33	0.4082	0.0918
0.87	0.3078	0.1922	1.34	0.4099	0.0901
0.88	0.3106	0.1894	1.35	0.4115	0.0885
0.89	0.3133	0.1867	1.36	0.4131	0.0869
0.90	0.3159	0.1841	1.37	0.4147	0.0853
0.91	0.3186	0.1814	1.38	0.4162	0.0838
0.92	0.3212	0.1788	1.39	0.4177	0.0823
0.93	0.3238	0.1762	1.40	0.4192	0.0808
0.94	0.3264	0.1736	1.41	0.4207	0.0793
0.95	0.3289	0.1711	1.42	0.4222	0.0778
0.96	0.3315	0.1685	1.43	0.4236	0.0764
0.97	0.3340	0.1660	1.44	0.4251	0.0749
0.98	0.3365	0.1635	1.45	0.4265	0.0735
0.99	0.3389	0.1611	1.46	0.4279	0.0721
1.00	0.3413	0.1587	1.47	0.4292	0.0708

TABLE 3.2 (cont.)

z_α	Area between zero and z_α	Area beyond z_α	z_α	Area between zero and z_α	Area beyond z_α
1.48	0.4306	0.0694	1.95	0.4744	0.0256
1.49	0.4319	0.0681	1.96	0.4750	0.0250
1.50	0.4332	0.0668	1.97	0.4756	0.0244
1.51	0.4345	0.0655	1.98	0.4761	0.0239
1.52	0.4357	0.0643	1.99	0.4767	0.0233
1.53	0.4370	0.0630	2.00	0.4772	0.0228
1.54	0.4382	0.0618	2.01	0.4778	0.0222
1.55	0.4394	0.0606	2.02	0.4783	0.0217
1.56	0.4406	0.0594	2.03	0.4788	0.0212
1.57	0.4418	0.0582	2.04	0.4793	0.0207
1.58	0.4429	0.0571	2.05	0.4798	0.0202
1.59	0.4441	0.0559	2.06	0.4803	0.0197
1.60	0.4452	0.0548	2.07	0.4808	0.0192
1.61	0.4463	0.0537	2.08	0.4812	0.0188
1.62	0.4474	0.0526	2.09	0.4817	0.0183
1.63	0.4484	0.0516	2.10	0.4821	0.0179
1.64	0.4495	0.0505	2.11	0.4826	0.0174
1.65	0.4505	0.0495	2.12	0.4830	0.0170
1.66	0.4515	0.0485	2.13	0.4834	0.0166
1.67	0.4525	0.0475	2.14	0.4838	0.0162
1.68	0.4535	0.0465	2.15	0.4842	0.0158
1.69	0.4545	0.0455	2.16	0.4846	0.0154
1.70	0.4554	0.0446	2.17	0.4850	0.0150
1.71	0.4564	0.0436	2.18	0.4854	0.0146
1.72	0.4573	0.0427	2.19	0.4857	0.0143
1.73	0.4582	0.0418	2.20	0.4861	0.0139
1.74	0.4591	0.0409	2.21	0.4864	0.0136
1.75	0.4599	0.0401	2.22	0.4868	0.0132
1.76	0.4608	0.0392	2.23	0.4871	0.0129
1.77	0.4616	0.0384	2.24	0.4875	0.0125
1.78	0.4625	0.0375	2.25	0.4878	0.0122
1.79	0.4633	0.0367	2.26	0.4881	0.0119
1.80	0.4641	0.0359	2.27	0.4884	0.0116
1.81	0.4649	0.0351	2.28	0.4887	0.0113
1.82	0.4656	0.0344	2.29	0.4890	0.0110
1.83	0.4664	0.0336	2.30	0.4893	0.0107
1.84	0.4671	0.0329	2.31	0.4896	0.0104
1.85	0.4678	0.0322	2.32	0.4898	0.0102
1.86	0.4686	0.0314	2.33	0.4901	0.0099
1.87	0.4693	0.0307	2.34	0.4904	0.0096
1.88	0.4699	0.0301	2.35	0.4906	0.0094
1.89	0.4706	0.0294	2.36	0.4909	0.0091
1.90	0.4713	0.0287	2.37	0.4911	0.0089
1.91	0.4719	0.0281	2.38	0.4913	0.0087
1.92	0.4726	0.0274	2.39	0.4916	0.0084
1.93	0.4732	0.0268	2.40	0.4918	0.0082
1.94	0.4738	0.0262	2.41	0.4920	0.0080

TABLE 3.2 (cont.)

z_α	Area between zero and z_α	Area beyond z_α	z_α	Area between zero and z_α	Area beyond z_α
2.42	0.4922	0.0078	2.89	0.4981	0.0019
2.43	0.4925	0.0075	2.90	0.4981	0.0019
2.44	0.4927	0.0073	2.91	0.4982	0.0018
2.45	0.4929	0.0071	2.92	0.4982	0.0018
2.46	0.4931	0.0069	2.93	0.4983	0.0017
2.47	0.4932	0.0068	2.94	0.4984	0.0016
2.48	0.4934	0.0066	2.95	0.4984	0.0016
2.49	0.4936	0.0064	2.96	0.4985	0.0015
2.50	0.4938	0.0062	2.97	0.4985	0.0015
2.51	0.4940	0.0060	2.98	0.4986	0.0014
2.52	0.4941	0.0059	2.99	0.4986	0.0014
2.53	0.4943	0.0057	3.00	0.4987	0.0013
2.54	0.4945	0.0055	3.01	0.49869	0.00131
2.55	0.4946	0.0054	3.02	0.49874	0.00126
2.56	0.4948	0.0052	3.03	0.49878	0.00122
2.57	0.4949	0.0051	3.04	0.49882	0.00118
2.58	0.4951	0.0049	3.05	0.49886	0.00114
2.59	0.4952	0.0048	3.06	0.49889	0.00111
2.60	0.4953	0.0047	3.07	0.49893	0.00107
2.61	0.4955	0.0045	3.08	0.49896	0.00104
2.62	0.4956	0.0044	3.09	0.49900	0.00100
2.63	0.4957	0.0043	3.10	0.49903	0.00097
2.64	0.4959	0.0041	3.11	0.49906	0.00094
2.65	0.4960	0.0040	3.12	0.49910	0.00090
2.66	0.4961	0.0039	3.13	0.49913	0.00087
2.67	0.4962	0.0038	3.14	0.49916	0.00084
2.68	0.4963	0.0037	3.15	0.49918	0.00082
2.69	0.4964	0.0036	3.16	0.49921	0.00079
2.70	0.4965	0.0035	3.17	0.49924	0.00076
2.71	0.4966	0.0034	3.18	0.49926	0.00074
2.72	0.4967	0.0033	3.19	0.49929	0.00071
2.73	0.4968	0.0032	3.20	0.49931	0.00069
2.74	0.4969	0.0031	3.21	0.49934	0.00066
2.75	0.4970	0.0030	3.22	0.49936	0.00064
2.76	0.4971	0.0029	3.23	0.49938	0.00062
2.77	0.4972	0.0028	3.24	0.49940	0.00060
2.78	0.4973	0.0027	3.25	0.49942	0.00058
2.79	0.4974	0.0026	3.30	0.49952	0.00048
2.80	0.4974	0.0026	3.35	0.49960	0.00040
2.81	0.4975	0.0025	3.40	0.49966	0.00034
2.82	0.4976	0.0024	3.45	0.49972	0.00028
2.83	0.4977	0.0023	3.50	0.49977	0.00023
2.84	0.4977	0.0023	3.60	0.49984	0.00016
2.85	0.4978	0.0022	3.70	0.49989	0.00011
2.86	0.4979	0.0021	3.80	0.49993	0.00007
2.87	0.4979	0.0021	3.90	0.49995	0.00005
2.88	0.4980	0.0020	4.00	0.49997	0.00003

The z score is the basic linear transformation used in psychological testing but often transformed scores are not expressed simply as z scores. The reason for this is that z scores are 'untidy' numbers, with negative as well as positive signs in front of them and decimal fractions following them. By a further linear transformation of the z score (which by definition leaves the z score distribution unchanged in just the same way as the z transformation left the original raw score distribution unchanged), a tidier set of numbers can be produced.

Instead of having the mean at 0 with a standard deviation of 1, which is what we have with z scores, we can set the mean to be, say, 100, and the standard deviation to be 15 and adjust all scores accordingly. The equation of the straight line is again of use:

$$Y = mX + c$$

But the X now is read not as the raw score, as it has been up to now, but as the z score we have calculated, and the weighting factor is the new standard deviation and the constant is the new mean:

$$Y = 15 \times z + 100$$

We have transformed a transformed score, but again linearly. You might try transforming the z scores in Table 3.2 using this equation. If you ignore the decimal points in your new transformed score a regular set of numbers results. Plotting the new set of numbers against the z scores results in a straight line and the equivalence of differences in the new and the z score distribution is maintained.

Rather than calculate the z scores and then transform them to the new distribution with mean 100 and SD 15, we could do this in one step, again using the equation of a straight line:

$$Y = mX + c$$

$$\text{New Score} = \frac{SD_{NewScores}}{SD_{OldScores}} \times (\text{Old Score} - \text{Mean of Old Scores}) + \text{Mean of New Scores}$$

For example:

$$100 = \frac{15}{1} \times (0 - 0) + 100$$

This is the procedure used originally by David Wechsler (1955) in developing his Adult Intelligence Scale (now the WAIS-III). He expressed an individual's score as a z score using the mean and standard deviation from a sufficiently large age-appropriate sample and then transformed these z scores to a distribution with a mean of 100 and a standard deviation of 15. He selected the mean to be 100 because, since from an earlier formulation of scores on Binet's test of intelligence by Terman, people had come to think of the average IQ as 100. Wechsler used the term Deviation IQ to capture the essential link between his metric for intelligence and the z score.

Within his original adult intelligence test, Wechsler used the z score to describe performance on each subtest (of which there were initially 11). In this case, a reference group of 500 cases aged 20 to 34 years was used to furnish a mean and standard deviation and the z score so computed was transformed to a distribution with a mean of 10 and a standard deviation of 3. Wechsler used the term standardised score to describe this form of z score.

Other test developers have used the z score as the basis for a transformed score. Hathaway and McKinley (1951) in developing the MMPI derived T scores as the way of expressing aggregate response on each of the subscales of the test. (Being a personality test, there are no right or wrong answers in the way there are on an ability or intelligence test. Answers either indicate the personality characteristic or interest or they do not and the raw score for each subscale is thus the sum of responses indicative of the personality characteristic of interest.) The mean of the T distribution was set at 50 and the standard deviation at 10. A score of 60 on a subscale is thus 1 standard deviation above the mean. Dahlstrom and Welsh (1960) suggested that, as a rule of thumb, a score of 65 (1.5 standard deviations from the mean) or greater should be considered as unusually high.

One other variation of the z score is that used by Cattell in developing the 16 PF. This is a 10-point scale with a mean of 5.5 and a standard deviation of 2, and is referred to as a sten score (see, eg, Cattell, 1957; Russell & Karol, 1994).

PERCENTILES AND TRANSFORMED SCORES BASED ON THEM

The z score, with its several transformations, is a widely used method of giving raw scores on psychological tests meaning. Almost as popular is the nonlinear transformation known as the percentile. This should not be confused with a percentage correct score, which is just the expression of the raw score as a proportion of the total possible score.

The percentile scale expresses each raw score in a distribution in terms of the percentage of cases that lie below it. Thus a raw score at the 50th percentile is larger than 50 per cent of the raw scores in the distribution of scores, a score at the 63rd percentile is larger than 63 per cent of cases and so on. Note that the percentile does not indicate the percent correct on the test but the percent of cases below the given value of the raw score. For example, a raw score that represents 50 per cent correct on the test would fall at the 63rd percentile, if 63 per cent of those tested obtained scores lower than 50 per cent correct. Percentile and per cent correct are quite separate concepts and must not be confused.

The term 'percentile point' is sometimes used to describe the point in the raw score distribution and the term 'percentile equivalent' to refer to the percentile score that expresses the raw score. That is, the raw score has a percentile equivalent, which is the point on the percentile scale. The distinction is correct but too subtle for most users, who recognise a raw score and the percentile corresponding to it. The term 'percentile rank' is more widely used and refers to the percentage of scores that fall below the percentile point.

The value of the percentile scale is that it allows scores to be ranked in such a way that their position in the distribution is immediately apparent. A percentile rank of 80 expresses a score that is larger than a percentile rank of 70, but as well as knowing this we know that 80 per cent of the cases lie below the percentile rank of 80 and

70 per cent below the rank of 70. That is, we know approximately where in the distribution the scores lie, as well as their standing relative to each other. Because of its intuitive appeal, the transformation is popular in educational and psychological measurement. It must be recognised, however, that the transformation is non-linear: it is not based on the equation of a straight line and it does not therefore preserve the equivalence of distances between scores in the raw score distribution. Scores in the middle of a normal distribution of scores are stretched apart on the percentile scale whereas those at the tails are pushed closer together to form what is sometimes called a rectangular scale. Think of it this way: in a distribution of scores that approximates a normal bell-shaped distribution, scores in the middle of the range of scores occur more frequently, by definition, and therefore we do not need to move far along the score range to aggregate any fixed percentage of scores, say 10 per cent. By comparison, in the tails where scores are less frequent we need to move further to aggregate the same fixed percentage of scores. Therefore, scores that are an equal number of percentiles apart are not necessarily an equal distance apart in the raw score distribution. In comparing differences in percentiles, we need to bear in mind where the percentiles are on the percentile scale.

Percentiles are determined in three main ways: graphic interpolation, arithmetic calculation, and by reading from the tables of the normal curve. Cronbach (1990, pp 110–11) provides a detailed example of determining percentiles by graphical interpolation and his demonstration will not be repeated here. Essentially, the procedure involves grouping the raw scores into convenient intervals (class intervals as they are called), counting the frequencies of scores in each of the intervals, cumulating the frequencies beginning from the lowest score intervals, and then expressing the cumulative frequencies as percentages. From a smooth curve fitted to the plot of the cumulative percentages against the midpoint of a class interval, the percentile corresponding to any particular raw score can be read. Quite accurate values can be obtained in this way.

Alternatively, the percentile for any particular raw score can be computed from the cumulative distribution by hand from a formula that is in little use in the days of the modern computer. Calculation requires the basic information used in plotting the cumulative percentage curve used in graphical interpolation, viz, frequencies of scores in class intervals and cumulative frequencies. Box 3.1 provides the formula.

BOX 3.1

Formula for calculating percentile

$$PR = \frac{cf_i + .5(f_i)}{N} \times 100\%$$

where:

PR   is the percentile rank

cf_i is the cumulative frequency for all scores lower than the score of interest

f_i is the frequency of scores in the interval of interest

N   is the total number of cases in the sample

A third way of determining the percentile equivalent of a given raw score is first to compute the z score of each raw score and then, if one can assume a normal distribution or one that is nearly so, to read off from the tables of the normal curve the proportion and hence the percentage of cases below each particular z score. Earlier we described the determination of percentage of cases below a given z score and the same procedure is involved here. Calculate z scores and then enter a table like that shown partly in Table 3.2 and read from Column 2 (for z score above the mean) or Column 3 (for z scores below the mean) the proportion (and hence percentage, proportion times 100) of cases below that z value. Although the z score is being used here to compute percentiles it does not follow that the percentile distribution is a linear transformation. A check of some actual values will show that equal distances between z scores do not correspond to equal differences in percentages of cases. For example, a difference of 0.2 between the following pairs of z scores does not convert into the same difference when the pairs of scores are expressed as percentiles. (Note you can verify the first transformation of z scores to percentiles by consulting Table 3.2.)

TABLE 3.3 Equal differences in z scores do not mean equal differences in percentiles

	z Score	Percentile
	0.25	60
	0.45	67
Difference	0.20	7
	2.00	98
	2.20	99
Difference	0.20	1

The fact that z scores can be used to calculate percentiles indicates the close relationship between the two, a point that is made more of below. Because whatever method is used to calculate percentiles is tedious (unless a computer is used), a test developer typically publishes a table of percentile equivalents for all possible raw scores on the test as part of the test manual. The user simply consults the table to find the percentile equivalent. The user must of course understand what a percentile is and its limitations to make intelligent use of the table.

The link between z scores and percentiles has led some test developers to use this to 'normalise' non-normal distributions of test scores. The normal distribution, as noted earlier, is a desirable distribution for test development because of the known properties of the normal distribution and because many psychological variables are distributed in a nearly normal way. Where a distribution of test scores departs from a normal distribution, some test developers are inclined to force the distribution into a normal form.

Normalised standard scores constitute an easy way of doing this. The first step is to determine percentiles for scores in the raw score distribution and then to calculate the z scores that correspond to the percentiles using, say, the tables of the normal curve. The process is the reverse of that used earlier in finding percentiles using z scores. In the earlier case, the user enters the tables of the normal curve with a set of z scores (calculated from the raw score distribution) and reads off the proportion of cases associated with each of these to express them as a percentage of cases below each, that is, a percentile rank. In the case now being considered, rather than enter the tables of the normal curve with z scores and read off percentages (proportions), the user enters the tables with percentiles (calculated from the raw score distribution) and reads off z score equivalents. The z scores are, by definition, normally distributed, but note that, because the starting point is with percentiles (a nonlinear transformation), the normalised standard scores that result from this procedure are nonlinear transformations of the original raw scores, and the limitations of this must be recognised.

A variant of the percentile that is used by some test developers is the stanine scale. This was developed to facilitate recording of scores because it required only nine numbers, all single digits, to describe all possible raw scores. (This was of value when recording and manipulating scores was done manually.) The 'standard nine' or stanine scale grouped percentiles into bands and assigned the numbers 1 to 9 to these bands as shown in Table 3.3 below. The stanine distribution has a mean of 5 and a standard deviation of approximately 2. Stanines (a nonlinear transformation) should not be confused with stens, see p 53 above (a linear transformation).

TABLE 3.4 Percentile ranges corresponding to stanine cores

Stanine	Percentile Range
1	Up to 4th percentile
2	4th to 11th percentile
3	11th to 23rd percentile
4	23rd to 40th percentile
5	40th to 60th percentile
6	60th to 77th percentile
7	77th to 89th percentile
8	89th to 96th percentile
9	96th percentile and beyond

Source: Based on Allen & Yen (1979)

RELATIONSHIPS AMONG THE TRANSFORMED SCORES

As noted above, there is a link between the linear and nonlinear transformations of raw scores in popular use and that link is the normal distribution. Where distributions are normal or nearly so, the properties of the normal curve can be used to express any particular raw score in that distribution in terms of its deviation from the mean in units of the standard deviation and then the resulting z score can be referred to the tables of the normal curve. From these tables the proportion of cases corresponding to a z score can be determined and this can be expressed as a percentage of cases below that point, ie, a percentile. Scores can be expressed using a value for a mean and a standard deviation of a user's choosing without distorting the essential meaning of the z score. Thus Deviation IQs, standardised scores, and T scores are all variations on the basic idea of the z score. Figure 3.3 demonstrates this relationship among transformations.

FIGURE 3.3 Relationships among linear and nonlinear raw score transformations

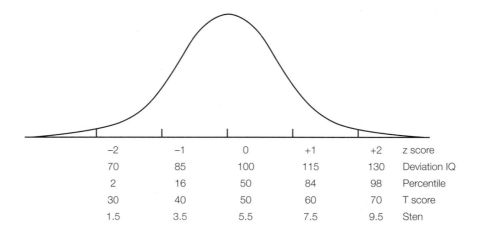

-2	-1	0	+1	+2	z score
70	85	100	115	130	Deviation IQ
2	16	50	84	98	Percentile
30	40	50	60	70	T score
1.5	3.5	5.5	7.5	9.5	Sten

NORMS

In all transformations of raw scores that use the idea of the z score, the mean and standard deviation that are used are critical to the meaning that is given to the score. In norm referencing, the raw score is referred to a relevant group for comparison purposes. If the comparison is not with an appropriate group, the transformation, although technically correct, fails to convey meaning or, worse yet, opens the score to misinterpretation. To say that a person's score is one standard deviation above the mean only has value if the mean is for a group the person is like in some way. For example, to say that an adult's score on reading is one standard deviation above the pre-schoolers mean for reading does not usually convey any information because we would expect this, unless we had some reason to suspect severe educational disadvantage. The pre-schooler group is not an appropriate point of comparison in most cases.

It follows that selecting an appropriate reference distribution and ensuring that the mean and standard deviation are well estimated are essential aspects of the norm referencing approach. What constitutes an appropriate reference group may vary even for the same test taker from time to time, depending on the interpretation of the individual's test score that is to be made. In testing for aptitude for business, for example, one might want to compare the individual's score to that of all students of the same age, or to just those students of the same age who are interested in business, or to business people who have a reputation for being good at business. The reference group that is appropriate varies depending on the use to be made of the score. More than one group is usually studied in preparing norms so that a number of interpretations become possible and a number of different individuals can be evaluated with the test.

The issue of an appropriate norm group helps make the point that the test score is not an immutable fact of the person but a sample of performance that needs to be interpreted in an appropriate context. The same performance can lead to different interpretations depending on the context. A score that earns the judgment that a student is in the top 20 per cent of their class mates in terms of business aptitude may lead to a judgment that they are below average if the reference group is that of a group of experienced business people.

Deciding on an appropriate norm group is an exercise of judgment, which takes into account the uses to be made of the test. Not all uses can be anticipated and the test user may be left with a situation for which an appropriate norm group is not provided. In such a case the test score needs to be interpreted cautiously or no interpretation offered and an alternative test with appropriate norms sought (see Box 3.2 and Box 11.1).

BOX 3.2

Using American norms with Australian populations

Test development is expensive and good psychological or educational tests require a substantial market for a test to justify the investment in its development. Not surprisingly, many of the tests used in Australia and other countries in the region are developed overseas, principally the USA, and used here with only minor modifications. For example, a question on a general knowledge test that asks the name of the American president might be altered to ask about the Australian prime minister. There is usually some pilot work done with the altered item to check that it is performing as expected but there is seldom any large-scale examination of a test in its new cultural environment.

This would seem a serious problem, given that we have made much in this chapter about using the correct norms for interpreting test results, and, indeed commentaries appear in the professional literature (eg, McKenzie, 1980) from time to time criticising the use in Australia of psychological tests with American norms. The reason should be obvious from this chapter; but to give a concrete example, consider the situation in which the Australian mean on, say, a test of intelligence is in fact higher than that of the mean for the American population. In these circumstances, a score for an individual on the test could be below the Australian mean but still above the American mean. The probability of this occurring increases as the distance between the Australian and American means increases. Consider now that an individual with a score sufficiently below the mean is eligible for some special form of intervention, eg, remedial education, and that failure to receive it is to their disadvantage. If the American norms are used in this situation, the person's score will be interpreted as being above the mean, whereas if Australian norms were to be used it could well be that their score may be sufficiently below the mean to warrant their access to the special program. In this situation, testing with the American norms has done the individual a disservice.

How likely is this scenario to occur? There are some data that point to Australian means on tests like the Wechsler differing from those reported in the American standardisation samples (see Holdnack, Lissner, Bowden, & McCarthy, 2004). As Holdnack et al point out, however, the Australian samples on which these observations are based are typically small, and unrepresentative in terms of the sampling design used for their collection. Where large samples with better claims to representativeness are employed (Howe, 1975), the means for Australian samples are on most factors of cognitive ability close to those reported for large American samples. Given the similarities in language and media exposure of the Australian and American populations, to find otherwise would be surprising. This is not, however, an argument for complacency. Where differences exist between cultures, in for example, educational practices, there may be reason to expect differences in means between American and Australian samples or some characteristics.

In the light of this discussion, we suggest the following rules of thumb:

1   Check the source of the norms for any test that one is using or evaluating the results from.
2   Ask whether the norms are relevant to the situation in which the test is being used or to which results might be generalised.
3   If there is concern about their relevance in terms of country of origin, ask what is known about the susceptibility of the measure to cultural differences.
4   Consider how the test result is being used. Is it being used with reference to a cutting score for describing the individual or determining a course of action with respect to the individual, and is it the primary or only basis for this?
5   Ask whether it is possible to check the result in some way using another test for which norms are available or by reference to non-test information, but beware small and unrepresentative samples.
6   Explain in any report the basis for the description or recommended action in terms of the norms employed, and any qualifications that should in prudence be considered.

Selecting an appropriate reference group (or groups) is the primary decision but once made there is a need to ensure that the mean and standard deviation that are determined for the group are accurate. Accuracy depends on two principal considerations: the manner in which the sample is drawn from the population in question and the size of the sample.

Sampling is a technically complex matter. A distinction is usually made between systematic and non-systematic methods of sampling from a population. The former allow estimates of error in sampling to be made, whereas for the latter there is no way to determine how much error is involved in the estimates that are derived from the sample obtained. For this reason, systematic methods are to be preferred.

Non-systematic methods include accidental or convenience sampling. In these cases, a sample is gathered in a way that is easy or convenient to do. For example, the test developer might stop individuals in a shopping mall and ask them to participate. There is no way of knowing how representative such a sample is or even what population it may be a sample from (people who frequent shopping malls, possibly).

Systematic methods involve drawing members from a defined population in a way that ensures representativeness. Random sampling is a case in point. Here members are drawn from the population but in such a way that every member of the population has an equal opportunity of being selected and the drawing of one member does not influence in any way the likelihood of any other member being selected. This is a stringent pair of requirements that is difficult to meet in practice, and for that reason systematic methods other than random sampling are typically used.

Wechsler (1955), for example, in norming his intelligence test devised a stratified sampling plan in which major demographic factors that might relate to intelligence (eg, education level, geographic region of residence) were first determined, then the percentage of the population falling into the various categories formed on the basis of these factors found from the United States census, and finally a sample gathered that matched faithfully these percentages. This was an ambitious attempt to draw a sample that carefully matched the population in terms of possible influences on the construct being measured. Not all norms are designed as well as these, largely because of the considerable cost involved.

A further consideration in developing norms is the size of the sample that is employed. Size is important because the requirement is to estimate the mean and standard deviation with precision and sample size has a potent influence on the standard errors of these statistics. In the case of estimating the mean, the standard error is proportional to the standard deviation of the distribution divided by the square root of the sample size:

$$SE = \frac{SD}{\sqrt{N}}$$

As sample size increases, the denominator becomes larger and the standard error smaller. Note, however, that the effect is not a linear one: doubling sample size does not half the standard error (double the precision). It is not sample size but the square root of sample size that is the denominator. Thus, to halve the sampling error one must increase the sample size by a factor of 8. What this means in practice is that, beyond a certain point, increasing the sample size will have little discernible effect on the standard error. On the basis of these considerations, Bartram and Lindley (1994) proposed the rules of thumb outline in Table 3.5 for evaluating samples for norming purposes.

TABLE 3.5 Bartram and Lindley's recommendations for sample sizes for purposes of test norming

Sample Size	Evaluation
Under 200	Inadequate
200–500	Adequate
500–1000	Reasonable
1000–2000	Good
2000+	Excellent

With these considerations in mind how well do some of the major psychological tests fare in terms of the norms they provide? Table 3.6 provides a brief summary. As inspection of the table indicates, the critic will find fault with even some of the best of tests currently available.

TABLE 3.6 Some examples of sampling methods and sample sizes for widely used psychological tests

Test	Sampling Method	Sample Size
WAIS-III	Stratified: gender, race, age, education	2450
MMPI-2	Convenience (7 US States)	2600
16PF	Stratified: gender, race, age, education	2500

One other consideration needs to be borne in mind in the use of norms for tests of general mental ability, and that is the age of the norms being used. The raw score mean on many of the commonly used tests of intelligence has been rising for at least the previous half century for reasons that are not well understood at present. This increase has been named the Flynn effect after the researcher who first observed it. What it means is that when a new or recently re-normed test is used to retest a person whose score has been previously determined, it may appear that the person's intelligence level is lower than it was. For example, testing with the WISC-III indicates on average a 5-point drop in IQ compared to initial testing with the WISC-R, because the norming process for the WISC-III, the more recent test, has adjusted for the upward trend in intelligence over time (Kanaya, Scullin, & Ceci, 2003). In view of the Flynn effect, the test user needs to be particularly vigilant in assessing what is and what is not a substantial change in IQ from one testing occasion to the next. If different tests with different norms are involved, the test user needs to allow for the Flynn effect in any inferences that are drawn from an apparent change in IQ.

CONCLUDING REMARKS

Test scores must be interpreted, either by direct reference to the behaviour they reflect (criterion referencing) or by reference to the performance of other individuals with whom a comparison is appropriate (norm referencing). In the case of the latter, test scores are transformed linearly (eg, the standard score) or nonlinearly (eg, percentiles) to aid in interpretation. There are important differences between these two sorts of transformations that need to be borne in mind, but when the distribution of scores is normal or nearly so, one form of transformation can be expressed in terms of the other.

Questions for consideration

1   Define: raw score, scaled score, standard score, standardised score, and percentile.
2   What are norms? Why are they needed for psychological testing?
3   What are the characteristics of a good sample for a psychological test?
4   Compare and contrast z score and percentile.
5   Find out the sample size used in norming the Wechsler Memory Scale, Wechsler Memory Scale – Revised, and Wechsler Memory Scale – Third Edition and evaluate them according to Bartram & Lindley's recommendation.

Exercises

1   For the following set of raw scores:

52   54   56   58   60   61   61   63   67   68

express each score as a z score, and then transform each to a score in a distribution with a mean of 100 and an SD of 15.

2   Assume that a large Grade 10 class took achievement tests known to be highly reliable and valid in the areas of Geography, Spelling, and Mathematics. The scores on all three of these tests were normally distributed, but the tests differed in the following respects:

	No. of Items	Mean	SD
Geography	75	60	10
Spelling	150	100	20
Mathematics	40	25	5

Assume that you are particularly interested in comparing the performance of three of the students who took these tests (David, John, and Brett).

First, you are interested in how each student has performed across the three tests, which is his best performance and which is his worst. Second, you are interested in comparing students in terms of their performance on each test. Third, you want to identify the student who performed best across all areas.

The students' scores are as follows:

	David	John	Brett
Geography	46	72	60
Spelling	110	100	97
Mathematics	30	33	37

a   Prepare a table showing the percentage correct scores for each student on each test. Note, however, that because the percentage correct scores on each test come from different distributions, they cannot be justifiably averaged across tests or otherwise compared.

b Prepare a table showing linearly derived z scores for David, John, and Brett. Note that although z scores can be averaged, the presence of decimals and negative values will make it more difficult to do so than it would otherwise be.

c Using the Table of Areas under the Normal Curve, determine the percentile equivalents for each z score.

d Convert each of the z scores into T scores (mean = 50, SD = 10) and prepare a table showing them and showing the average T score for each student. The initial goal of obtaining scores that are intra- and inter-individually comparable will have been achieved most suitably with this final step.

3 Assume that 100 students took a test and that the test scores were normally distributed with a mean of 20 and a SD of 2.

a What are the z scores for the following raw scores?

16   18   19   20   21   22   24

b Using the Table of Areas under the Normal Curve, with the z scores you have just obtained, determine the percentage of the scores that fall between the following raw score ranges:

18 and 22   19 and 21   16 and 24

4 The percentile of a score with a z score of 1.0 is _____
The z score of a score at the 98th percentile is _____
The T score for a score with a z score of 2.0 is _____

5 Given that a test has a mean of 30 and an SD of 10, complete the following table.

Raw Score	z Score	Percentile
40	…	…
…	0.5	…
…	…	75

Further reading

Crocker, L, & Algina, J (1986). *Introduction to classical and modern test theory*. New York: Holt, Rinehart and Winston.

Kline, P (1998). *The new psychometrics: Science, psychology and measurement*. London: Routledge.

Nunnally, J, & Bernstein, I H (1994). *Psychometric theory* (3rd edn). New York: McGraw Hill.

Rust, J, & Golombok, S (1999). *Modern psychometrics: The science of psychological assessment* (2nd ed). London: Routledge.

Wasserman, J D, & Bracken, B A (2003). Psychometric characteristics of assessment procedures. In J R Graham, & J A Naglieri (Eds), *Handbook of Psychology: Vol 10, Assessment Psychology* (pp 43–66). Hoboken, NJ: John Wiley & Sons.

chapter four

Reliability

> A young man who has suffered a motor cycle accident is experiencing some memory loss and those managing his recovery want to track the severity of this problem using standard memory tests as he rehabilitates.

> In a compensation case, evidence is presented that the litigant has shown a deterioration in scores on measures of planning ability from before to after the accident that is the source of the claim. The legal counsel for the insurance company asks for evidence that not only have the scores changed but that the change is greater than that to be expected if the accident had not intervened.

> A psychologist notes that there is a discrepancy between a client's scores on measures of verbal and spatial ability taken from the same test of general mental ability and wonders whether the difference should be taken seriously.

> Two tests are being considered for use in a situation where decisions will have a substantial impact on what happens to those involved. Although the tests, on the data available, appear similar in many of their features, one is much shorter than the other and is being favoured for use for this reason.

INTRODUCTION

Psychological tests are used in a number of different situations and we need to know in any situation how appropriate use of the test is. Answering this general question involves consideration of a number of issues and this chapter begins an examination of these. Chapter 5 will take the exploration further, but for the present we focus on the reliability of psychological tests for use for particular purposes. Note we talk of the reliability of a test for a particular purpose and not of the reliability of a test in general, because the latter is not correct although we might find ourselves saying that for economy of expression. Reliability, as with validity, which we take up in the following chapter, is not a property of a test itself but a property of a test as used in a particular situation.

In this chapter we discuss the meaning of the concept of reliability, how it is expressed in particular situations, how it can be estimated, and how it can be applied in considering the appropriateness of a test when used in a particular way.

THE MEANING OF RELIABILITY

The word reliability has as its ordinary meaning, dependability. To say that a person or a car is reliable is to say that they can be depended on. The person will be true to their word; the car will run and not let you down. The term reliability in psychometrics has much the same meaning. To ask about the reliability of a psychological test score is to ask about how much it can be depended on. When, for example, an intelligence test yields a score for a person that indicates their mental ability to be well above average, how much confidence can we have in this finding? Because of the importance of reliability, theorists and researchers have paid a good deal of attention to working out how the reliability of a test can be determined. The important ideas that have emerged from this century-old exercise are the subject of this chapter.

Tests, like cars, can be unreliable for two sorts of reasons. Imagine one of the tyres on your car deflates over the course of the day. The first time this happens you cannot use the car when you want to. But once you have become aware of the problem you can deal with it by building time into your schedule to pump the tyre up each day. Alternatively, your battery may gradually lose its charge but again, once you know, you can arrange to have it recharged during the evening so that the car is drivable when you want it in the morning. These defects make the car unreliable but they are predictable, regular, or systematic, once you become aware of them. Compare this with, say, a problem in the electrical system of the car that is difficult to trace and intermittent in its effects. The car is rendered inoperable at various times over which you have no control. This is an unsystematic source of unreliability.

So too, psychological tests have both systematic and unsystematic sources of unreliability. Unlike cars, however, the systematic sources of unreliability in a test may be hard to detect unless a lot is known about it. The test may appear to be functioning well but it is not really testing what you want it to be testing. You may think, for example, that your test is one of 'anxiousness' but what it is really testing is a mixture of anxiousness and the desire of the test taker to present himself or herself in a favourable light to the tester, social desirability bias as it is called. The test is systematically wrong in the assessment of anxiousness because of the confounding with social desirability. This problem is taken up again in Chapter 5 when we examine threats to the validity of tests. The major concern of the present chapter is with the unsystematic sources of unreliability in tests.

THE DOMAIN-SAMPLING MODEL

One of the earliest ways of thinking about the problem, and one that is still of considerable value, is founded on the idea that a psychological test is a sample of responses or behaviours from a much wider population of responses (Nunnally, 1967). For various reasons, not the least of which is practicality, an assessor interested in an individual's status on some trait or condition can only ask a limited number of questions or present a limited set of tasks. The test or assessment device thus draws from a larger possible set of items to give a score for the person on the trait or condition. It is recognised that, because the sample is limited, the score obtained is an estimate of the person's actual or true position on the trait rather than a direct expression of that position. If all possible questions had been asked we would have the true position, but we have in fact a sample of questions and hence an estimate that is likely to be in error. How good an estimate do we have? That is, how close is the score obtained from the sample to the score that would have been obtained if all possible questions had been asked?

Put this way, the question of test reliability becomes a problem of sampling, but not one of sampling people from a specified population but items from a domain of possible items. The 'domain-sampling' model, as it is called (Nunnally, 1967), is one important way of thinking about the question of reliability. In applying it, we can think of the score a person receives on a test as one of the scores that would be obtained if samples of the items were put to the person repeatedly. That is, imagine drawing a finite set of items, say 20, from the domain of all possible items that might be asked, and presenting them to the test taker. Once those have been completed, you draw another sample of 20 items and administer those, and then another 20, and so on. The patience of the test taker is not infinite and this is an illustration of what is implied by the model rather than the beginning of a real study. The scores obtained from each of those 20 item tests would not be the same; there would be some variation due to sampling. The mean of the scores from all possible samples would tell us, however, the true position of the person on the trait in question, the person's 'true score' as it is called in classical test score theory. The standard deviation of the distribution of scores from all possible samples about the true score would tell us about the likelihood of obtaining any particular sample score. It is referred to as the standard error of measurement and indicates the precision of our estimate of the true score.

The situation is hypothetical but serves to illustrate the essential idea. In practice, we have only samples and the true score eludes us, but we can use what we know from the sample to make estimates of the likely true score for an individual and the interval in which it lies, with a stated degree of confidence. If the interval is very large, clearly we have a great deal of imprecision in the measurement process and we cannot depend on any score we obtain with this sample of items. The value of thinking about the problem in this way is that it leads to two quantitative indexes of reliability that allow us to be more precise than verbal labels allow. To say that a test is 'not very reliable' or has 'satisfactory reliability' is to make a statement that is open to misinterpretation. Quantitative indexes, when their meaning is understood, provide for a more precise form of communication.

One of the indexes we have encountered already, namely, the standard error of measurement (SEM). The other is the reliability coefficient (r). They are intimately related but serve slightly different purposes in practice. Their actual mathematical derivation is beyond the scope of this chapter but the interested reader is referred to Nunnally (1967) for a statistical treatment of domain-sampling theory and its implications. The relationship between the two indexes is:

$$SEM = \sqrt{(1-r)}$$

for scores expressed as standard normal deviates (z scores). For ordinary scores we simply multiply the right hand side of the equation by the standard deviation of the obtained score distribution. We leave it in deviation score form for the present to illustrate the essential relationship.

The fact that drawing samples repeatedly from a domain gives rise to variation in obtained scores can be understood in terms of the mixture of true score and error score variability that makes up the observed score. When this variability is defined in a particular way (as variance, ie, the sum of the squared deviation of each score from the mean of the scores), we can say that the observed score variance is equal to true score plus error score variance. (We are assuming here that there is no relation between true and error components of the observed score.) How much true score variance makes up the observed score variance is of course of considerable interest to us. If it constituted the whole, our measure would give us the true score we ideally want to know and we could claim it was perfectly reliable. We can define the reliability coefficient then as the proportion of observed score variance that is due to true score variance. In practice the proportion will be less than 1.0 and in some cases a good deal less. If the proportion is only 0.5 (ie, r = 0.5), 50 per cent of the variance in the scores obtained with the test is due to variance in true scores and the other 50 per cent to errors of measurement. For some, 0.5 would be a minimal level of reliability, beyond which point the test is reflecting more of what we are not interested in than what we are.

If we return to the formula above, we see that, in the unlikely situation that r = 1.0 (perfect reliability), the SEM is zero; that is, there is no error in estimating the true score. If, on the other hand, the proportion of true score variance is zero (r = 0) then the SEM = 1, which is the standard deviation for a standard normal distribution. That is, our obtained score gives us no more information about the true score than any other score we might have obtained at random.

In practice the two indexes have different applications. The reliability coefficient is, in general terms, used in forming judgments about the overall value of a particular test (eg, is this a better test for some given purpose than another test?), whereas the standard error of measurement is used in making judgments about individual scores obtained with the test (eg, how much error might be associated with this score as an estimate of the trait in question?). The reliability coefficient is determined from data obtained with the test and the standard error is then calculated using the above formula.

CALCULATING RELIABILITY COEFFICIENTS

The reliability coefficient is determined in three main ways. The oldest is in terms of the correlation between equivalent forms of the test. Knowing that the problem of reliability has to be faced at some stage, the test developer from the outset devises two tests rather than one, ie, draws two samples from the domain of possible test items. The two forms will have the practical benefit of minimising practice effects if, subsequently, a person is to be tested on two separate occasions, because one form can be used on the first occasion and the equivalent form on the second. For present purposes, however, the existence of equivalent forms allows the test developer to examine how well two samples of items from the same domain agree in the scores they yield. This is a far cry from all possible samples but it is a good beginning. If the two samples do not yield comparable scores, the test, or at least one form of it (although we do not know which one), cannot be depended on.

The product moment correlation between scores on equivalent forms of the test for a reasonably large sample of test takers gives an estimate of the reliability coefficient. If equivalent forms of a test are not available, the reliability can be calculated by splitting the test into two equivalent forms. For example, all the even numbered items are used for one form and all the odd numbered items for the other. By correlating the scores obtained on the two halves for a sample of test takers of reasonable size, one again obtains an estimate of reliability. This is called the split-half reliability. The coefficient is usually corrected for the fact that, when the test is used as a whole, it is twice as long as either of the two halves and larger samples are better estimates of a population mean than smaller samples. (In the limiting case, when the sample is the same size as the population, its mean is the population value.) The formula for estimating the reliability of a test that is longer than the original test by some factor is given by a formula named after the two people who derived it independently of each other, Spearman and Brown. The Spearman-Brown formula is sometimes termed the Spearman-Brown prophecy formula because it purports to tell us about an otherwise unknown state of affairs. The formula is given later in this chapter.

How to split the test into two to determine its split-half reliability is something of a problem. The odd-even method is a practical solution that at least ensures that any factors that may influence scores late in the test (eg, fatigue) have an equal influence on both halves. Even with this proviso, however, when speeded tests are being examined (those that must be completed within a time limit), this method of estimating reliability is not recommended. But the odd-even method is arbitrary and different reliability estimates can result from the one test split in different ways. In terms of the domain-sampling model, this outcome is not at all surprising because each sample provides only an estimate and estimates are likely to vary.

Cronbach (1951) suggested one way around the problem. He proposed that the test be split into subtests each one item in length. That is, think of the test as made up of k tests, where k is the number of items in the test. All subtests are then correlated with all other subtests and the average correlation calculated. This average correlation becomes the estimate of reliability. This method is often described as determining the internal consistency of a test. The formula for calculating it is simple (see Box 4.1) and is referred to as Cronbach's alpha. It is the same as a formula, arrived at in a somewhat different way, by Kuder and Richardson and known after them as the KR20 formula (Kuder & Richardson, 1937). Because Cronbach's alpha is so easy to calculate, with major software suites providing a program for it, it is frequently calculated in determining reliability. It does, however, have its limitations. A test can be developed to have a high internal consistency by having items with highly similar content. Although faithfully sampling a domain, the domain itself may be so constricted as to be trivial. On the other hand, high internal consistency does not of itself guarantee that the items are all reflecting the one thing. What is being measured by a test with high internal consistency needs further investigation, which is the problem of validity to be discussed in the next chapter. High internal consistency is an important attribute in a psychological test but it is not of itself a 'seal of approval'.

BOX 4.1

Cronbach's alpha

Assume a 5-item true/false test has been administered to 10 participants, who have responded as shown in the first table below. 1 indicates a 'true' response and 0 indicates a 'false' response.

   The data are artificial but serve to illustrate a point. Note from the table that all items are consistent in the responses they elicit across participants. For half the sample, all items elicit a 'true' response and for the other half a 'false' response. Knowing how an individual has responded to one of the items we know how they have responded to all other items. Cronbach's alpha is calculated using the standard formula. It requires that we know the number of items in the test (5 in this case), the items' variances, and the variance of total score on the test. The variance of a dichotomously scored item is simply the product of the proportion of individuals (p) who answer in one way (say, True) and the proportion who answer in the opposition direction $(1 - p)$. The variances are shown for each item. The variance of total score on the test is calculated in the usual way for calculating the variance for a sample (not the population estimate that uses $N - 1$). It is shown as the average of the squares of the deviations of each total score from the mean of the total scores.

   When the formula is applied to the calculated values, alpha is shown to be 1. That is, the test shows perfect internal consistency, which is not surprising as it was designed with this in mind. Consider now what happens to alpha if just one of the items does not allow prediction of response to the other items. In the second table, the response pattern for Item 2 has been altered to create this situation, and the necessary values recalculated. Item variances remain the same as in the first table (although with a different pattern for Item 2 its variance could have changed) but the variance of total score on the test has altered. The result is that alpha is less than 1; the test is no longer perfectly internally consistent. As greater discrepancies occur across items, alpha falls.

TABLE 1 Calculating Cronbach's Alpha for a 5-item test

Person	Item 1	2	3	4	5	Total Score	(x–M)	(x–M)²
1	1	1	1	1	1	5	2.5	6.25
2	1	1	1	1	1	5	2.5	6.25
3	1	1	1	1	1	5	2.5	6.25
4	1	1	1	1	1	5	2.5	6.25
5	1	1	1	1	1	5	2.5	6.25
6	0	0	0	0	0	0	–2.5	6.25
7	0	0	0	0	0	0	–2.5	6.25
8	0	0	0	0	0	0	–2.5	6.25
9	0	0	0	0	0	0	–2.5	6.25
10	0	0	0	0	0	0	–2.5	6.25
Sum								62.5
Mean	0.5	0.5	0.5	0.5	0.5	2.5		
Variance	0.25	0.25	0.25	0.25	0.25			6.25

Alpha is then given by the following formula:

$$\alpha = \left(\frac{k}{k-1} \right)\left(1 - \frac{\sum \sigma i^2}{\sigma t^2} \right)$$

where:

α is coefficient alpha

k is the number of items in the test

σ_i^2 is the variance of an item

σ_t^2 is the variance of total score on the test

In this example,

$$\alpha = \left(\frac{5}{5-1} \right)\left(1 - \frac{1.25}{6.25} \right)$$

$$= 1.25 \times (1 - 0.2)$$

$$= 1$$

TABLE 2 Calculating Cronbach's Alpha for another 5-item test

Person	Item 1	Item 2	Item 3	Item 4	Item 5	Total Score	(x–M)	(x–M)²
1	1	1	1	1	1	5	2.5	6.25
2	1	0	1	1	1	4	1.5	2.25
3	1	1	1	1	1	5	2.5	6.25
4	1	0	1	1	1	4	1.5	2.25
5	1	1	1	1	1	5	2.5	6.25
6	0	0	0	0	0	0	–2.5	6.25
7	0	1	0	0	0	1	–1.5	2.25
8	0	0	0	0	0	0	–2.5	6.25
9	0	1	0	0	0	1	–1.5	2.25
10	0	0	0	0	0	0	–2.5	6.25
Sum								46.5
Mean	0.5	0.5	0.5	0.5	0.5	2.5		
Variance	0.25	0.25	0.25	0.25	0.25			4.65

Alpha is then given by the following formula:

$$\alpha = \left(\frac{k}{k-1} \right)\left(1 - \frac{\sum \sigma i^2}{\sigma t^2} \right)$$

where:

α is coefficient alpha

k   is the number of items in the test

σ_i^2 is the variance of an item

σ_t^2 is the variance of total score on the test

In this example,

$$\alpha = \left(\frac{5}{5-1} \right)\left(1 - \frac{1.25}{4.65} \right)$$

$$= 1.25 \times (1 - 0.27)$$

$$= 0.91$$

It needs to be pointed out again that the statements being made about reliability and standard error are for the test when used in a particular way. A test, once constructed, is not reliable in all situations in which it may be used. The variance of observed scores on the test is likely to differ depending on the particular sample of individuals we choose to study, and we cannot assume that the reliability will remain constant across different samples. Studying creativity in a group of people purposely selected because they are high in intelligence means that variability in creativity is likely reduced compared to what it was when the creativity test was developed in an unrestricted sample from the population. Artificially restricting the range of scores on creativity means that reliability will need to be calculated again. It is better to think of the reliability coefficient and the SEM as applying to a test when applied to a particular type of sample and not as a property of the test itself. This may seem a highly conditional way of speaking, but it is more accurate and makes us pay particular attention to the circumstances under which the claim of reliability is being made.

EXTENDING THE DOMAIN-SAMPLING MODEL

Thus far we have talked about the domain-sampling model of reliability and the ways this leads us to assess reliability. Although very important, it is not the last word on reliability and some other ideas about it need to be understood.

The first is that reliability can be thought of in relation to the time of testing. Having determined a score today, how likely is it that the same score would be obtained by the test taker if the test were administered tomorrow, or next week, or in a month, or 12 months time? Test-retest reliability is a long-standing way researchers have sought to evaluate reliability because its meaning is intuitively obvious. If the characteristic we are attempting to measure is in fact likely to be stable over time (mental ability is likely to be; mood is not because by definition it varies from day to day or even within the same day), then scores obtained on two different occasions should correlate highly, and reliability is assessed by the product moment correlation between test scores on two occasions. To the extent that the two sets of scores do not correlate, the test lacks reliability.

Note that, in this case, the sample of items employed is the same on the two occasions and hence there has not been sampling from a domain of items as required by the domain-sampling model. There has been, however, a sampling from a domain of occasions, in that the choice of tomorrow, or next week, or 12 months as the second occasion for testing is arbitrary. There would be the same interest in the outcome if the second occasion were, for example, one week and one day as if it were one week. Occasions are sampled from a wider possible set of occasions. But this is not what domain-sampling theory is about. Cronbach proposed that the original theory be extended to include not just items but occasions, in what he termed generalisability theory (Cronbach, Gleser, Nanda & Rajaratnam, 1972). In obtaining a score on a test, the user, according to Cronbach and colleagues, seeks to generalise beyond the particular score to some wider universe of behaviour. Generalisability theory asks the user to specify what generalisation they are seeking to make and then ask whether there are data that support such a generalisation. The detail of the theory is challenging and the ways that it is implemented in practice require a good understanding of the statistical technique of analysis of variance, but the essential idea that extends domain-sampling theory is a valuable addition to our perspective of what reliability of measurement is about.

Its value can be shown when we extend our thinking about reliability to include cases in which human judgment is the basic assessment tool, for example, a diagnosis of a psychiatric condition or the rating of a person on some characteristic (eg, leadership ability). Here the question of reliability arises in terms of whether or not a different judge of similar expertise would make the same diagnosis or rating. In this case, correlating scores across judges provides a means of estimating reliability. Reliable judgments are those that involve high inter-rater agreement. The contingency coefficient, a version of the product moment correlation when applied to categorical data, is one index of reliability in these circumstances. Another is kappa (see eg, Howell, 2002).

In terms of Cronbach's generalisability theory, the problem of estimating reliability is now one of generalising over judges rather than over occasions or items. The logic remains: what grounds do we have for generalising from this particular sample, the judgment of one individual, to the wider universe in which we are interested, for example, the judgment of psychiatrists in general when presented with this patient or the judgment of leadership experts in general when observing this individual's leadership behaviour. The particular statistical techniques used to assess reliability in any particular instance should not hide the fact that the question being asked is basically the same.

Put in this wider context of generalisability, a question that sometimes is asked about reliability is shown not to be a good way of thinking about the issue. The question is: Given all these various ways of indexing reliability, which is the correct way? The answer depends on the generalisation, in Cronbach's terms, that you wish to make. Often the interest is in generalising to a domain of items, not all of which it is practically possible to administer. In this case, the methods first discussed (equivalent forms, split-half, internal consistency) are the appropriate ones. But for some purposes the question of generalising over occasions of testing may be quite important and reliability needs to be assessed in terms of some version of the test-retest procedure. Consider, for example, a patient who has suffered a head injury that has produced some cognitive deficits. Those responsible for the care and management of the patient need to know whether these cognitive deficits are getting worse, remaining the same, or perhaps improving as the result of the passage of time or some remedial intervention. In this situation, test-retest reliability of the measure being used is a prime concern. If a test is known to have scores that drift over time, then it is of little use for this type of assessment.

SOME SPECIAL ISSUES

How reliable does a test need to be? Again this is not a good question, because it depends on the circumstances in which the test is being used. If the result of the test has serious consequences for an individual, then a very high level of reliability is required. If, however, the test is in the process of being developed, then one might be content to persevere with a much lower level of reliability, expecting that in time one may be able to improve the low figure obtained. Nunnally (1967) gave the following rule of thumb for assessing reliability: 0.5 or better for test development; 0.7 or better for using a test in research; better than 0.9 for use in individual assessment. Like all rules of thumb this one needs to be treated cautiously, as Pedhazur and Schmelkin (1991) cogently argue.

How good are the reliabilities of tests in use? The best answer to this question can be found by checking the manual that comes with each commercially produced psychological test or diagnostic procedure, because reliabilities vary considerably. Some conclusions are, however, possible. Tests of cognitive abilities have the highest reliabilities followed by self-report tests of personality. Jensen (1980) reviewed the reliabilities of widely used individual and group tests of general mental ability and reported that the Stanford–Binet showed a median alternate forms reliability over 21 samples of 0.91. The Wechsler tests, which cover the age span 4 to 74 years show reliabilities for Full Scale IQ of from 0.95 to 0.97. For 30 individual tests of general mental ability the average reliability reported by Jensen was 0.9. At the other end of the scale are projective measures of personality. Entwisle (1972) summarised findings on the reliability of measures of achievement motivation based on the Thematic Apperception Test, which has been used extensively in research although seldom for decision making in the individual case. Her review indicated that test–retest reliability over periods of one to two months was no better than 0.26, split–half reliability about 0.27, and equivalent forms at best 0.48 and in some cases as low as 0.29. Some advocates of projective techniques (eg, Atkinson, Bongort & Price, 1977; Winter & Stewart, 1977), it should be noted, would dispute the application of psychometrics to an evaluation of these techniques. The reliabilities of self-report tests are closer to those of cognitive tests, of the order of 0.75 to 0.85 for commercially produced tests (Fiske, 1966).

What are the implications of differing levels of reliability across different tests? One is in terms of assessment of the individual case. Consideration of the standard error of measurement helps to make the point. Suppose we have an individual's IQ result of 105 and wonder whether this means that the person is of at least average intelligence. If the test has a reliability of 0.9, the SEM is 0.31 and if it is 0.7 the SEM is 0.54 (for raw scores expressed as standard scores; to express the SEM in raw score form we simply multiply the standard scores by the standard deviation of the raw score distribution). That is, the interval within which the individual's true score lies is almost twice that at the lower reliability. If the raw score standard deviation is, say, 15 for both tests this means that for one test the true score is likely to lie within the range 105 ± 5 on 68 occasions in 100 on which we check it, whereas for the other the range is 105 ± 8. We can have more confidence with the first test than with the second that the person's IQ is at least 100, although both test scores involve error. Note that a more accurate assessment would involve calculating the predicted true score and setting the confidence intervals about it rather than about the obtained score because the error is about the true score. For most practical purposes there will be little substantive difference in the judgments made, unless the test has a very low level of reliability.

A second reason for being concerned about varying reliabilities among tests is that the reliability of a test affects the magnitude of the intercorrelation of the test with any other variable. The logic of this is straightforward. Thought of in terms of equivalent forms reliability, an unreliable test is one that does not correlate with itself. How then can it be expected to correlate with anything else? The effect can be made explicit in terms of the following formula:

$$r_{xy} = \sqrt{r_{xx} \times r_{yy}}$$

where r_{xy} is the intercorrelation between tests x and y, and r_{xx} and r_{yy} are the reliabilities of the two tests.

Although the theoretical maximum correlation coefficient is 1.0, as the reliability of one test, or both, the maximum possible correlation falls too. With low reliabilities we may conclude that two variables are unrelated when in fact the magnitude of the correlation has been attenuated by poor measurement of one or other of the variables.

Can reliabilities be improved if found wanting in any particular case? The answer here depends on the nature of the reliability being considered and practical constraints on what is possible in any particular situation. Where one is sampling from a domain of items, reliability can often be improved by extending the sample, that is lengthening the test. The Spearman–Brown formula referred to earlier can be used to give an indication of the number of items that need to be added to a test to bring its reliability from a given level to some desired level.

$$k = \frac{r_{yy}(1 - r_{xx})}{r_{xx}(1 - r_{yy})}$$

Where k is the factor by which the test has to be lengthened to take the reliability from its current level (r_{xx}) to the desired level (r_{yy}) (Allen & Yen, 1979). The formula makes important assumptions about the nature of the items being added (eg, that the interrelationships among them duplicate those of the original set of items), which in practice are not always easily achieved. Brief reflection on the formula will show that the relationship between increasing the number of items and changes in reliability is not linear; doubling the number of items for example does not double the reliability.

CONCLUDING REMARKS

Reliability is an important property of a test or any assessment device because it allows the user to generalise from the score obtained to some wider domain of interest. It is estimated in a number of ways depending on the generalisation one is interested in making, but usually results in an estimate in the form of a correlation coefficient or a standard error of measurement. The former indicates the proportion of variance in the measure that is dependable and the latter allows the user to set a confidence interval on an obtained score to specify the range within which the test taker's true score is likely to lie at the given level of confidence.

Questions for consideration

1   Define reliability. Why is it an important concept for psychological testing?
2   Compare and contrast systematic and unsystematic sources of unreliability and give some possible reasons for each.
3   Name the different types of reliability and briefly explain how they can be calculated.
4   Compare and contrast SEM and Cronbach's alpha.
5   Compare the test–retest reliability and SEM of the WAIS-III and Stanford-Binet 4.
6   A study indicates that the variance due to stable individual differences in a test is 0.36 and that the variance due to other random sources is 0.14. What is the reliability of the test?
7   What is the best estimate of the average intercorrelation of the items of a test?

Exercises

1   A psychological test has 16 items. The mean and SD for each are as follows: 0.13, 0.33; 0.11, 0.32; 0.11, 0.37; 0.06, 0.24; 0.21, 0.41; 0.08, 0.28; 0.08, 0.27; 0.19, 0.39; 0.11, 0.31; 0.23, 0.42; 0.01, 0.12; 0.10, 0.30; 0.15, 0.36; 0.01, 0.13; 0.11, 0.31; 0.01, 0.09.

   Mean score on the test was 2.0 with a standard deviation of 1.91. What is the coefficient alpha for the test?

2   The standard error of measurement (SEM) of a psychological test score, as its name suggests, is an index of measurement error. It tells us something about the reliability/accuracy of scores obtained by that test. The scores of a test are more reliable/accurate if the SEM of that test is small (small error, more accurate).

   This statistic can be calculated if we know the reliability coefficient and standard deviation of a test.

   The following table summarises the reliability coefficients and standard deviations of four psychological tests.

Test	Reliability Coefficient	Standard Deviation	SEM
A	0.85	15	
B	0.85	5	
C	0.55	15	
D	0.55	5	

   a   Before calculating the SEMs for the above four tests, try to guess which one of these tests has the most reliable/accurate test scores.
   b   Use the following formula to calculate the SEMs and see if your guess is correct:

$$SEM = SD\sqrt{1-r}$$

   Hint: There is a trick in this question. Think very carefully about it.

c   Sometimes psychologists want to know if the score on one subtest is significantly higher/lower than the score on another subtest. To do so, one needs to calculate the *standard error of the difference* between two scores. The equation for this statistics is as follows:

$$SE_{diff} = \sqrt{(SEM_1)^2 + (SEM_2)^2}$$

Looking at this equation, do you think the SE_{diff} is larger or smaller than the SEM of the two subtests?

3   Entry to the University of Old England requires a score of at least 115 on the Australian version of the Scholastic Aptitude Test (ASAT). The ASAT has been found to have a standard deviation of 15 and reliability of 0.90 using an applicant sample.
a   How would you interpret the reliability of this test?
b   Would you admit a person with a score of 112 on the test?

Further reading

Crocker, L, & Algina, J (1986). *Introduction to classical and modern test theory*. New York: Holt, Rinehart and Winston.

Kline, P (1998). *The new psychometrics: Science, psychology, and measurement*. London: Routledge.

Nunnally, J, & Bernstein, I H (1994). *Psychometric theory* (3rd edn). New York: McGraw Hill.

Rust, J, & Golombok, S (1999). *Modern psychometrics: The science of psychological assessment* (2nd edn). London: Routledge.

Wasserman, J D, & Bracken, B A (2003). Psychometric characteristics of assessment procedures. In J R Graham, & J A Naglieri (Eds), *Handbook of Psychology: Vol 10, Assessment Psychology* (pp 43–66). Hoboken, NJ: John Wiley & Sons.

chapter five

Validity

- A counsellor who specialises in vocational assessment is interested in knowing how well a test of aptitude for computer programming predicts results in a technical college course in programming in Visual Basic.

- A group working with young boys asks if there is any relationship between the score on a test of 'delinquency proneness' and the likelihood of coming to the attention of the criminal justice system.

- A personnel manager has introduced a selection test for those working in clerical positions in his organisation and is interested in knowing whether decision making about whom to employ in these positions has improved as a result.

- A psychologist is surprised to find that a test that is reported in the literature as highly valid does not seem to be useful in the hospital in which she is working.

- A journalist is planning to write a magazine article about a new measure of 'ecological intelligence' but has cold water poured on the idea by a psychologist friend who questions whether there is any evidence to show that 'ecological intelligence' is any different from intelligence as it has been traditionally measured for over 100 years.

- An experienced manager is firmly of the view that by reading a psychological test carefully you can always tell whether it is any good.

INTRODUCTION

In this chapter we explore some practical issues about the use of psychological tests. How do we evaluate how well they predict socially relevant outcomes to do with performance or well-being that society might be interested in, such as success in school or university courses, the likelihood of suffering from a psychological disorder or in engaging in delinquent or criminal activity? What sorts of errors can be made with psychological tests if they are used to make decisions and are they all equally important? How can we be sure a test is measuring what its authors claim it is measuring or appears to be measuring? These are questions that form part of the literature on psychological testing that is usually considered under the heading of validity. The literature on validity is extensive because the issues can be approached in a number of different ways. The purpose of the present chapter is to acquaint you with the major issues that need to be thought about when examining validity.

THE MEANING OF VALIDITY

The validity of a test has been traditionally defined as the extent to which the test measures what it purports to measure (eg, Nunnally, 1967). Test developers make claims about their tests; the most obvious are the labels they place on them. The question of validity asks about the justification for the claims made. For example, a test developer publishes a new test of 'social intelligence'. The test community, those who use or develop tests, and the community more generally have the right to ask the developer of the new test about the extent to which it is in fact a measure of social intelligence and not a measure of, say, 'verbal intelligence' or general education level. The onus is on the developer to justify the claim. Statements of the sort, 'I know a lot about social intelligence, more than most, and I say it is' are not adequate. What is required is an empirical demonstration, and preferably more than one. That is, are there observations about scores on the test that are consistent with the claim that it is a measure of social intelligence? It is in this spirit that the Standards for Educational and Psychological Testing define validity as 'The degree to which accumulated evidence and theory support specific interpretations of test scores entailed by proposed uses of a test' (AERA, APA, NCME, 1999, p 184).

Validity is a central requirement for the use of a psychological test. Without it we have a set of items (questions, tasks) without meaning. The sets of data the developer and, subsequently, other interested test users gather about the test and its relationship to other measures help to give meaning to the test scores. Note that the earlier and the more recent definitions speak of 'the extent to which' and 'the degree to which', which implies that the question 'is the test valid or not' is never one that can be answered 'Yes' or 'No'. Rather the answer is always conditional. For example, we might conclude that on the basis of *what we currently know* this test is a good measure for the purpose for which it is to be employed, but this is not to say that the test cannot be found wanting as new evidence accumulates and it does not mean that it is necessarily valid when used for a new purpose. How we form views about test validity requires some statistics and a lot of critical thinking. The statistics help to crystallise some of the thinking but, as with most important issues, ultimately an exercise of judgment is involved.

The need to evaluate test validity was recognised early in psychology and has been an ongoing topic of discussion in the test community as ideas are refined and added from the broader domains of psychology and social science. Binet and Simon, for example, in their pioneering work on the assessment of intelligence saw the need to justify their test for the purpose for which it was to be used. Although Binet had been called on by the Office of Public Instruction in Paris to develop the test because of his expertise in the field, he did not base the value of his test on his reputation: 'because Binet says it is a good test then it must be so'. Instead he applied two criteria to establish its worth. If the test measured intelligence, then children identified by their teachers as 'bright' children should perform better on it than those identified as 'dull'. Second, older children should perform better than younger children. Only items that met both these criteria were included, irrespective of the merit Binet or his coworkers saw in them.

Binet's criteria were practical and, for several decades after his work became widely known, test developers focused on the practical aspect of test validity. The way it came to be framed was in terms of the extent to which scores on the test predicted some criterion measure external to itself (teachers' judgments and children's age were the criteria Binet employed). The use of tests for selection in World War I and subsequently in industry supported this widespread interpretation of validity. If a test is being used to select which of a pool of applicants will perform best in a particular job, it makes sense to ask about the validity of the test in terms of the prediction of job performance from test score. This remains an important aspect of discussions of validity, but it was subsequently seen as too limiting in terms of the types of tests for which it is relevant and in terms of its limited integration with developments in the mainstream science of psychology.

The term construct validity was introduced to capture a wider core of meaning for validity than predictive validity provided. A construct is a concept, a way of talking about features of the world that may make them more comprehensible. Constructs may be found to be unhelpful and are then discarded. In psychology, constructs are 'invented' by theorists in an effort to make sense of aspects of people's behaviour. Intelligence is a construct, anxiety is another. Because we see certain commonalities in the way people solve problems or adapt to their surroundings, we speak of intelligence. It is not a thing in the way a chair or a computer is a thing. It is an idea that potentially makes sense of differences in the way people solve problems. In the same way, anxiety does not exist other than in the responses that individuals make in certain situations, eg, when they are under threat. Regularities in these responses lead theorists to use anxiety as a convenient way of talking about them and linking them to other phenomena. Constructs as ideas are tied to the world of observation by certain 'operations', things that we do to identify them. Answers to a word quiz can be used as one operational way of tying down the construct of intelligence, but constructs have surplus meaning and are not reducible to sets of operations. To show that one particular test of intelligence lacks validity is not to show that this is true of the construct.

Construct validity sees the test as an operation for giving a construct meaning and asks how well it does that. The value of this approach is that it moves test development into the mainstream of psychology rather than having it as a technology on the periphery. The general approach to theory development in psychology thus becomes available to evaluate the quality of psychological tests, and they in turn can inform psychological theory. To find that scores on a presumptive test of intelligence do not behave as a theory of intelligence predicts may mean that there is a fault with the test (it is lacking validity) or, and this would not be the first alternative accepted, that there is a problem with the theory. It is this interaction between test and theory that attracted psychologists to the thinking about construct validity, and some argued that predictive validity could be seen as a special case of construct validity.

In this chapter, we consider predictive validity separately from construct validity, although some would see this expository convenience as potentially hiding the important relation between the two. But before either of these we need to comment on the idea of content validity.

CONTENT VALIDITY

The content of the items that constitute a test give rise to inferences about the nature of the test and there is some evidence that individuals can guess reasonably well what some tests are attempting to assess from reading through the items (Fiske, 1971). In some areas of testing, content validity is a sufficient basis for justifying use of a test. An end of semester examination in a psychology course, for example, is validated by demonstrating that the questions asked are drawn from the material set for the course and only from this source, and that the course material is adequately sampled. Beyond achievement testing, content validity is often a poor guide to test validity. Although test developers often use items that 'look' as if they are appropriate so that the layperson can guess their purpose, the use of such questions does not provide the evidence necessary to demonstrate test validity. Tests that 'look' valid, that have what is sometimes called 'face validity', may not be valid when subjected to the more rigorous requirements of predictive and construct validity, and some tests can be useful even when they include items that have little if any face validity (eg, the Minnesota Multiphasic Personality Inventory).

PREDICTIVE VALIDITY

As noted above, the essential idea of predictive validity is that the claim about the nature of what the test measures is evaluated in terms of the extent to which scores on the test allow us to estimate scores on a criterion external to the test itself. If the estimates the test provides are good, then we are likely to accept the test as a valid measure of the criterion in question. Thus, a scholastic aptitude test should allow us to estimate to some degree how students will perform in an academic examination. For example, those who obtain high scores on the test should perform well in the examination and those who obtain low scores should perform poorly. As another example, scores on a test of anxiety should predict the ratings of anxiety that psychiatrists make of patients in therapy. Psychiatrists' ratings, as with examination results, are criteria external to the test, which should be estimated from scores on the two types of tests, if they are in fact valid measures.

The examples imply that there is some difference in time between administration of the test one is seeking to validate and assessment on the criterion measures. The scholastic aptitude test is administered, for example, at the beginning of the semester and the examination at the end, or the anxiety test is administered before therapy begins and the ratings are made, say, at the end of the first session. This is often the case but it is not necessarily so. The test and criterion can be administered at the same point in time and the logic still holds. This is often the case when the criterion external to the test is another test. In developing a short form intelligence test, the test developer may administer the short form along with a test that can be considered a well-validated test, such as the WAIS. The term 'predictive validity' is sometimes restricted to those instances where the test is administered before the criterion is evaluated and the test is then predicting a future event, a common meaning of prediction. The term 'concurrent validity' is then used to characterise those situations in which the test and criterion are administered jointly.

It is important to recognise this difference, if only because prediction introduces potentially more error than is the case in concurrent assessment of validity. Events, which have nothing to do with the validity of the test, may intervene in the interval between test and criterion and these can reduce artificially the validity of the test. A family crisis can mean that a student does not do as well in an examination as he or she might and hence their actual performance is less than that predicted, but this is not what the test purports to measure (reactivity to a family crisis). Although it is important to use the terminology of predictive and concurrent validity correctly, it is important to note that concurrent validity is a special case of the more general idea of predictive validity, ie, prediction when the time interval is minimal.

The regression approach to predictive validity

The way predictive validity has traditionally been indexed is in terms of the regression coefficient or its close relative, the Pearson product moment correlation coefficient (see Box 5.1). Pearson drew on the insights of Galton in his studies of the heritability of intelligence to develop an index that would indicate, on a scale that ranged between −1 and +1, the strength and direction of association between two variables. If we have a set of values on each of two variables X and Y, we can regress Y or X, that is, plot Y as a function of X as in the first plot in Box 5.1, and use the line drawn to best fit the plotted points (see second plot in Box 5.1) to estimate a value of Y from any given value for X. We simply read along the X-axis to the value of X we are interested in, go up to the plotted line at that point, then across to the Y axis, and read off the corresponding value of Y. If the estimation is 'good', we can use the estimated values of Y in samples for which we do not have actual Y scores but only Xs (test scores but no criterion scores). Before we discuss what warrants good estimation, a few other points need to be noted.

BOX **5.1**

An example that illustrates the calculation of predictive validity

Consider a situation in which we have scores on the test we are seeking to validate and scores on an appropriate criterion for ten persons. We would of course seek a considerably larger sample than this, but for purposes of illustration we will use an N of 10. The test could be one of General Mental Ability that yields scores with a mean of 100 and a standard deviation of 15 and the criterion is a rating of performance on a 7-point scale, from 1 indicating a low score on the criterion to 7 indicating a high score. Suppose the scores are as follows.

Person	Text (X)	Criterion (Y)
1	100	1
2	102	4
3	108	2
4	109	4
5	112	3.5
6	115	4
7	117	5
8	120	4.5
9	122	5
10	124	6.5

First we plot the criterion score as a function of the test score, with both expressed as z scores.

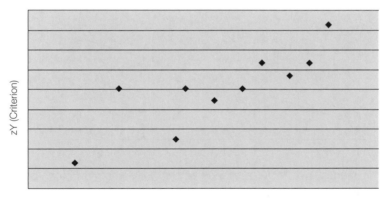

zX (Test)

Next we fit a straight line to the points. This line has been fitted by eye to make the distances of the points above the line about the same on average as the distances below the line.

Instead of fitting the line by eye, we can use a mathematical solution, known as the 'least squares' solution. This fits the line in such a way that the sum of the distances of the points from the line when squared is a minimum.

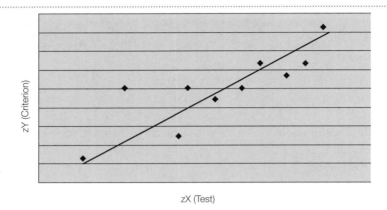

zX (Test)

One needs to understand calculus to fully appreciate this, but an intuitive grasp of what is being done is sufficient for present purposes. Because the line fitted by eye above is only one of a number of lines that can be fitted in this way, we need a way of choosing which is the best. We could compare them in terms of which one comes closest to all of the points. This would be the line for which the sum of the distances of each of the points from the line is the smallest. Because some distances will be positive (above the line) and some negative (below the line) and hence would cancel each other out if we were simply to sum them, we square them first and then add them. The mathematical solution does all this directly.

With a line fixed to the points, we can find its slope: how much do Y values change per unit change in X values (when X changes by 1, by how much does Y change)? We could do this manually by measuring distances on the figure:

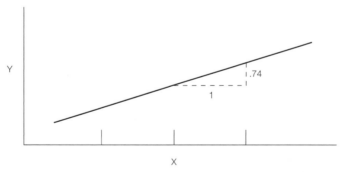

That is, Y changes by 0.74 for a change of 1 in X. Alternatively, it can be solved mathematically using the following formula:

$$r = \frac{\Sigma(ZxZy)}{N}$$

This is the basic equation for the product moment correlation, which, when applied to the values in the example problem, gives

$$= \frac{7.35}{10}$$

$$= 0.74$$

We can now predict a value of Y for any given value of X, because we have found that

$$zY = 0.74zX$$

Whether this is a reasonable thing to do depends on considerations outside the mathematics (eg, is our sample sufficiently large and representative to warrant generalisation to cases not included in the sample). If it is then we can say that the test has a predictive validity of 0.74 for this purpose.

First, the values plotted are in fact z scores (see Chapter 3), because this means that the straight line drawn through the plotted points will pass through the origin (the point where the X and Y axes intersect). If we use raw scores rather than z scores, we need to take into account the metric of the scores (no longer standard deviation units as with z scores) and the line will not necessarily pass through the origin. Second, it is the slope of the line that allows the estimation of Y scores from X scores, the slope being the rate of change in Y scores per unit change in X; that is, how much the Y score changes when the X score increments by 1. (Note the Y scores may not increment but in fact decrement if the relationship between Y and X is negative. Tests are usually scored in such a way, however, that relationships with important criteria are positive rather than negative.) Third, the slope of the line when the two variables are expressed as z scores is the product moment correlation (r), and is defined as the average of the cross products of the two variables. Thus:

$$r = \frac{\Sigma(ZxZy)}{N}$$

That is, we find the correlation between the two variables by first expressing each of the scores as z scores (using the respective mean and standard deviation for each variable), multiplying the paired z scores for each participant in the sample, and then finding the average of these cross-products. The index that results has many interesting features, apart from the fact that it can only take a value between +1 (perfect positive correlation) and −1 (perfect negative correlation). For example, its square indicates the amount of variance common to the two variables (when the variables are other than ranks). Because of these features, the measure has been used as a staple in psychometrics.

Just how good the estimate is that a test provides can be evaluated partly by the magnitude of the product moment correlation between test and criterion, with larger values giving better prediction (all other things equal, which as we will see below they seldom are). There is an argument for considering the magnitude of the correlation as a direct index of the accuracy of the estimate (Ozer, 1985). Considered in this way, a test with a validity of 0.3 improves the prediction of the criterion by 30 per cent (0.3×100) over prediction by chance and a validity of 0.6 improves prediction by 60 per cent. Prediction, however, is seldom by chance and one usually needs to consider what method of prediction would be used if a test was not used for this purpose. Thus one could use years of education rather than score on a psychological test to predict job performance and the accuracy of the estimate would then be better evaluated in terms of the improvement in prediction the test affords over that provided by the demographic information. The improvement is sometimes referred to as the incremental validity of the test (Hunsley & Meyer, 2003). Although the absolute magnitude of the validity coefficients for psychological tests is not high (eg, 0.3 for personality tests, 0.6 for cognitive tests) they often add to the estimate available without them.

A further consideration in evaluating the estimation a test provides is the magnitude of the error involved in any particular instance. We predict from score on the test (the X) that the individual's score on the criterion (Y) will be a particular value. We might expect in a fallible world that the prediction will not, however, be exact, that it will involve some error. The actual scores will be somewhat larger or smaller than we predict. If we inspect the plot in diagram 2, Box 5.1, it is clear that the line does not fit the plotted points exactly and that no line could. The one we have drawn by eye is an attempt to get the best fit. The rule used for this in calculating r is that the sum of the squares of the deviations of the points from the line is a minimum. The 'least squares' rule, as it is called, requires that the line be plotted in such a way that this sum is a minimum.

Although it is a minimum by virtue of the way it is plotted, it is not zero; some error is involved. An index of this error is to take the average of the difference between the estimated and the actual values. Where this is large, we can expect in any particular case a good deal of variation of predicted score from actual score. This index is termed the standard error of estimate and can be determined from knowledge of the correlation between test and criterion and the standard deviation of the criterion:

$$SEe = SD_Y(1 - r^2)$$

The standard error of estimate (SEe) can be thought of as the standard deviation of the distribution of the differences between actual and predicted scores, with a large SEe indicating considerable difference and hence the greater likelihood of error in any particular case. Although the SEe is a useful index for some purposes, it is more common in test evaluation to use the correlation coefficient, or validity coefficient as it is sometimes referred to in this context.

The decision-theoretic approach to predictive validity

As noted above, interest in predictive validity was encouraged by the widespread use of psychological tests in industrial and educational settings after World War I. This use centred on the value of tests in decision making, itself an issue that came into prominence during and after World War II, because of its significance in a number of military contexts, from signal detection by the radar operator to choice of a particular plan of attack. One of the earliest members of the test community to recognise the importance of the expanding relevance of decision theory to psychological testing was L J Cronbach. With Gleser (Cronbach & Gleser, 1965), he wrote an important but difficult text on the application of decision theory to the evaluation of tests. (A more accessible source is Wiggins, 1973.) Some of this thinking informs what follows.

The simplest decision, relatively speaking, that can be made with a test is when it is used to decide which of two categories a person belongs to: successful worker versus unsuccessful worker; a prisoner who is likely to re-offend if released on parole versus a prisoner who is not likely to re-offend; a patient who is psychotic versus a patient who is not psychotic. There are only two categories possible. More complex decision problems involve more than two categories, but we will stay with the simple case. To make the two-choice decision, a cutting score on the test is determined (by prior research) and those with scores that fall above the cutting score are assigned to one of the categories and those with scores below the cutting score are assigned to the other. The problem can be summarised in the following diagram. (See Box 5.2.)

The X-axis represents the range of test scores and the Y-axis the range of outcomes on the criterion variable. Rather than concentrate on the continuous range of scores as in the previous presentation of validity, we think now in terms of grouped scores. A cutting point is established on the X-axis, with scores above indicating one type of predicted outcome and those below the other type of predicted outcome (see diagram 2 in Box 5.2). The actual state of affairs is either consistent with prediction or contrary to it. Framed in this way, it is clear that the use of the test may lead to correct and to incorrect decisions. There are two sorts of correct decision. Valid positive decisions are those where the person is predicted to show the characteristic of interest (successful worker, patient with the condition in question) and this is in fact the case. Valid negative decisions are those in which the prediction is that the person does not show the characteristic of interest and this is the case. There are, as well, two sorts of errors. False positive decisions are those in which the prediction is that the person has the characteristic but in fact does not, and false negative decisions, in which the prediction is that the person does not have the characteristic of interest but does.

BOX 5.2

An example that illustrates the decision-theoretic approach to predictive validity

We begin with the example in Box 5.1 of scores on test and criterion for a sample of N = 10, and plot Y against X as before.

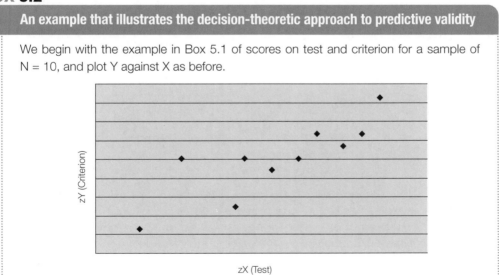

This time we will not use the scores as continuous variables but rather categorise them, first in terms of a cutting score on the predictor variable, X.

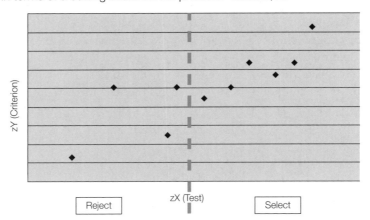

And then in terms of a cutting score on Y.

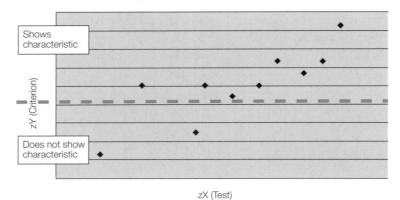

When both categorisations are combined, we have four cells: A, B, C, D.

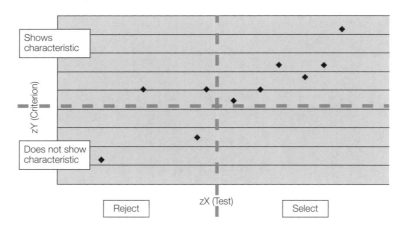

These have the following names:

A   False negatives (predicted not to have the characteristic but actually does)
B   Valid positives (predicted to have the characteristic and does)
C   Valid negatives (predicted not to have the characteristic and does not)
D   False positives (predicted to have the characteristic but does not)

The 2 x 2 contingency table formed by splitting the plot into four quadrants based on predicted and actual outcomes has marginal totals. For example, the frequencies in A and B can be added to find a marginal total, or A and C likewise.

Some of these marginal totals reflect factors operating in the context of decision making over which the test user has little if any control. This means that the entries in the table are in fact constrained and are not free to take on all possible values.

A	B
C	D

A + B = Base Rate (of criterion behaviour in the population of interest)

C + D = 1 – Base Rate

B + D = Selection Ratio (under the prevailing conditions)

A + C = 1 – Selection Ratio

If the marginals are fixed then only one value in the table is free to vary.

A	B	BR
C	D	1 - BR
1 - SR	SR	N

If BR is 0.5, and SR is 0.4, then only one of A, B, C, D can vary.

If B = 0.4, for example, then

D must be 0.1 (0.5 – 0.4)

A must be 0.1 (0.5 – 0.4)

and C must be 0.4 (0.5 – 0.1)

What is the benefit of thinking about the validity of a test in this way? First, it takes us closer to one way tests are used in practice. To say that a test has a predictive validity coefficient of 0.3 does not tell us a great deal about the test in use. To say, on the other hand, that with the test 60 per cent of the predictions on average will be correct is more immediately meaningful. Second, it makes us think about the errors that will be made with the test, the false positives and the false negatives. Although both are errors, they are not always of the same significance. If one is predicting success in pilot training, for example, the false positives are, from the point of view of the organisation doing the selecting, far more important than the false negatives. To say that a person will be a successful pilot and to find that this is not the case will involve the organisation in an expensive training program without a result and could lead to the loss of an expensive aircraft. To say that a person will not be a successful pilot and then find that he or she would may have a consequence to the individual but, unless there is a great shortage of applicants for pilot training, no adverse result for the organisation.

In another context, the relative costs or the two types of errors may be reversed. Imagine a situation in which a test is being used to screen for a central nervous system malignancy. If the test predicts the person falls into the category of persons with the malignancy, then there is an extensive neurological examination; if the test predicts the person is clear then there is no follow-up. In this situation, a false positive has only minor consequences: the person must undergo a neurological examination, which admittedly takes time and may involve some inconvenience, but which has a relatively small cost. On the other hand, a false negative is of considerable significance. The person does not undergo the examination that would identify the potentially life-threatening malignancy. The decision theory approach draws our attention to the fact that errors are made in using tests, none are perfect, and makes us think about the consequences of these errors in the way the test is used. For example, any false negative rate, in the screening for malignancy, may lead us to dispense with the screening approach even though it has a high valid positive rate.

There is a further good reason to consider the decision-theoretic approach to test validity. To demonstrate this we need to first consider the relationship between the classical approach to validity and that based on decision theory. In the classical approach, in which we consider predictor and criterion continuous, we examine the slope of the line relating the two and use the slope as a basic index of validity. In the decision-theoretic approach we set up a 2×2 contingency table, in which we cross-tabulate scores above and below a cut-off on the predictor with one of two outcomes on the criterion. A 2×2 contingency table permits an index of association to be computed that describes the relationship between the two variables that are cross-tabulated. The index of association frequently used in these cases is the phi coefficient, which is a form of the product moment correlation used in the classical approach. That is, we could compute a form of validity coefficient from the 2×2 approach if we wished.

What the decision-theoretic approach adds, however, is the recognition that the magnitude of the association, the validity coefficient, is constrained by the marginal totals in the 2×2 table (see Box 5.2). In practice these marginal totals are often not under the control of the users of the test. One of the marginal totals (the sum of the valid positives and the false negatives) is referred to as the base rate of the characteristic in the population where the test will be used. Without any test being administered, there is a certain number of individuals in the population who have the characteristic of interest (eg, can do the job, are recidivists). A second of the marginal totals (the valid positives plus the false positives) is termed the selection ratio, the number who can be assigned to the category of persons showing the characteristic, and is defined by practical considerations unrelated to testing. In the case of personnel selection, for example, the selection ratio is the number of workers the organisation can employ divided by the number who apply. If there are, for example, only 10 jobs to fill, then the selection process cannot yield 20 successful outcomes. Similarly, if there are only a fixed number of beds in a psychiatric facility, more patients cannot be admitted to the facility than there are beds to take them.

The base rate and the selection ratio are often fixed by the population on which and the conditions under which the test is to be used. These values, the marginal totals, of the 2×2 contingency table constrain the values in the cells because the 2×2 contingency table has only one degree of freedom: once one of the cell frequencies in the table is set, the remaining cell frequencies cannot vary (see Box 5.2). What this means is that the association between predictor and criterion, the validity coefficient, is set by the conditions under which the test is used and is not some property of the test that holds irrespective of the situation. A test of anxiety proneness that is validated by comparing equal numbers of patients diagnosed with a neurotic disorder and those not so diagnosed has a validity coefficient for a situation where the base rate of anxiety proneness is artificially set at 0.5 (equal numbers in the two groups). If the test is now used in a situation in which the base rate is much lower (or higher) than this, for example, it is employed in an unselected sample from the normal population, the validity coefficient will necessarily be lower.

It is important therefore to know the base rate of the characteristic in the population in which the test is to be used, a consideration that does not necessarily arise with the classical approach to predictive validity.

A similar consideration applies to the selection ratio. This at times can be manipulated and if it can then a higher valid positive rate can be obtained even with a test of low predictive validity. This phenomenon was described many years ago and Taylor and Russell (1939) compiled a table that specified the change in effectiveness possible with tests of varying validities when selection ratios of different magnitudes apply. Gregory (2000) gives a specific example of the use of the Taylor and Russell table.

One final consideration before we leave the decision-theoretic approach to validity. In the clinical literature, the valid positive rate is only one of a number of indexes employed in describing a test's validity. It is the number of valid positives divided by the total number of persons tested. Rather than considering all who are tested we might narrow our consideration to just those who have the characteristic of interest and ask how well does the test do in identifying them. That is, we divide the number of valid positives by the base rate (expressed as the number of cases in the sample and not as the proportion in the population). This index is termed the test's sensitivity. Alternatively we can ask how well does the test do in ruling out those who do not have the characteristic. In the example given earlier where a test was being used to screen for a malignancy, the point was made that the false negatives were of great importance. If we express the number of valid negatives as a ratio of the number of those who do not have the characteristic (as a proportion of $1 - BR$), we have the index we want. This is termed the test's specificity. For more indices of this sort, see Bland (2000).

CONSTRUCT VALIDITY

To this point we have considered the practical context in which the validity of tests is studied. In a landmark paper, Cronbach and Meehl (1955) shifted the emphasis in discussions of validity from the practical to the theoretical and argued that the validity of a test depends on the extent to which it truly reflects the construct that it purports to measure. If a test developer claims a test measures intelligence, how well does it do that job? Because constructs are theoretical entities, an answer depends partly on the power of the theory in which the construct resides. A weak theory will have poorly defined constructs which are poorly operationalised and in these circumstances it will be difficult to conclude with any precision on the validity of a presumed measure of the construct.

The approach is theoretical but moves consideration of validity of a test very much within the mainstream of psychology. Psychological tests become tests of theory in the sense that the ability to develop a valid test of a construct adds some confidence to the theory from which it is drawn. The failure of a test to behave as predicted may bring into question the theory or suggest amendments to it, if the test has been developed along sound lines. Badly constructed tests have no value for testing theories but well constructed ones do. With this approach the testing enterprise is no longer a technology, but very much part of theory development.

Cronbach and Meehl proposed ways in which construct validity can be evaluated. They introduced the idea of the multitrait–multimethod matrix as a tool for evaluating validity. The basic idea is that scores on a test are a mixture of method variance, ie, variation arising from the method used to obtain the scores (eg, self-report, problem solving, self-rating) and variation due to the underlying disposition that the test user wants to assess. The variance due to the disposition should manifest itself irrespective of the method used, whereas method variance by definition is bound to the method employed. To untangle these two sources of variance, Cronbach and Meehl proposed that we examine simultaneously more than one underlying disposition assessed by more than one method. Tests which use the same method will correlate to some degree because of their shared method variance, but tests of the same construct using different methods should correlate to an even greater extent if the underlying dispositional variance is properly reflected by the tests.

Cronbach and Meehl introduced one further idea: a test can be called into question as a measure of a construct if scores on it correlate to any considerable extent with a measure of a different construct. That is, validity is demonstrated not just by the correlation of a test with another measure, the classical view of validity in terms of prediction of a criterion, but by the lack of correlation of a test with a measure of a theoretically different construct. We need discrimination of measures, as well as their convergence, to demonstrate validity. This was a major step forward in understanding validity, because it uses the counter instance as a method of establishing a claim, in the way a researcher seeks to build confidence in a hypothesis by attempting to demonstrate its falsity.

For example, there was considerable interest in the 1950s and 1960s in the construct of creativity and various 'creative' measures of creativity were developed. The research program stalled, however, when it proved difficult to show that the various measures of creativity correlated more highly with each other than they did with measures of intelligence (see eg, Brody, 1972). That is, they generally correlated more strongly with measures of a supposedly different construct (intelligence) than they did with each other.

The name convergent and discriminant validity was given to this method of construct validation. It involves calculating a correlation matrix based on scores for a sample of individuals for whom two or more independent constructs are measured using two or more methods (see Box 5.3). When all possible correlations are calculated and the matrix formed, the researcher can evaluate it in terms of three principal guidelines. First, coefficients in the validity diagonal should be positive, substantial, and statistically significant. Second, their magnitude should exceed the magnitudes of those in the same row or column, ie, correlations between different constructs measured by the same or different methods. Third, the pattern of correlations with a measure of a construct should be the same across variations in the method of measurement.

BOX 5.3

An example of a multitrait–multimethod matrix

The multitrait–multimethod matrix requires measures of two or more (hence, 'multi-') constructs (traits) obtained using two or more methods of measurement. The purpose is to examine whether (a) different measures of the same trait converge (correlate) over methods, and (b) whether the same measures of different traits can be differentiated (discriminated) from each other (fail to correlate). Consider, for example, three traits that according to theory are independent of each other: Sociablity (Soc), Cheerfulness (Cfl), and Impulsivity (Imp).

Imagine measuring these traits using two different methods of measurement, eg, objective test and peer assessment. Scores on each trait are obtained using both methods for a reasonable sample of participants, and the scores intercorrelated. A hypothetical matrix of intercorrelations is presented in the following table.

The coefficients in brackets are reliability (internal consistency) coefficients that are provided to establish the magnitude of the correlations that are possible with the various measures. The values in the triangles at the top and right of the matrix are the intercorrelations of different traits measured with the same method (in the case of the

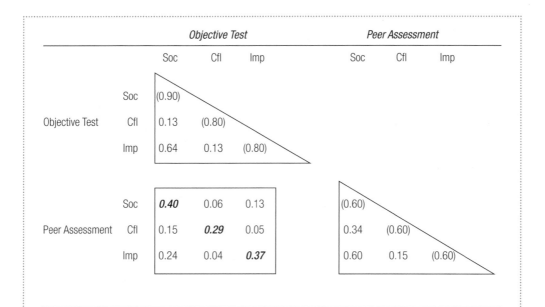

triangle at the top, the method is objective test; in the case of the triangle on the right, the method is peer assessment). The values in these two triangles, which are termed heterotrait-monomethod (different trait, same method) triangles should not be too large, because they involve measures of supposedly independent constructs. There will be some correlation, because a method is common in each triangle, but it is a question of their size relative to other correlations in the matrix.

The values in the diagonal of the square, termed the validity diagonal (shown in bold italics in Box 5.3) are those obtained when a single construct is measured using different methods. These values should be large, if there is convergent validity, and larger than any of the values in the same row or column, which do not involve the same construct, if the measures have discriminant validity. The final requirement is that the correlations in the two triangles, although these will be relatively small, should show the same pattern. Subsequently more sophisticated statistical methods, such as factor analysis, have been used to make these evaluations more rigorous, but the logic remains the same: measures of the same construct should relate more strongly than measures of different constructs using the same or different measures. Cronbach and Meehl's work has been subject to criticism (see Pedhazur & Schmelkin, 1991), not the least because of the difficulties of determining in advance the independence of methods, but the approach provides a valuable addition to thinking about construct validity.

Although the work on the multitrait-multimethod matrix is important, it would be wrong to conclude that this is the only way that construct validity can be examined. In essence, construct validity involves theory testing and this can be done in many ways, which means that there is no fixed set of operations that define construct validity. That said, some procedures are more common than others (Thorndike, 1982). Groups considered to differ in terms of a construct may be compared, or an intervention expected on the grounds of theory to affect a construct may be introduced to see if the presumptive measure of the construct varies as a consequence. Wherever the researcher posits a relationship or an effect and sets out to test it, there is the opportunity for evaluating the construct validity of the measure employed.

CONCLUDING REMARKS

Tests can be conceived as tools to be used in practical situations such as selection or classification or as tools of theory. The approach to evaluating validity will vary depending on the focal interest, with predictive validity and utility being of primary concern in practice and construct validity being of more interest when the theoretical meaning of a test is the concern. But it would be incorrect to see these differences in approach as being absolute. Analysis of a practical problem in terms of theory can suggest appropriate constructs to measure and identification of measures of these may provide the practical solution needed. Alternatively, a theory about a construct may lead to the hypothesis that a measure of it will predict a given criterion; construct validity may be shown by the predictive validity of a test. In all cases we are interested in reasoning from the test scores to some non-test context, practical or theoretical, and the essential question is what warrant do we have for going beyond the test.

Questions for consideration

1. Compare and contrast reliability and validity.
2. Explain why validity is an important property for a psychological test.
3. Give some examples of criteria commonly used in predictive validity.
4. What is the difference between concurrent and predictive validity?
5. Define content and construct validity.
6. What is a multitrait–multimethod matrix? Discuss its significance.

Exercises

1. A new test has been developed to predict whether members of a prison population will be diagnosed as psychopathic. Results for a sample of prisoners are as follows:

Test Score	Diagnosis	Test Score	Diagnosis
40	psychopath	26	Non-psychopath
20	Non-psychopath	30	Non-psychopath
21	Non-psychopath	32	Psychopath
25	Non-psychopath	25	Non-psychopath
35	Psychopath	26	Non-psychopath

Looking at this table, what do you think is a good cut-off score for this new test?

   a   If this cut-off score is used, what is the validity coefficient for this sample?

   b   If this cut-off score is used, what is the Valid Positive Rate?

   c   Would a psychologist on the basis of these results be confident in using the test with a sample of adolescents drawn from the community?

2   The selection ratio to be used in a testing situation is set at 0.3 and the base rate for the behaviour in question is known to be 0.3. If the Valid Positive Rate is 20 per cent what is the Valid Negative rate? What are the error rates in using the test in this situation?

3   A new test of emotional intelligence has been developed for executive selection. It has an internal consistency reliability of 0.75. As part of the validation process, the test is administered to a sample of 500 managers with a standard test of intelligence (reliability 0.92). Ratings of the general ability level of all managers in the sample and of their emotional intelligence are obtained from their supervisors. Ratings of this sort have a reliability of no more than 0.45. Draw up a multitrait–multimethod matrix (by using the information provided and coming up with other correlation coefficients) that would point to the validity of the new test.

Further reading

Crocker, L, & Algina, J (1986). *Introduction to classical and modern test theory*. New York: Holt, Rinehart and Winston.

Kline, P (1998). *The new psychometrics: Science, psychology, and measurement*. London: Routledge.

Nunnally, J, & Bernstein, I H (1994). *Psychometric theory* (3rd edn). New York: McGraw Hill.

Rust, J, & Golombok, S (1999). *Modern psychometrics: The science of psychological assessment* (2nd edn). London: Routledge.

Wasserman, J D, & Bracken, B A (2003). Psychometric characteristics of assessment procedures. In J R Graham, & J A Naglieri (Eds), *Handbook of Psychology: Vol 10, Assessment Psychology* (pp 43–66). Hoboken, NJ: John Wiley & Sons.

Test Construction

- When medical schools in Australia established postgraduate programs in Medicine open to entry by graduates with a range of different degrees, they needed a selection process that could cope with large numbers of applications but not rely on the information source used for undergraduate medical school selection, viz, high school performance. A new test of aptitude for medical training was required.

- A concern by government that the achievement of Australian school students in mathematics and science was falling behind that of students in comparable countries led to the call for repeated testing for numeracy throughout the years of primary and secondary schooling and with it the need for age-appropriate tests of ability in mathematical understanding.

- Professional staff in a counselling service dealing with large numbers of clients experiencing grief and loss as a result of crime formed the view that the capacity to accept and forgive are essential to client progress and asked for assistance in developing a test that would track this through the therapeutic encounter.

- A psychology student proposed for her Honours project to test the hypothesis that school children's altruism is linked to the adequacy of their self-concept, and needed measures of both these characteristics.

- A large business firm wanted to evaluate the morale of its staff and called in a consultant to do this for them systematically and objectively.

INTRODUCTION

New ideas in education, health, business, and government bring with them the need for more information about human behaviour and experience on which to base decisions and for new or modified psychological tests. The present chapter is about the work that is done in constructing a psychological test. What are the procedures employed? What sorts of decisions need to be made? Is it all based on human judgment or is empirical evidence brought to bear on the task and if so how? In describing the procedures that are typically followed, the intention is not to prepare you for actual test development but to give you a greater understanding of the processes involved in developing a psychological test. This should make you a more critical user of psychological tests, either as a professional administering or interpreting tests or as a consumer to whom a psychological test is administered.

THE RATIONAL APPROACH

A psychological test is a set of items that allows measurement of some attribute of an individual. The items may be problems to which the individual must find correct answers, as in the case where the attribute is an ability of the person, or they may be questions about the way the individual typically behaves, feels, or thinks, as in the case where the attribute is a personality characteristic. Other types of items may be appropriate for other types of attributes, for example, an expression of a sentiment where an attitude the person holds is the attribute, or a statement of preference where the attribute is an interest. The term 'item' has been traditionally used as a generic way of referring to the various forms the content of a psychological test can take.

The set of items is in no sense random or accidental, because it must permit some form of measurement of the attribute. Often one sees in popular magazines collections of items that purport to indicate some attribute of the magazine reader: 'Are you a good partner?' The reader is invited to complete the items and then some 'diagnosis' is offered, eg, 90 per cent correct and you are a 'good partner', 60 per cent and you 'could improve', 30 per cent and 'there is a lot wrong with the way you are approaching your relationship'. Seldom, however, has there been any rigorous development of the 'test' that permits any reasonable inference being drawn. There is nothing particularly wrong with these 'tests' as long as they are taken as entertainment, which is what the editor of the magazine intends. They have the look of a psychological test in that they are a collection of items, but without the developmental work necessary there can be no claim that any form of measurement of the attribute in question, in this case 'being a good partner' is possible.

The approach outlined in the sections that follow has been termed the rational approach, as distinct from the empirical approach, to test construction (Kline, 1993). In the interval between the two world wars, a number of tests were constructed using the empirical approach. Items were selected on the basis of how well they correlated with a criterion of interest. The constructors of the MMPI, for example, used this approach. An item was selected if it was shown to discriminate between a criterion psychiatric group and a normal group (hospital visitors), irrespective of its content. Patients diagnosed as suffering from schizophrenia were found to be more likely than normals to endorse an item such as 'I like horseback riding'. As a consequence, this item was included in the schizophrenia scale of the MMPI. Such 'blind' acceptance of item discrimination indices was questioned by a number of commentators who argued for a more rational basis for the development of psychological tests, in which theory about the construct or constructs of interest guides the process (eg, Jackson, 1971). Although the superiority of one approach over the other is itself an empirical question (which one provides the better tests?), many test developers today opt for the rational approach.

For purposes of exposition the development process is set out in a number of steps. In practice the process may not always be as linear as this account implies; some steps may be collapsed on to each other or steps repeated or the process looped at certain points. In general, however, test developers work through a process similar to that described here and briefly summarised in Figure 6.1.

FIGURE 6.1 Steps in test construction

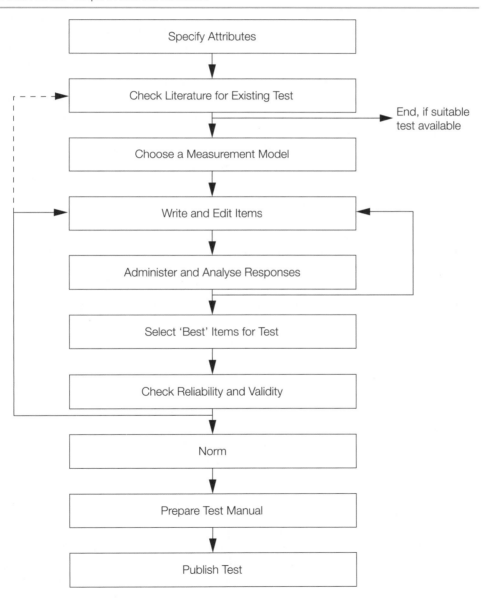

The description is purposely made as general as possible rather than have it focus on the development of one particular type of test, but examples of particular tests are provided from time to time. The process has itself developed from the earliest work of Binet and colleagues and has been refined by practice and by developments in psychometrics, the mathematics of psychological measurement. The account given here rests heavily on the work of Nunnally (1967; Nunnally & Bernstein, 1994), whose text could be read by the student seeking a more advanced treatment of topics covered here.

SPECIFICATION OF THE ATTRIBUTE

The first question to be asked concerns the attribute that the test developer is seeking to measure. Test construction requires a clear specification of the attribute to be measured and what is known about it. Although both definition and understanding may change as a consequence of test development, the test developer needs to begin with as clear a specification as possible. Knowledge of the attribute is needed to generate the items that will form the test, both their format and content, and for testing the validity of the test once it has been developed. Without sound knowledge of the way the attribute is supposed to behave it is not possible to check the test's validity. Although test development sometimes begins with only a rudimentary theory of the attribute to be measured, attributes embedded in rich theories, ones with lots of testable implications, make for better starting points for test construction.

Because often more than one person will be involved in the various stages of test construction, the specification needs to be a written one. This has to include a clear definition of the attribute and the outcome of a literature search that identifies the central theoretical claims about it and any research findings bearing on it. If the test is to measure more than one attribute the specification needs to be done separately for each and a section provided on why and in what ways the attributes are separable (cf, the discussion of discriminant validity in the preceding chapter).

LITERATURE SEARCH

Once it is clear what it is that a test is supposed to measure, the would-be test constructor needs to establish whether or not a satisfactory test of the attribute exists. There are now a large number (in the thousands) of tests in the psychological literature, as reference to the *Mental Measurement Yearbooks* indicates. It would not be sensible to add to this list, and expend a good deal of effort and money (as these exercises are costly), without being assured that the test is needed. A literature search, beginning with the latest *Mental Measurements Yearbook*, is required to establish what tests of the attribute in question have been published and what their properties are. It may be that no test has been developed, but this is unlikely and may result from a failure to search the literature carefully enough or because the attribute has not been clearly specified. The would-be test constructor may be calling the attribute X (eg, intelligence), whereas it has been referred to in the literature as Y (general mental ability). Ambiguities of this sort are less likely if the attribute has been clearly specified from the outset.

It is more likely that a test has been developed but that it has less than adequate properties for the purpose for which it is required (eg, there are no norms for the population with which it is to be used). Further work with an existing test (copyright permitting) may be a better investment than development of a new test. The point being made is that the test developer needs to justify the test development project. In so doing, the expected use of the test (eg, for research, for decision making in the individual case) will be made clear.

CHOICE OF A MEASUREMENT MODEL

Having decided on the attribute and the theory about it and having determined that no suitable test is currently available, the next choice is the type of measurement required and the model to be used to attain it. Measurement is simply defined as the assignment of numbers to objects according to a set of rules. With a tape measure we assign numbers to objects, eg, strips of cloth, to indicate the quantity, length. Although we do not normally reflect on what we are doing here, there are in fact a set of rules implicit in this simple process.

Types of measurement

S S Stevens (1951) introduced a four-fold classification of measurement that has been widely used (and abused) in textbooks in psychology. According to Stevens, measurement may be nominal, ordinal, interval, or ratio. Nominal measurement (see Figure 6.2) is hardly measurement at all and simply involves naming objects to indicate their discreteness. Players in a sporting team wear numbers on their clothes to identify them for the referee. They could be identified by having their names on their shirts but if two players happened to have the same name there would be some confusion. Numbers are unique. The rule applied here is simply that each player receives one and only one number and no two players can receive the same number.

Ordinal measurement improves on this by assigning numbers in a way that permits some inference about relationships among objects. Objects are ranked in terms of the quantity and numbers are assigned from more of the quantity to less (or from less to more, it does not matter as long as a consistent approach is adopted). Larger numbers mean more of the quantity in question than smaller numbers (or vice versa if ranking has been done in the reverse order), but how much more is unknown. There may be very little difference, for example, between performers ranked first and second in a competition but a considerable difference between these two and the person ranked third. That is, the distance between 1 and 2 in this case is not equivalent to that between 2 and 3. Ordinal measurement does not carry any information about the distance between objects in terms of the quantity of interest.

FIGURE 6.2 Types of measurement

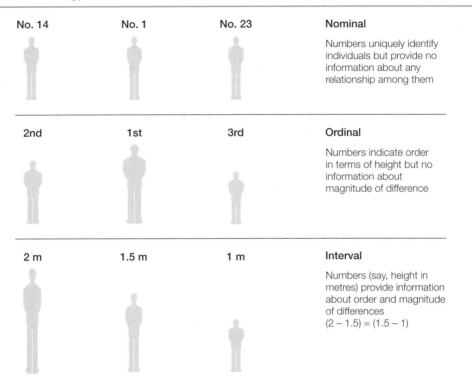

Interval measurement, on the other hand, does. We now know the relative positions of two objects with respect to the quantity in question but we also know how far apart they are in intervals of a certain magnitude. We know that a boy with a height of 70 cm is taller than a boy of 65 cm but we also know that the difference in height of these two boys is the same as that for boys of 84 and 89 cm. The scale, in this case length, is informative because the intervals are of equal magnitude.

If as well as this property, equal intervals, the scale has a true zero, that is, there is a point at which the quantity is said not to exist, then Stevens described this as a ratio scale. Length and mass as we commonly measure them are ratio scales. Temperature as measured in degrees Celsius or Fahrenheit is not a ratio scale because at 0° C or 0° F there is still heat in an object (the molecules of which it is constituted are still moving). The zero on the Celsius Scale is the freezing point of water, a useful but arbitrary reference point.

Psychometricians have sought various procedures for generating the highest form of measurement of psychological attributes possible, because of the greater precision that better forms of measurement allow for theorising and decision making. However, there are still few measurements in psychology that allow even interval measurement and none ratio measurement. Tests of general mental ability are, at best, interval scales and some would dispute that they are even this. (Can we really be sure that the difference between IQs of 90 and 100 is the same as that between 100 and 110?).

It is important to be clear about the rules that underpin the measurements being made, but sometimes too much can be made of differences between types of measurement. Some writers on the topic would prohibit the use of arithmetic with anything but ratio scales, thereby excluding statistical procedures with virtually all psychological measures. This fundamentalist approach overlooks the role of convention in measurement. As long as the conventions are understood and claims are not made beyond the limits of the conventions, then reasonable inference is possible. Thus we can reasonably compute a student's Grade Point Average by summing their grades over different subjects and dividing by the number of subjects, even though we might not wish to defend the proposition that the differences between HDs, Ds, and Cs (or As, Bs, and Cs) are all equal.

Models of measurement

Given that the level of measurement likely to be attained in developing a psychological test is, at best, interval, there is a further consideration: which is the model of measurement to be used in test construction (Allen & Yen, 1979; Hulin, Drasgow & Parsons, 1983)? The model widely used to date for developing psychological tests is that sometimes referred to as the weak true score model. To understand this and the model that is coming to rival it, we need to talk about the way individual items on psychological tests are considered to operate. One way of making this discussion clearer is graphically in terms of what is called a trace line. This relates the likelihood of endorsement of the item (in the simplest case, whether the respondent says 'Yes' or 'No' to a question, or gets a problem right or wrong) to the person's position on the underlying attribute of interest (see Figure 6.3). Because much of the early work involved general mental ability, it is appropriate to use an

FIGURE 6.3 An example of a trace line

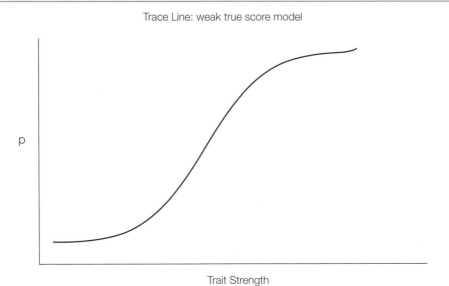

Trace Line: weak true score model

p

Trait Strength

example from that literature. Given that we are attempting to measure general mental ability, we assume that any individual in question will have a position somewhere along the underlying distribution of ability. They might be of high ability, somewhat less than that, below average, or anywhere along the assumed underlying dimension. We are attempting to identify their true position, their true score, using the fallible set of items. Each item we use might not be a good marker of this true position and we need to know how individual items behave. If the item is a good one, then, most of the time, those high in ability will pass the item and those low in ability will fail. That is, the trace line will rise showing an increasing probability of endorsement as ability increases. If we have, say, 100 people and we know their true scores on general mental ability, then we could plot the number getting the item right for various true scores. Weak true score theory says only that the relationship between the two is monotonic. That is, the direction of the relationship does not change at any point in the distribution of true scores. It is called 'weak' by some commentators because it makes no further claims about the relationship.

More recent models attempt to fix the trace line by specifying certain parameters of the mathematical relationship. The most complex of these, Item Response Theory (IRT) models, specify three parameters: the height of the curve with respect to the Y axis (how high or low on the page does the curve sit), the distance along the X axis before there is an inflection point, and, once the curve is inflected, the rate of change of the curve (its steepness). Figure 6.4 identifies these parameters of the trace line and Figure 6.5 shows a variety of curves, which vary in these different parameters. The parameters are not simply of technical interest to psychometricians. They have expressions in the behaviour of respondents taking the test. An item that

FIGURE 6.4 Three parameters of a trace line

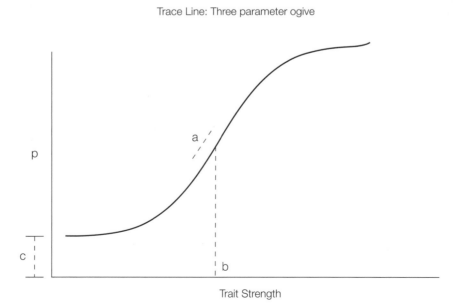

Trace Line: Three parameter ogive

Trait Strength

FIGURE 6.5 Examples of curves with different parameters

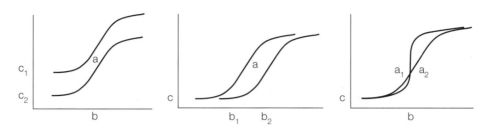

begins at a high rate of endorsement (at c1, in the curve to the left in Figure 6.5) may be one for which individuals for some reason can guess the right answer reasonably easily. An item that has an inflection point low on the underlying distribution of true scores (b1, in the middle curve of Figure 6.5) is a relatively easy item. We say it has low 'item difficulty'. The steepness of the slope reflects the sensitivity of the item to a change in an underlying true score; does it make a sharp discrimination (a1, in the curve to the right in Figure 6.5) or a gradual one. This was originally referred to as the discriminability of an item. If at a certain point on the underlying distribution, the proportion getting the item right versus those getting it wrong suddenly shifts, the item is discriminating well at that point; it is making a sharp discrimination between those of less and those of more ability at that point on the ability scale.

In developing a test, we would ideally like to have good data on all these parameters (a, b, and c). Getting such data is not easy and calls for some assumptions to be made and for quite large samples for test development. A first assumption has to do with the underlying true score distribution. This cannot be estimated directly, and so test developers assume some proxy for it, such as the total score of an individual across all other items selected to measure the attribute. Unless the developer is totally misguided, a good number of the items selected will probably be reasonably good items and so aggregating across them will give a usable estimate. There is error in the process, but by using different sets of items and not expecting that the test developer will develop a perfect test the first time the problem is not as large as it might first appear.

Estimating the various parameters is a complex business, and it is because of this complexity that the model proposed in weak test score theory has remained in vogue for a long time. Advances in information technology (eg, computer capacity, software application development) have meant that these complexities are being overcome and tests in future are likely to be constructed using stronger assumptions than those of weak true score theory. For example, the Rasch model (a single parameter IRT model) is increasingly being used in the development of tests. For present purposes, we will remain with the simpler model.

With this model, two basic statistics are required for each item, the difficulty (or popularity) of the item and its validity. These statistics are similar to the parameters that define the more specific models but in this case we are not fixing these but merely deciding whether they fall within acceptable limits. We will see how that is done in Box 6.2 below.

The weak true score model and the IRT models are not the only models for test development. Two of the others that have been applied in the history of test development are briefly described in Box 6.1.

BOX 6.1

Alternative models of measurement

Monotonic trace lines are not the only form that has been proposed for the behaviour of test items. Two important alternatives in the history of test development are the deterministic model underlying Guttman's (1944) approach to scaling attitudes and before that the non-monotonic probabilistic model of Thurstone (1929). Examples of these are presented in the accompanying figure. On the left is a trace line that indicates that the probability of responding in one way (eg, 'No') is constant at zero until some point on the attribute scale is reached, at which point the probability of responding in the opposite direction becomes 100 per cent. That is, all those with scores on the attribute below the point of inflexion say 'No' to the item and all those with scores above say 'Yes'. The model is deterministic in the sense that the probability is either 0 or 1.0 (100 per cent) and no intermediate probabilities are possible. If, for example, a test is composed of a series of questions about a person's height ('Are you shorter than 150 cm?', 'Are you shorter than 151 cm?'...), then a person will endorse all the items below their height and the item representing their height by saying 'No' and all those above their height by saying 'Yes'. Responses above and below the point that represents their height are perfectly consistent but are in the opposite direction. Finding items that scale in this way for psychological characteristics has proved difficult and for that reason Guttman developed a method for estimating the degree to which a set of items approached such a model (the reproducibility coefficient, as it is called) rather than fitted it precisely. But, for some, postulating as a model one that is totally unrealistic for psychological attributes seems a strange way to undertake a measurement exercise.

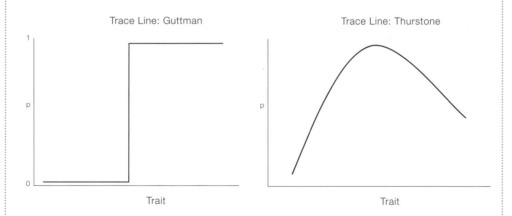

The trace line on the right of the figure is different again to the monotone trace line. It shows the probability of responding to the item in a particular way as increasing up to some point on the attribute scale and then, once that point is reached, as decreasing.

The turning point is shown in the middle of the attribute scale but it could be anywhere along the scale. Thurstone sought to measure attitudes using such a model and developed a technique for doing so based on a procedure used for scaling attributes of physical stimuli. The methods he developed are interesting, but again the question arises about how realistic the model is for psychological attributes. Thurstone proposed that some features of religious attitudes fitted such a model. For example, a conventionally religious person may say 'Yes' to an item that indicates a preference for the public display of a Sunday church service, whereas a truly religious person and a person with little or no religious sentiment are more likely to say 'No'. As strength of religious commitment rises from zero to an intermediate level, the probability of expressing a preference for the Sunday service increases, but as religiosity increases still further to high levels of commitment the probability may well decrease because a genuine concern for matters religious is not compatible with public show.

The value of this model has been debated by those concerned with attitude measurement, but for practical purposes nowadays a much simpler model and method is adopted. Rensis Likert (1932) showed how attitude scales with reasonable properties could be constructed by having people respond to statements relevant to the targeted attitude by indicating on a 5-point scale (from strongly disagree to strongly agree) where their preference lay. By summing over a number of such statements a good form of measurement was obtained. But this has taken us full circle and we are back with the weak true score model that has been used in so much of the construction of psychological tests.

ITEM WRITING AND EDITING

At this stage, items to tap the construct must now be prepared. The format of the items relates to the original decision about the nature of the attribute that the test is to tap. Tests of abilities usually take the form of multiple-choice items in which a question or problem is broached and the respondent needs to identify which of a number of options are correct (see Figure 6.6). Typically four or five options are provided because the more the options, the less the influence of guessing. For example, if there are only two options, the chances are 50/50 that a random choice without regard to content will be correct, whereas with four options the chance of a correct answer being generated by a random process falls to 25 per cent.

Tests of typical behaviour take a variety of forms, with the Yes/No, True/False format being widely used for tests of personality and rating scales being more common in tests of attitudes. There is a considerable literature on how many alternatives to allow in these types of tests (eg, should a 'not sure' option be allowed in a True/False format? Should five, seven, or more points be allowed with a rating scale)? The details are beyond the scope of this introductory discussion.

With the format settled, the next task is to develop a pool of items. More items than are considered necessary for the final version of the test need to be prepared because a number will be lost at the stage of item analysis. Content experts are

FIGURE 6.6 Examples of item formats

Ability

Complete the following series: 2, 4, 8, 16, ...

What is the capital of the Northern Territory? (Tick the correct option)

a. Alice Springs
b. Darwin
c. Tennant Creek
d. Katherine

Typical Behaviour

Indicate which of the response options best reflects your beliefs or feelings:

I like motorbike racing.   True   False

Children should be seen but not heard.   Yes   No   Unsure

Without any reason, I find myself in tears.

Frequently   Sometimes   Rarely   Never

frequently employed to provide a fund of face valid questions for selection. For example, in attempting to develop a test of mathematical ability, a group of high school mathematics teachers might be recruited because of their expert knowledge of mathematics. In the case of a construct such as anxiety or depression, clinical psychologists might be the group that can provide the necessary expertise. Even though the item writers are expert, the construct needs to be explained to avoid each working with a somewhat different idea of the attribute.

The items are then edited to a standard form. For example, two to three lines of text is usually the maximum length of items and very long or very short ones should generally be avoided. Readability of the items needs to be appropriate for the population on which the test will be used, and wording should be clear and concise to aid comprehension.

The item is usually pilot tested with small groups with the same demographic characteristics as the population of interest. Respondents are asked to answer subsets of questions and comment on how they experience them. Do they find them clear, relevant to their background, and so on? Qualitative evaluation of items is an important aspect of test development to ensure the items are 'working' as wanted.

ITEM ANALYSIS AND SELECTION

With a pool of items that appear satisfactory for assessing the attribute, the test developer collects data from a sample of the population on how the items 'behave'. The sample size needs to be fairly large (100+) to enable stable statistics to be calculated for each item. Once the respondents' answers are available, a data table of the sort in Box 6.2 is drawn up to provide the necessary statistics described and discussed in the box.

BOX **6.2**

Item analysis

Consider you have prepared a five-item multiple-choice test (four options for each question) and have administered it to a sample of 10 participants. The problem is hypothetical and for the purposes of demonstration only. An actual item analysis would involve a larger item set (20 plus typically) and a larger sample (100 plus). The item data from the imaginary exercise are summarised in the first table below.

TABLE 1 Fictitious item data for a 5-item test each with four options administered to 10 individuals (option a is the correct option in all cases)

Person	Item 1 Options				Item 2 Options				Item 3 Options				Item 4 Options				Item 5 Options			
	a	b	c	d	a	b	c	d	a	b	c	d	a	b	c	d	a	b	c	d
1	1	0	0	0	1	0	0	0	0	1	0	0	0	1	0	0	0	1	0	0
2	0	1	0	0	1	0	0	0	0	1	0	0	1	0	1	0	0	0	1	0
3	1	0	0	0	1	0	0	0	0	1	0	0	0	0	0	1	0	1	0	0
4	1	0	0	0	1	0	0	0	1	0	0	0	0	0	0	0	1	0	0	0
5	1	0	0	0	1	0	0	0	1	0	0	0	1	0	0	0	1	0	0	0
6	0	0	1	0	1	0	0	0	0	1	0	0	0	0	1	0	0	0	0	1
7	1	0	0	0	1	0	0	0	1	0	0	0	1	0	0	0	0	0	1	0
8	1	0	0	0	1	0	0	0	1	0	0	0	0	0	0	1	0	0	0	1
9	1	0	0	0	1	0	0	0	1	0	0	0	0	0	0	0	1	0	0	0
10	0	0	0	1	1	0	0	0	0	1	0	0	1	1	0	0	0	0	0	1
Mean	0.7	0.1	0.1	0.1	1	0	0	0	0.5	0.5	0	0	0.4	0.2	0.2	0.2	0.3	0.2	0.2	0.3
σ^2	0.21				0				0.25				0.24				0.21			

The table lists the responses of each person to each option for each item. The numeral 1 indicates an option has been selected and 0 that it was not. Thus Person 1 answered the first item by endorsing option a, the second item by endorsing option a, the third question by option b, and so on. At the bottom of the table are the mean endorsement for each option for each item and the variance (sample value and not population estimate) for the options that are being scored as 'correct'. If this were an ability test, for example, one of the options would have been determined at the time of item writing as the right answer. If it were a personality test, one of the options for each item would have been included to attempt to reflect the attribute being measured.

The first step in the analysis is to examine (a) the popularity of each of the responses, and (b), for a multiple-choice test such as this one, the attractiveness of the options that are used as 'distracters'. They are called distracters because they are not correct but have been included because they raise some level of uncertainty. Put another way, the options are written so that they are not so far from the correct answer that no one who knows the right answer would choose them.

For Item 1, the correct answer has proved quite popular (endorsement of 70 per cent) and the participants who did not choose the correct answer have spread their responses over the remaining three options equally. This is a relatively easy item (high proportion of correct answers) and one for which the distracters are working well. Item 2 is a very easy item (the correct answer has a 100 per cent endorsement), but as it stands would be rejected because of its high endorsement. The beginning assumption in test development is that individuals differ. The purpose of development of the test is to assess these differences. An item that does not show differences (as with Item 2) is therefore not useful. Where endorsement is too high (more than 90 per cent of respondents) or too low (less than 10 per cent), the item is usually rejected.

Item 3 is a more difficult question, with a response rate of 50 per cent for the correct option, but two of the distracters have not been chosen at all. This item needs further consideration, because as it is currently written there is one option that is attractive but wrong. This could be because there is some ambiguity in the wording. Item 4 is a slightly more difficult item than the previous one, but here the distracters are all working well (all options are achieving reasonably equal endorsement). The same could be said for the final item. At this stage, one item (Item 2) would be rejected, three accepted, and one held for further consideration.

The next step is to analyse the intercorrelations of the items and the correlations of each of the items with the sum of all of the items. The intercorrelation analysis is straightforward (each item is correlated with every other item) but the item-total correlation analysis deserves some comment. The correlation is between the item and the sum of all the items. This sum is the best estimate of what is common to all the items in the set. It is assumed that while there are likely to be some problem items in the set, the sum over all items is a reasonable first approximation to the attribute to be measured. The item writers, working from a reasonably tight specification, should have been able to generate at least a reasonable number of good items and summing over the complete set should even out to some degree the limitations of individual items. In calculating the sum, each item is in turn deleted, to give what is sometimes called the corrected item total. If in correlating an item with the total of all the items, the item itself were included there would be an artificial inflation of the correlation, because the item would be part of that with which it is being correlated and this must produce some level of correlation. So, in determining the item total correlation for each of the items, each item is in turn deleted from the total of all the other items.

The second table presents the corrected (item deleted) and uncorrected item total correlation. (The intercorrelations of the items themselves would also be examined but in the interests of space have been omitted. You may wish to calculate them.) The uncorrected correlations are included simply to make the point that they are different (and, with such a small item set and N, not surprisingly, substantially so).

TABLE 2 Corrected and uncorrected item-total correlations for the data in Table 1

| Item | Item-Total Correlations | |
	Uncorrected	Corrected
1	0.66	0.36
3	0.9	0.75
4	0.23	−0.17
5	0.77	0.52

Note in Table 2 Item 2 has been omitted. Recall that this was the item that all 10 participants answered correctly. There is no variance for this item and therefore no correlation is possible with any other variable.

Inspection of the corrected item total correlations in Table 2 provides the next significant piece of information in item analysis. Item 2 has already been discarded. Items 1 and 5, easy and more difficult items at the first stage, are found to correlate reasonably well with the sum of all the other items. They show reasonable item validity. Item 3, which was suspect because of its pattern of responding across distracters, is found to have quite high item validity. This suggests that it should be kept and the distracters reformulated or reworded. Item 4, which appeared a reasonable item at the first stage, is found here to have zero item validity (the correlation is in fact negative). This item is not measuring what the other items in the set are measuring and therefore will have to be discarded.

Thus we finish with three items, one of which requires further work. If we wanted a five-item test we will now need to go back to the item writing stage and then do a further item analysis. Items are typically lost in item analysis and hence the pool of items is made larger at the outset to allow for this.

You may wish to calculate the alpha coefficient for this 3-item test and then apply the Spearman-Brown formula to determine the number of items you would need to add to take the alpha to, say, 0.9.

Textbooks on testing often include discussions of a number of indices that have been proposed over the years for item analysis. We have concentrated on the ones that we consider are of central importance to contemporary item analysis but our treatment of the topic is not meant to be exhaustive.

Gregory (2000), for example, describes what he terms the reliability index for an item, which should not be confused with the reliability of a test. It is the product of the standard deviation of the item and its item-total correlation. For a dichotomously scored item (True/False) as in many personality tests, the standard deviation of the item is the square root of the product of the proportion (p) endorsing the item (what we have termed its popularity) and the obverse of that proportion $(1 - p)$. Indices, such as item reliability, that are the product of other indices are, in our view, open to misinterpretation. Two items may obtain the same item-reliability index but for different reasons, one because the item standard deviation is high and the other because the item correlation is high. We suggest that it is better to make decisions about items on the basis of a consideration of each of the indices separately than in terms of a combination of the two.

Another index that Gregory and others discuss is the item validity, or the correlation between an item and score on an external criterion being used to validate the test. By selecting items with high item validity, the correlation between score on the final version of the test and the external criterion should be maximised. This was a common strategy when validity was thought of only in terms of criterion validity and external keying was the method of choice for test construction, neither of which is true any more. If a test is being developed for one highly specific use, then attention to item validity may make sense, but to the extent that one seeks to maximise the correlation with one criterion measure one may be reducing the correlation of the test with another criterion that is only moderately correlated with it and thereby reducing the value of the test. To develop an aptitude test for success in first year university psychology by selecting on the basis of the correlation of items with the result of a first year psychology examination may produce a test with reasonable predictive value against this criterion. However, to the extent that results in psychology do not correlate well with results in, say, first year cultural studies then one could be doing a disservice to those seeking advice on their aptitude for university study. Again one needs to specify in advance the construct that one is seeking to measure before the exercise begins and let this specification guide all the decisions that are made along the way. Viewed from this perspective, item validity may have only curiosity value.

There is an exception, and that is the use of the item validity index to reduce social desirability variance in personality tests. We noted at the beginning of Chapter 4 that psychological tests were subject to systematic and unsystematic forms of bias. To the extent that people in completing a test respond to an aspect of the test that is irrelevant to the construct of interest, systematic bias is introduced into scores on the test. For example, a test of neuroticism (simply put, tendency to neurotic illness) would include items about thoughts, feelings, or behaviours experienced by people suffering from neurosis. The test developer is expecting that those taking the test will respond to the content of the items, but it may be that responses to some degree are prompted not by the content of the items but by the desire of persons completing the test to present themselves in a favourable light to others. Put bluntly, we usually do not want other people to think we are mad! This understandable human tendency to make a good public impression is not what the test developer wants to assess, but the items may inadvertently prompt this. Social desirability bias, as it has been called, is a feature of most self-report tests of personality and introduces a systematic bias into scores on these tests.

One way of combating social desirability bias, as Jackson and his colleagues demonstrated, is to pay attention to it in test construction and to do this at the item level. In developing his Personal Research Form (a self-report test of personality that sought to capture 20 of the needs identified by Henry Murray in his theory of personality), Jackson (1970) examined the correlation of each of the items with a measure of social desirability. Crowne and Marlowe (1964) showed how such a measure itself is developed by using items that reflect altruistic but improbable behaviours (eg, 'I never gossip'). Jackson developed his own measure of social desirability and required that an item to be selected for inclusion in his test show a correlation with total score on the test that was larger, and substantially so, than its correlation with the measure of social desirability. Such a requirement ensured that the final version of the test would have a higher saturation of construct relevant variance than social desirability variance. The correlation with social desirability used here can be thought of as an item validity, but in this case it is negative validity (a systematic form of bias that one is seeking to eliminate rather than a source of construct variance that one is seeking to maximise).

Even here one needs to be cautious. A reasonable level of concern about how one presents oneself to one's peers would be considered by many a sign of a good self-concept and of mental health. Aggressive attempts to eliminate its influence from a test of neuroticism might leave the test developer with a poorer test of the construct than otherwise would be the case. Worse yet, it may produce a set of items that reflects defensiveness in respondents, that is a tendency to deny they have symptoms when in fact they do. Thus, in seeking to eliminate one confound, the test developer may have unwittingly introduced another. Is there any escape from this maze? The only real protection is to have a good map, in this case, a good specification of the construct to begin with. The richer the conceptualisation of the construct in terms of the constructs with which it is related and those that it is not, the better one can undertake the test construction exercise.

One other index for item analysis work that should be mentioned, although it is not strictly speaking a new index, is the one termed by Gregory the 'item discrimination index'. This was commonly used in the days before high-speed computers were available to compute the correlation matrices for large item sets and was a way of generating an estimate of the item-total correlation. Nowadays it presents the test developer with not less but more work and is seldom employed. The index is calculated by dividing the total sample available for analysis into two groups in terms of total score. The two groups can be those with the top 25 per cent and the bottom 25 per cent of total scores on the item set, or the top 27 per cent and bottom 27 per cent. Each item is then considered in terms of how well it discriminates between the two groups, on the grounds that a good item is one that makes a clear discrimination between those with high scores and those with low scores on the construct of interest. The actual index is the difference in the frequencies of respondents in the two groups endorsing the item expressed as a ratio of the total number of cases in the two groups. Items with larger values for the item discrimination index would be selected in preference to those with smaller values, all other things being equal.

Originally the item discrimination index was used to estimate the biserial correlation between the item and total score on the item set, which is related to the item-total correlation that we have recommended as the estimate of discriminability. The two are not the same, and there are arguments for considering the biserial correlation to be the better index of correlation for test theory purposes. It is not, however, a product moment correlation and as such does not fit with a number of other forms of analysis of item data (eg, factor analysis). If we need to know the biserial correlation it is easily calculated from the point biserial correlation by the formula:

$$r_{bis} = r_{pbis} \left(\frac{\sqrt{pq}}{y_i} \right)$$

where:

r_{bis} and r_{pbis} are the coefficients for the biserial and point biserial correlations respectively

p and q   are the percentage of cases in the two groups

y_i is the ordinate of the normal curve corresponding to p and is found from the tables of the normal curve.

On the basis of an evaluation of the item statistics and qualitative information about the items, a subset will be selected as the most useful for the test. If the subset is smaller in number than the number considered desirable for the final version of the test, then more item writing and item analysis will be necessary.

ASSESSING RELIABILITY AND VALIDITY

The subset of items that have been selected is then evaluated for reliability using the most appropriate form for the construct of interest (see Chapter 4). The data gathered for item analysis can used for this purpose, but it is important to collect data using independent samples to ensure that chance effects are not confounding the conclusions being drawn about the test. With only a moderate number of items, there is the possibility that, with the number of correlations being calculated, some of these are due to sampling error. Using a number of representative samples allows one to check the replicability of the findings and provides increased confidence that the decisions being made about the test are sound.

If the item set does not reach the standards of reliability usually applied (again see Chapter 4), then further test development is necessary.

Data on validity of the test can be collected from the independent samples being used to check the item analysis and reliability findings. Some data may have already been collected. It is usual, for example, in developing self-report tests of personality to include measures of response sets such as social desirability (see earlier discussion under Item analysis and selection) when administering the original item pool.

NORMING THE TEST

With a test of satisfactory reliability and validity for the purpose for which it was devised, the test developer has two further tasks to complete, if the test is to be used professionally. It may be that the purpose of constructing the test is to use it in research and in this case the next two steps are not required. But if the test is to be used by others for decision making then relevant and representative norms for the uses to which the test will be put need to be developed and a manual for using the test needs to be prepared.

The features of norms were discussed in Chapter 3. Representativeness is of course the key consideration, and this depends on a clear answer to the question: Representative of what? What is the population to which the test user is likely to want to compare a score on the test for an individual? With some constructs, general mental ability, for example, the comparison is often to the population at large. For other constructs, there may be a particular sub-population that is important. A test of suicide potential, for example, might be developed for use with patients with diagnosed mental disorder in an in-patient setting, or the test might be for memory in patients with dementia. The norms in these cases should represent the respective patient populations rather than the general population.

In developing norms it is often the case that factors known to correlate with score on the test are explicitly included. Gender and age are two variables that correlate with measures of a number of psychological constructs, albeit only at a modest level, and for that reason are often explicitly included in preparing norms. When we say 'explicitly included' we mean that norms are prepared in such a way that these variables are identified in the tables that are prepared. They will almost always be implicitly included in developing a sampling plan for collecting norms. When age and gender are explicitly included, the test user can base interpretation of the extremity of a score on its deviation from the mean for the age group most similar to and the gender of the individual tested. Although this is helpful for the user, it does increase the work involved in norming the test. It is not one mean that is now of interest but a set of means, one for each of the groups formed by the cross-break of the two variables. For example, if separate norms are to be developed by gender and age, at a minimum the means for four groups will need to be found. Gender is fixed at two levels and age could be reduced to two levels (old and young). Therefore, there are 2×2 or four groups. But a split into old and young is a very coarse treatment of the age variable for most purposes and three to five levels are more realistic, which would make for up to 10 groups (2×5). It was noted in Chapter 3 that from 200 to 500 participants are needed to estimate the mean with reasonable accuracy; Kline (1993) proposed 300. This means that a total of from 4×300 (1200) to 10×300 (3000) participants will be needed, depending on how coarse a grouping on age is acceptable. If separate norms are not provided for age and gender, then 300 participants would be sufficient, although one would normally need to sample in such a way that these variables are adequately represented in the norming sample.

The reader is referred to the discussion in Chapter 3 and to more advanced texts (eg, Pedhazur & Schmelkin, 1991) regarding the issues that need to be considered in developing a sampling plan for the collection of normative data. Careful development of test items and comprehensive work on the validity of the test for given purposes will be compromised by poor sampling for the establishing of norms. Serious users will quickly identify problems relating to poor or inadequate sampling and use an alternative or wait until these problems are corrected.

With normative data to hand, the decision needs to be made on how best to present it. That is, what form of transformation of the raw scores on the test need to be made to best communicate the required information (refer to Chapter 4). Frequently, standard scores or some whole number transformation of them and percentiles are both provided to maximise the information available to the user. Tables are then prepared with the transformed values for all possible raw scores so that the user can read off the appropriate transformation once the raw score on the test has been computed.

PUBLICATION

The final task, if the test is to be used professionally, is to prepare the test for publication. If this is being done commercially the test publisher will be of considerable assistance at this stage, but even here the test developer remains responsible for the decisions made. Some of these decisions concern how the test will be made available to potential users. For example, what materials will be used for the test items to maximise their readability, durability, and professional format? Will they be included in a kit and if so what form will it take? Will the test user be able to carry it about easily? In the age of computer testing, a somewhat different set of questions arise about the optimal presentation of material on computer screens and the ways answers are recorded, and security of test material becomes an even more significant issue. These are not psychological decisions as such but can have an important bearing on test use and are therefore important.

A second set of questions arise with respect to the manual that needs to accompany the test. This will outline the way in which the test was developed, indicating the theoretical account of the construct relied on, how items were constructed, the item analysis procedures followed and criteria employed in selecting items, and the data currently available on reliability and validity, as well as, of course, the normative data obtained. The manual must provide instructions for administration of the test, including any time limits that need to be observed and how the test is to be scored. The populations for which the test is appropriate need to be specified, including any requirements of those taking the test, eg, the upper and lower chronological ages for which the test is appropriate, the reading age necessary to understand items. The qualifications necessary for test users to interpret test scores need to be clearly stated. The limitations of the test should be admitted and caution expressed about any ways in which it could be foreseen the test could misused. If there are published data on the test, reference to these should be included, or an indication given that summaries of unpublished work are obtainable from the author of the test. Preparation of an adequate manual is a significant exercise in psychological writing and could run to the length of a small book. As Cronbach (1970, pp 118–19) put it: 'The manual must be clear enough that any qualified user can comprehend it—and clear enough that the reader who is not qualified will realize that he is not. Yet the information must be precise enough to satisfy specialists in test research'.

CONCLUDING REMARKS

The steps followed in constructing a psychological test have been outlined and discussed. To provide an example of the procedures in practice, a test construction project undertaken by two of the authors is outlined in Box 6.3. This is not meant to illustrate test construction at its very best but does serve to show how the steps come together when a real question is posed.

BOX **6.3**

A test of retrograde amnesia

Loss of memory has an impact on well-being and the enjoyment of life and can be an indication of central nervous system (CNS) damage or disease. Diagnostic tests of memory loss have concentrated on identifying what is termed anterograde amnesia, that is, memory loss resulting from insult to the CNS that involves events occurring in the patient's life subsequent to the damage or onset of the disease process. For example, following a motor vehicle accident, a person may have difficulty remembering day-to-day events that happen to them. Retrograde amnesia, on the other hand, involves loss of memory for events prior to the CNS insult, for example, events in the early years of the person's life well before the accident.

Shum and O'Gorman examined the literature on retrograde amnesia and found no published tests suitable for use in Australia. Although psychological tests can often be used with good effect in countries other than where they were first developed, given a common language and similar culture, in the case of tests of retrograde amnesia the problem of cultural difference becomes particularly acute. Although one could ask about particular events in a person's early life, these will differ from individual to individual and there is frequently no one who can verify the answers the person gives. For this reason, tests of retrograde amnesia commonly use statements of events or faces of people that would generally be known to those who have lived through a particular period. Choice of the events or faces is critical, because, if they are too obscure, failure to recognise them may reflect lack of knowledge in the first place rather than loss of memory. If, on the other hand, they are too well-known, recall of them reflects general knowledge rather than a specific memory. For example, the face of a past president of the USA may be a useful item for checking memory for previous events in a citizen of that country but may not be of use for an Australian population.

Having specified the construct of interest and checked the literature thoroughly, Shum and O'Gorman embarked on an exercise in test construction, some of the details of which are reported in Shum and O'Gorman (2001). A pool of 90 famous faces and 90 public events relevant to the decades between the 1930s and 1980s was compiled from a number of sources, chiefly published photographs from newspaper or magazine stories. The item pool was administered to a sample of 47 participants for item analysis. A number of criteria were used, including the difficulty level of the items and their item-total correlations. From this large pool, 54 famous faces and 54 public events were selected for the final version of the test. The Cronbach alpha for the Famous Faces and Public Events part of the test were 0.92 and 0.91 respectively.

Validation of the test relied on two principal criteria. The first was the relationship between age and memory in a group of participants without known CNS damage or disease. It was expected that memory for events in the remote past would be poorer than that for more recent events, but that this would depend on the age of the person tested. Older compared to younger participants should have better recall of events and faces from the decades through which they have lived but the younger people had not. Shum and O'Gorman (2001) were able to show that this was the case. The second criterion was the sensitivity of the test to CNS disease known from other studies to affect memory for past events. The performance of patients with Alzheimer's disease or Korsakoff's syndrome, disorders different in aetiology, was compared to that of disease-free volunteers of approximately the same age. As predicted, the patient group showed greater memory loss on both parts of the test.

Work is progressing on norming the test for clinical use with aged people and those with dementia. An as yet unpublished manual for the test has been prepared and there is also a plan to computerise the test.

Questions for consideration

1   Define and give examples for the four levels of measurement.
2   What parameters of Item Response Theory does the Rasch Model specify?
3   What are the major steps to undertake in developing psychological tests?
4   What are some of the factors that one needs to take into consideration when developing a psychological test?
5   What is item analysis? What are some of the indices commonly used in item analysis?

Exercises

1   In the exercises for Chapter 3 the following data were provided:

A psychological test has 16 items. The mean and SD for each are as follows: 0.13, 0.33; 0.11, 0.32; 0.11, 0.37; 0.06, 0.24; 0.21, 0.41; 0.08, 0.28; 0.08, 0.27; 0.19, 0.39; 0.11, 0.31; 0.23, 0.42; 0.01, 0.12; 0.10, 0.30; 0.15, 0.36; 0.01, 0.13; 0.11, 0.31; 0.01, 0.09.

In addition, the item-total correlation for each are found to be: 0.03, 0.29, 0.34, 0.21, 0.36, 0.15, 0.02, -0.19, 0.16, 0.15, -0.23, 0.25, 0.01, 0.28, 0.24, 0.03.

You were asked to compute coefficient alpha. Assume that these are 'True/False' items and perform an item analysis of the test, to the extent that this is possible with the data available.

If the desired reliability of the test is to be 0.9, would you need to add items to it after your item analysis, and if so how many?

2   Write a five-item test of social desirability. How would you set about testing its validity?

3   The following have been offered as items for a test of general mental ability for use in Australia? Would you use them and if not why not?

    a   What is the population of the southern-most town in New Zealand? 10,000 or more than 10,000 people?

    b   The prime minister before the prime minister who was the prime minister before the present prime minister was or was not John Hewson?

    c   It is not the case that a ball is not out in tennis if it is not outside the line. True or False

    d   Complete the following number series: 20, 30, 40, 50, …

Further reading

Crocker, L, & Algina, J (1986). *Introduction to classical and modern test theory*. New York: Holt, Rinehart and Winston.

Kline, P (1998). *The new psychometrics: Science, psychology, and measurement*. London: Routledge.

Nunnally, J, & Bernstein, I H (1994). *Psychometric theory* (3rd ed). New York: McGraw Hill.

Rust, J, & Golombok, S (1999). *Modern psychometrics: The science of psychological assessment* (2nd edn). London: Routledge.

Wasserman, J D, & Bracken, B A (2003). Psychometric characteristics of assessment procedures. In J R Graham, & J A Naglieri (Eds), *Handbook of Psychology: Vol. 10, Assessment Psychology* (pp 43–66). Hoboken, NJ: John Wiley & Sons.

part three

Areas of
Professional
Application

3

chapter seven

Clinical and Mental Health Testing and Assessment

7

- Since her divorce three months ago, a 30-year-old female has been feeling very sad and has lost interest in activities she normally enjoys. She was referred by her family doctor to a clinical psychologist for assessment of depression.

- A 60-year-old male who has been drinking heavily for the last 25 years was referred to a rehabilitative service for assessment and treatment of alcohol abuse.

- Since witnessing a bank robbery, a young bank teller has not been able to return to work. She was anxious, agitated, and has nightmares. The bank referred her to a clinical psychologist for assessment and counselling.

- A young man in his early 20s has been acting strangely over the last two months. He reported that he was being unfairly treated by his family and workmates and he also reported hearing voices. He was admitted to a hospital for psychiatric assessment and treatment.

- Partners who have been married for 10 years are having difficulties maintaining the relationship. They referred themselves to a clinical psychologist to seek help.

INTRODUCTION

In Australia and other parts of the world, mental health services, public and private, are one of the largest employers of psychologists. Clinical psychologists in this setting assess, diagnose, and treat mental disorders (eg, schizophrenia, depression, anxiety, and personality disorders) as well as problems in everyday living (eg, relationship problems, low self-esteem, and stress). In all cases, the starting point for the psychologist is usually the referral questions, which may be as broad as: is the client suffering from a mental disorder? What is the likely cause of the client's problem? What is the client's current level of psychological functioning? What is the appropriate treatment for a client and how should the treatment be evaluated? In this chapter, we introduce the assessment techniques most commonly used by clinical psychologists in the mental health setting. These techniques include history taking, clinical interview, mental status examination, and psychological testing. For the psychological tests, we concentrate on the commonly used tests for intelligence, personality, psychopathology, depression, anxiety, and stress. To conclude the chapter, we discuss the content and structure of a clinical psychological report and provide an example of such a report.

CLARIFYING THE REFERRAL QUESTION

In the mental health setting, the need for psychological testing and assessment for a client is usually triggered by a referral question. This question provides the justification or rationale for testing and assessment. If the client is referred by another professional (eg, a psychiatrist or general practitioner), the referral question will have been formulated by them. If the client is self-referred, there is a need to formulate the problem to be addressed. In either case, there may be a need to spend some time clarifying or refining the referral question so that it becomes realistic or answerable in terms of what current knowledge in psychology can provide (Maloney & Ward, 1976). The question may be too broad (eg, why does my daughter have an eating disorder?) or generate expectations that cannot be met (eg, please assess and treat this client's depression in three sessions) and there needs to be a negotiation of the expected outcome with the referring agent. The formulation of a clear and specific referral question will facilitate the derivation of hypotheses about a case, selection of psychological assessment instruments, interpretation of results, and provision of recommendations. This process can be facilitated by the use of a standard referral form with explicit questions about the reason for referral, use of assessment results, and the client's willingness to undertake the assessment (Bagby, Wild & Turner, 2003).

CASE HISTORY DATA

After clarifying or agreeing on the referral question for a client, a psychologist who works in the mental health setting usually commences a case by collecting demographical and biographical data about the client. These data are useful for providing the context in which to understand the referral question, to interpret results of other data collection procedures, and in preparing the psychological report. Although most of the data can be obtained during a clinical interview with the client, sometimes it is useful to collect them from a number of sources for verification purpose. For example, for clients who lack self-awareness or those with memory problems, it might not be possible to find out details of their educational or vocational history. In most mental health settings, standardised forms have been designed to summarise these demographic and biographical data. Having access to these forms facilitates the collection of information. An important consideration here is the need to be aware of and familiar with the privacy policies of various organisations (eg, hospitals and private companies) or government departments, and the legal requirements (eg, the *Freedom of Information Act*) and ethical guidelines for obtaining and using information of this sort.

CLINICAL INTERVIEW

One of the oldest psychological assessment techniques to collect information about a client or a patient and most widely used by psychologists who work in a mental health setting is the clinical interview. Basically, during the interview, a psychologist will ask the client a number of questions (both open- and closed-ended) that are related to the client and to the referral question. Sometimes questions are used to elicit information that is not readily available from the client's record or file. For example, although there may be some information on educational history, the interviewer may need to ask the client directly about the level of educational achievement or favourite subjects in school. Similarly, information on a client's file may indicate that a client is married, but the interviewer will need to ask about the quality of the marital relationship. At other times, questions are used to test a hypothesis that the psychologist has formulated about the client's condition. For example, if the psychologist suspects that the client is suffering from a depressive disorder, questions about the person's recent level of activities, sleeping and eating habits, and prevailing mood become pertinent.

The clinical interview also provides the psychologist with a good opportunity to establish rapport with the client, to provide important information, and to establish whether the client has a reasonable understanding of what is happening to them and why. If the psychologist considers that the client does not feel comfortable during the initial stage of the clinical interview, she might want to spend more time putting the client at ease. Information the psychologist can convey during the interview includes:

(a) the purpose and nature of psychological assessment;
(b) what the client or patient is expected to do;
(c) confidentiality of information collected during assessment;
(d) the need for informed consent (examinee consents to testing after being made aware, in language she can understand, of the nature and purpose of testing);
(e) who will have access to the information collected and how it will be used.

To conduct a successful clinical interview, the psychologist needs to establish good rapport with the client by being sincere and supportive (Giordano, 1997). To engage the client in the interview, techniques are used such as trying not to dominate the interview, reflecting what is said, paraphrasing, summarising, clarifying, confronting, using eye contact and a positive posture, and nodding (Groth-Marnat, 2003; Maloney & Ward, 1976).

Although most of the information collected by the psychologist during a clinical interview is verbal in nature (ie, answers to questions), non-verbal information is provided by the client's demeanour during the interview, by how particular questions are answered, and at times by what is not said. For example, a matter-of-fact or flippant style of responding may be inconsistent with the seriousness of the content being revealed.

Psychologists who work in the mental health setting, typically obtain the following information during a clinical interview:

- demographic data
- medical history (self and family)
- family history
- educational and vocational history
- psychological history.

Although much of this information is of the sort that would be obtained by psychologists working in other settings (eg, organisational or educational), an important additional source of information comes from the mental status examination and this is unique to the mental health setting (Bagby et al, 2003).

THE MENTAL STATUS EXAMINATION

Similar to the physical examination conducted by a doctor, the mental status examination is a comprehensive set of questions used by a psychologist or by other professionals in a mental health setting to systematically assess the mental state of a client. These questions include the following:

- **Appearance:** How does the client look? What kind of clothing does the client wear? What is the personal hygiene of the client?
- **Behaviour:** How does the client behave during the examination? Does the client show unusual verbal and non-verbal behaviour?
- **Orientation:** Is the client aware of who or where he is? Does the client know what time (year, month, date, day, and time) it is?
- **Memory:** Does the client show any problems in immediate, recent, and remote memory?
- **Sensorium:** Is the client able to attend and concentrate during the examination? Does the client show problems in hearing, vision, touch, or smell?
- **Affect:** Does the client display a range of emotions during the examination? What are these emotions and how appropriate are they?
- **Mood:** What is the general or prevailing emotion displayed by the client during the examination?
- **Thought content and thought process:** What does the client want to focus on during the interview? Does he only want to talk about these things? Is the client able to clearly explain his ideas during the interview? Does he show problems such as talking rapidly, jumping from one topic to another, being circumspect and tangential, using illogical reasoning and arguments?

- **Intellectual resources:** Does the client have good verbal ability? Can he answer questions that call for general information or arithmetical operations?
- **Insight:** Is the client aware that he has a problem? Does the client know what is causing the problem? Does the client know why he was referred to see a mental health professional?
- **Judgment:** Does the client have the ability to make decisions about himself? Can the client make plans and solve problems?

Based on information gained during the clinical interview and mental status examination, the psychologist can begin to formulate or conceptualise the client's problem by referring to systematic classification systems such as the Diagnostic and Statistical Manual of Mental Disorders published by the American Psychiatric Association (see Box 7.1) or the International Classification of Diseases published by the World Health Organisation (1992–94). To further clarify ideas and narrow down or test hypotheses, the psychologist may administer psychological tests to finalise the assessment.

BOX **7.1**

Diagnostic and Statistical Manual of Mental Disorders (DSM)

The DSM is a standard classification of mental orders published by the American Psychiatric Association for use by mental health professionals. It is the most commonly used system adopted by professionals in the USA, Australasia, and Asia. The first edition, *DSM-I* was published in 1952 and the latest version, *DSM – Fourth Edition – Text Revision (DSM – IV – TR)* was published in 2000. The main purpose of the *DSM* is to facilitate communication among mental health professionals and the diagnostic terms and codes included in the manual provide a shorthand for professionals to communicate information about clients and their conditions. Because the diagnostic system of the *DSM* is based on observed behavioural symptoms rather than on a particular theoretical perspective, it can be used by professionals with different theoretical orientations.

The *DSM – IV – TR* contains a list of psychiatric disorders and their corresponding diagnostic codes. Each disorder is accompanied by a set of diagnostic criteria and text containing information about the particular disorder including associated features, prevalence, familial patterns, age-, culture-, and gender-specific features, and differential diagnosis. No information about treatment or ætiology is included. In addition, each client is not just given a single label. Rather the client is classified in terms of a set of five axes or clinically important factors:

- Axis I—Clinical disorders (eg, dementia, substance-related disorders, schizophrenia, mood disorders, anxiety disorders, eating disorders)
- Axis II—Mental retardation and personality disorders (eg, antisocial personality disorder, paranoid personality disorder, borderline personality disorder)
- Axis III—Physical or medical conditions that may be relevant to mental disorders (eg, epilepsy, cancer, Alzheimer's disease, Parkinson's disease)
- Axis IV—Psychosocial and environmental problems (eg, stress, financial, marital,

occupational) that may affect the diagnosis, treatment, and prognosis of mental disorders

- Axis V—Global assessment of functioning from 1 to 100

Although the *DSM* has been criticised for being atheoretical, adhering too closely to the medical model, and for having low reliability and validity, it is still commonly used by professionals who prevent, diagnose, and treat mental health problems (Jensen & Hoagwood, 1997; Nathan & Langenbucher, 2003).

PSYCHOLOGICAL TESTS

Because of space limitations, we will confine our description to a selected number of instruments commonly used in the clinical and mental health area for the testing and assessment of intelligence, personality, psychopathology, depression, anxiety, and stress. Interested readers can consult sources such as Goldstein and Hersen (2000) and Groth-Marnat (2003) for a more comprehensive treatment of instruments used in the mental health setting.

Intelligence

Since Binet's pioneering development of ways of assessing intelligence in children, psychologists in a number of settings have made use of measures of ability. A substantial advance in the clinical area came with the publication of a battery of tests for the appraisal of adult intelligence following the work of David Wechsler at Bellevue Hospital in New York. The facility had a large outpatient unit that saw a broad spectrum of patients. From superficial features of the way the patient presented it was difficult to decide if the problem was, for example, an illness such as schizophrenia, or a deficit such as mental retardation, or the result of alcoholism. Wechsler devised a series of tests that would allow classification of the patient's intelligence level but, as well, would aid in narrowing down the particular nature of the patient's problem. The tests he developed were subsequently extended to children and pre-schoolers and have been revised several times since their first publication.

Wechsler's own definition of intelligence was that it is 'the aggregate or global capacity of the individual to act purposefully, to think rationally, and to deal effectively with the environment' (1939, p.7). There are, of course, many other definitions of intelligence in the literature (see Cianciolo & Sternberg, 2004), but this captures well a practitioner's view of the construct. The definition implies that overall intelligence is a compound of a number of abilities. The question of whether intelligence is one dimension or many has exercised psychologists since Binet's time. The use of a single number, the intelligence quotient or IQ, implies that it is a unitary construct but common experience suggests that individuals show a profile of abilities with strengths and weaknesses. A person may have good general knowledge but be only average on spatial ability. The consensus among researchers is now that both positions are correct: a general factor can be found across a wide variety of cognitive tests but there are as well more discrete abilities. Carroll's (1993) exhaustive re-analysis of a very large number of previous studies (briefly mentioned in Chapter 8) points inescapably to this conclusion. In practice this outcome justifies attention to general as well as particular abilities, depending on the question the practitioner is seeking to answer.

Wechsler Adult Intelligence Scale—Third Edition (WAIS–III; Wechsler, 1997a)

This classic test is one of the most commonly used psychological tests throughout the world (Camara, Nathan & Puente, 2000; Knight & Godfrey, 1984; Ryan, Dai & Zheng, 1994; Sharpley & Pain, 1988; Watkins, Campbell, Nieberding & Hallmark, 1995). The original version was published as the Wechsler-Bellevue Intelligence Scale in 1939. Other editions of this test include the WAIS (1955) and the WAIS – Revised (WAIS–R; 1981). Developed for adults aged between 16 and 89 years old, the WAIS-III was published in 1997 and, similar to its predecessors, its aim is to assess intellectual ability in adults. It is also used for assessing psychoeducational disability, neuropsychiatric and organic dysfunction, and giftedness.

The WAIS–III is an individually administered test battery that comprises seven verbal and seven performance subtests (one performance subtest is optional). According to the manual, it takes about 65–95 minutes to administer, depending on which subtests are included. Table 7.1 lists all the subtests of the WAIS–III and the abilities they measure and Figure 7.1 provides some examples of these subtests. A training video and computerised scoring and report-writing CD can be purchased separately.

TABLE 7.1 Subtests of the WAIS–III

Subtest	Description	Abilities Measured
Verbal		
Vocabulary	Test taker is required to provide meaning of words of increasing difficulty	Knowledge of word meaning
Similarities	Test taker is provided with pairs of words that represent objects, facts, and ideas and asked in what way they are similar	Verbal concept formation
Arithmetic	Test taker is presented with mathematical problems orally and asked to solve them mentally	Attention and arithmetic skills
Digit Span	Test taker is presented with series of randomised digits at one digit per second and asked first to repeat them as given and then backwards	Attention and working memory
Information	Test taker is required to answer a number of factual questions relating to persons, places, and common phenomena	General knowledge

TABLE 7.1 (cont.)

Subtest	Description	Abilities Measured
Comprehension	Test taker is asked to answer questions relating to common sense and social and cultural convention	Social intelligence
Letter-Number Sequencing	Test taker is orally presented with a series of letters and numbers that are random in order and is asked to repeat the numbers and letters separately but in order	Attention and working memory
Performance		
Picture Completion	Test taker is shown pictures with important parts (one per picture) missing and asked to identify what is missing	Attention to visual details
Digit Symbol—Coding	Test taker is shown an array that pairs numbers with symbols and asked to fill in a separate array with numbers, using the matching symbols, in two minutes	Attention and visuo-motor coordination
Block Design	Test taker is asked to arrange red and white coloured blocks according to specific designs	Spatial reasoning and problem solving
Matrix Reasoning	Test taker is shown patterned pictures with one part missing and is asked to choose which of the five choices provided would fit in the missing part	Visual-spatial reasoning and problem solving
Picture Arrangement	Test taker is shown cartoon pictures that are presented in the wrong order and is asked to reorganise them so that the picture will tell a logical story	Visual-spatial problem solving and logical reasoning
Symbol Search	Test taker is asked to search for a target symbol among a group of symbols in two minutes	Visual-motor processing speed
Object Assembly (optional)	Test taker is asked to assemble the pieces of jigsaw puzzles to form a common object	Perceptual analysis and organisation

One of the strengths of the WAIS-III is the size and representativeness of the standardisation sample used in test development. A total of 2450 individuals were included, ranging in age from 16 to 89 years across thirteen age groups. A stratified sampling plan was used to match the final sample as closely as possible to the population of the USA in 1995 in terms of demographic characteristics known to influence intelligence scores: namely, gender, socio-economic status, ethnic background, educational attainment, and geographical location. In 1995 a census had been completed that provided the test developers with accurate information on the proportions of individuals in each of the demographic groupings and these proportions were reproduced in selecting participants for the standardisation sample.

FIGURE 7.1 Simulated examples of WAIS–III subtests items

Picture Completion

Matrix Reasoning

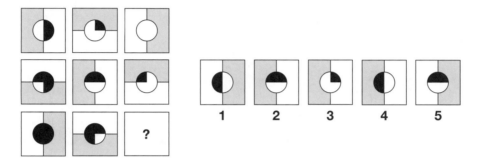

Digit Symbol-Coding

1	2	3	4	5
>	‡	//	<	#

5	3	2	4	5

Comprehension

What does this saying mean: 'A man is known by the company he keeps'?
What would you do if a shopkeeper gives you more change than she should?

Information

Who wrote Lord of the Rings?
Who is Alan Bond?
Lake Taupo is in the North or South Island of New Zealand?

Arithmetic

John has $300 and spent $45 on petrol. How much money has he got left?
Five children were given 40 lollies. How many does each child get if they were divided equally?

Scoring the test involves two steps. The raw scores on the subtests are converted to scaled scores (with a mean of 10 and a standard deviation of 3) based on the appropriate age group of the standardisation sample. The subtest scores are then summed and transformed into three IQs (viz, Full Scale, Verbal, and Performance) and four Index Scores (viz, Verbal Comprehension, Perceptual Organisation, Working Memory, and Processing Speed). Figure 7.2 shows which subtests make up the three IQ and four Index Scores. The IQ and Index Scores all have a mean of 100 and standard deviation of 15.

FIGURE 7.2 Subtest composition of the three WAIS–III IQs and the four indices

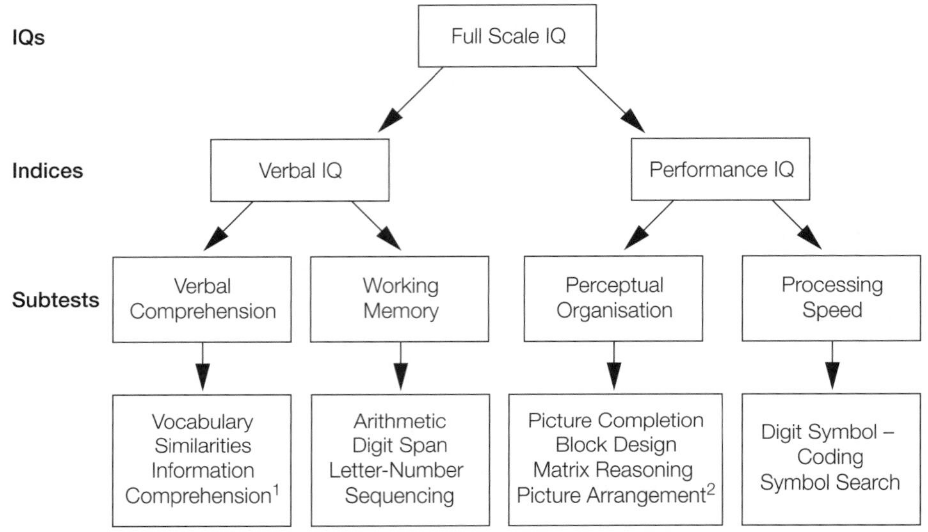

IQs	Full Scale IQ

| Indices | Verbal IQ | Performance IQ |

| Subtests | Verbal Comprehension | Working Memory | Perceptual Organisation | Processing Speed |

| Vocabulary Similarities Information Comprehension[1] | Arithmetic Digit Span Letter-Number Sequencing | Picture Completion Block Design Matrix Reasoning Picture Arrangement[2] | Digit Symbol – Coding Symbol Search |

Note 1. the Comprehension subtest is part of the VIQ but not the Verbal Comprehension Index
Note 2. the Picture Arrangement subtest is part of the PIQ but not the Perceptual Organisation Index

Table 7.2 summarises the split-half and test-retest reliabilities of the subtests, Indices, and IQ scores of the WAIS–III. The test-retest reliabilities were obtained based on a subgroup (394 adults) of the standardisation sample and the retest period ranged from 2 to 12 weeks (average = 34.6 days). The manual also reports high interscorer agreement on some subtests that require the exercise of judgment in scoring (r for Vocabulary, Similarities and Comprehension = 0.95, 0.92, and 0.91 respectively). This, together with the coefficients summarised in Table 7.2, indicates that the WAIS–III has high reliability.

The test manual of the WAIS–III also presents an impressive amount of evidence to support its validity. First, it has been shown that the WAIS-III can discriminate between those with and without neurological, psychoeducational, and developmental disorders. Second, results of exploratory and confirmatory factor analyses support the four-index model. Third, the WAIS–III has been found to correlate significantly with other tests of intellectual ability (viz, the WISC–III, the WAIS–R, and the Stanford-Binet).

TABLE 7.2 Reliability of the WAIS–III

Scores		Reliability	
		Split-Half	Test-Retest
IQ	Verbal	0.97	0.96
	Performance	0.94	0.91
	Full Scale	0.98	0.96
Indices			
	Verbal Comprehension	0.96	0.95
	Perceptual Organisation	0.93	0.88
	Working Memory	0.94	0.89
	Processing Speed	0.88	0.89
Subtests			
	Vocabulary	0.93	0.91
	Similarities	0.86	0.83
	Arithmetic	0.88	0.86
	Digit Span	0.90	0.83
	Information	0.91	0.94
	Comprehension	0.84	0.81
	Letter-Number Sequencing	0.82	0.75
	Picture Completion	0.83	0.79
	Digit Symbol-Coding	–	0.86
	Block Design	0.86	0.82
	Matrix Reasoning	0.90	0.77
	Picture Arrangement	0.74	0.69
	Symbol Search	–	0.79
	Object Assembly	0.70	0.76

Note: split-half reliability for Digit Symbol-Coding and Symbol Search could not be calculated because of the timed nature of these two subtests.

Despite its strong psychometric properties, it has been suggested that the WAIS–III has some limitations. These include, for example, the relatively long time required to administer the eleven or thirteen subtests required to obtain the necessary IQ or Index scores, failure to include new subtests to assess recently emerging concepts in the area of intelligence such as emotional and social intelligence, and the comparatively low test-retest and split-half reliabilities of some subtests (eg, Letter Number Sequencing, Picture Arrangement, and Object Assembly) (Hess, 2001; Kaufman & Lichtenberger, 1999).

Personality

The assessment of personality has been an area of some controversy in psychology in the past (eg, Mischel, 1968), because of concerns about the validity of many of the tests developed for this purpose. There is now less concern on this point, for three main reasons. First, the cumulation of a very large number of individual studies using a technique termed meta-analysis has pointed to validity coefficients for personality tests that are modest in size but replicable and useful for assessment purposes. Second, factor analytic work with personality tests has helped to clarify the similarities and differences between them. Third, there are now much more realistic expectations about what information these tests can provide and of their limitations. Personality measures do not provide highly specific predictions about what individuals will do; they provide information about what people are generally like or what they usually do.

There are a number of different systems or theories of personality and these lead to different approaches in practice to personality assessment (see, for example, Wiggins, 1973). The choice of a system for assessment depends partly on the theoretical orientation of the assessor and partly on the referral question. Because there are a large number of personality theories currently discussed in the literature, space does not permit an extensive treatment of various approaches. Instead, we confine ourselves to some of the most widely used tests for this purpose.

Minnesota Multiphasic Personality Inventory—Second Edition (MMPI–2; Butcher, Dahlstrom, Graham, Tellegen & Kaemmer, 1989)

This 567-item self-report inventory is one of the most commonly used psychological assessment instruments in the USA, Australia, and New Zealand (Camara et al, 2000; Knight & Godfrey, 1984; Sharpley & Pain, 1988; Watkins et al, 1995). The original MMPI was developed to measure major patterns of personality and emotional disorders in adults 18 years and older using a technique called the criterion keying approach. In criterion keying, test items are selected from a pool of items if responses to them discriminate between a group presumed to show the characteristic of interest and a group who do not. In the development of the original MMPI, patient groups previously diagnosed by a panel of expert psychiatrists and groups of visitors to a large hospital were used. Items that differentiated between, for example, a group of patients diagnosed with schizophrenia and a group of 'normals' (ie, hospital visitors) were included in the schizophrenia scale. Content of the item is not important in criterion keying. The only consideration is the empirically demonstrated capacity of the item to discriminate.

The MMPI–2 can be administered individually or to a group and it takes about 90 minutes to complete. Test takers are asked to consider each of the items of the inventory and indicate whether the statements are 'True' or 'False' for them. The responses of the test takers can be hand- or computer-scored and T scores for seven validity indicators (Cannot Say, Lie, Infrequency, Correction, Back F, Variable Response Inconsistency, True Response Inconsistency) and ten clinical scales (Hypochondriasis, Depression, Conversion Hysteria, Psychopathic Deviate, Masculinity-Femininity, Paranoia, Psychasthenia, Schizophrenia, Hypomania, and Social Introversion) and a number of supplementary scales (eg, Anxiety, Repression, Ego Strength, Social Responsibility) can be obtained. The standardisation sample of the MMPI-2 comprised 2600 non-clinical individuals and 423 individuals with psychiatric problems.

The internal consistency of the MMPI-2 scales is typically in the 0.70s and 0.80s but some coefficient alphas as low as 0.30 have been reported for some scales in some samples. In terms of test-retest reliability, correlation coefficients ranging from 0.50 to 0.90 have been reported for retesting after one week.

The validity of the MMPI–2 has been supported by high correlation between scores on the second and the first editions. In the literature, a large amount of research has been conducted examining the validity of the MMPI, and Graham (1993) reported an average validity coefficient of 0.46. The MMPI–2 is a sensitive instrument but it should be pointed out that the scales are highly correlated and it is not based on a firm theoretical base. In addition, it has not been revised based on a recent classification of psychopathology (eg, the DSM–IV).

Rorschach Inkblot Test (Rorschach, 1921)

This is a projective technique for assessing personality and assisting in clinical diagnosis. Projective techniques present the test taker with a set of ambiguous stimuli, such as designs or photographs deliberately selected to be vague in their reference, and ask the test taker to give them meaning (see Figure 7.3 for an example of an ambiguous stimulus). Because the stimuli are ambiguous, a number of interpretations are possible and the one offered by the test taker is considered to have meaning in terms of the individual's own needs and wishes. The hypothesis is based on psychodynamic theorising which sees the person's thought and behaviour influenced by motivations of which they are not fully aware. Because the objective environment of the projective test provides little if any clue to interpretation, it is argued, the test taker is thrown back on their own internal motivational life in

FIGURE 7.3 A simulated example of a Rorschach inkblot

offering an interpretation of the test materials, and so reveals something of their psychodynamics.

Although the Rorschach Inkblot Test is not commonly used in Australasia (Knight & Godfrey, 1984; Sharpley & Pain, 1988), it is still a very popular test in the USA (Camara et al, 2000; Watkins et al, 1995). For this reason and because of the historical significance of the test, we have included a description of it here. The Rorschach is an individually administered test that was designed for use with individuals 5 years and older. The test materials comprise 10 cardboard plates (24.6 cm × 17 cm) with a symmetrical inkblot on each. Five of the inkblots are black and white in colour, two are black, white, and red in colour, and three are composed of pastel colours (see Figure 7.3 for an example of an inkblot). Test takers are presented with the plates one at a time and asked to report 'What might this be?' If a test taker provides only one response to the first inkblot, they are encouraged to offer a further response. After responding to all ten plates, the test taker is asked to revisit the responses given and explain to the test administrator the reason for each. There is no recommended time limit for the test but it can take up to an hour to complete.

A number of different methods exist in the literature for scoring and interpreting the Rorschach and there is no agreement as to which of these is to be preferred. In an effort to improve the reliability of scoring, Exner (1974) introduced what he termed the Comprehensive System. Basically, this system involves scoring responses according to the location of the blot that is referred to, whether there is reference to movement and the content of the response. Although this system has improved reliability, questions are still raised about the validity of the test. Some critics consider the interpretation of the responses subjective and the validity of the test questionable, and not much research evidence has been provided to support its validity.

Psychopathology

Unlike the WAIS–III or the MMPI–2, a number of instruments have been developed to provide a comprehensive assessment of mental health problems. One of the main advantages of this type of instrument is a systematic and comprehensive coverage of all major areas of potential problems. In this section, we review one example of this type of instrument.

Personality Assessment Inventory (PAI; Morey, 1991)

This is a 344-item self-report scale designed to provide information relating to clinical diagnosis, treatment planning, and screening for psychopathology in adults 18 years and older. It can be administered individually or in a group and usually takes 40–50 mins to complete. Test takers are asked to consider each of the 344 items and endorse each one of them according to a four-point scale (False, Not At All True, Slightly True, and Mainly True). Some examples of the PAI items include: My health condition has restricted my activities; often I think and talk so quickly that other people cannot follow my train of thought; I have some ideas that others think are strange.

Hand or computer scoring can be used and results summarised in T-scores. There are four validity scales (Inconsistency, Infrequency, Negative Impression, and Positive Impression), eleven clinical scales (Somatic Complaints, Anxiety, Anxiety-Related Disorders, Depression, Mania, Paranoia, Schizophrenia, Borderline Features, Antisocial Features, Alcohol Problems, and Drug Problems), five treatment scales (Aggression, Suicide Ideation, Stress, Nonsupport, and Treatment Rejection), and two Interpersonal Scales (Dominance and Warmth). The standardisation sample of the PAI comprised a census-matched sample (n = 1000; stratified according to age, gender, and race), a clinical sample (n = 1246), and a university student sample (n = 1051). Scores can be compared to means and standard deviations for the subsamples based on gender, race, and age groups (viz, 18–29, 30–49, 50–59, and 60+ years old).

The internal consistency of the 22 PAI scales has been found to range from 0.22 to 0.94 across the three-standardisation samples (median = 0.85). The test-retest reliability of the full scale of the inventory over 24 days using a community sample (n = 75) has been found to range from 0.67 to 0.90.

In terms of validity, the four validity scales have been found to correlate significantly with the validity scales of the MMPI–2 and the Marlow-Crown Social Desirability Scale. Questions about the validity of the PAI have been raised because of moderate correlation of the clinical scales with other tests of psychopathology. Given its recent development, more research and data are needed before the validity and utility of the PAI can be more clearly demonstrated (Boyle, 1995).

Depression and anxiety

According to Mathers, Vos, Stevenson, and Begg (2000), mental health problems account for about 30 per cent of the non-fatal disease burden (viz, years lost due to disability) in Australia. Among these mental health problems, depression and anxiety are the two that contribute most to this burden. It is, therefore, not surprising that these are the two most commonly referred problems in mental health settings in Australia. It is estimated that about 20 per cent of adults will experience a major depressive episode in their lives (Hassed, 2000). Those suffering from depression experience feelings of intense sadness for a considerable time; those suffering from anxiety are affected frequently by a state of severe and distressing nervousness. Although the symptoms of depression and anxiety are different, both of these conditions, if left untreated, can lead to debilitating and life-threatening consequences. In this section, we discuss a number of commonly used tests of depression and anxiety.

Beck Depression Inventory—Second Edition (BDI–II; Beck, Steer, & Brown, 1996)

The BDI is a commonly used scale for assessing depression and the BDI–II is a major revision of the BDI. The test was developed for age levels 13 years and older to assess symptoms corresponding to criteria for diagnosing depressive disorders based on the DSM–IV. The BDI–II can be administered individually or in groups and it takes about 5–10 mins to complete. Test takers are asked to use a four-point scale (0 to 3) to indicate whether they are experiencing depressive symptoms and their intensity. A total score can be obtained by hand or by using computer software. The standardisation sample of the BDI–II included a group of 500 outpatients and a group of 120 university students.

The internal consistency of the BDI–II as reported to date is high (viz, 0.92 for the clinical sample and 0.93 for the non-clinical sample) and its test-retest reliability is 0.93 for a one-week retesting period. In terms of validity, scores on the BDI–II have been found to correlate significantly and substantially with other measures of depression (eg, the Hamilton Psychiatric Rating Scale for Depression – Revised, and the Symptom Check List-90-Revised Depression subscale). In addition, it has been found to discriminate between individuals who suffer from clinical depression and those who do not. Results of factor analyses also provide support for the validity of this inventory.

Beck Anxiety Inventory (BAI; Beck & Steer, 1987a)

The BAI is a twenty-one-item self-report inventory designed to measures the presence and extent of anxiety in adults and adolescents. It takes only 5–10 mins to complete and can be administered individually or in a group. Test takers are asked to indicate how much they have been bothered by the symptoms listed during the past week using a four-point (0–3) scale that ranges from 'Not at all' to 'Severely; I could barely stand it'. The total score for the BAI is simply obtained by summing the points endorsed by the test takers on each of the twenty-one items. The norms for the inventory are based on 810 outpatients with a variety of diagnoses.

The reported internal consistency of the BAI is high, ranging between 0.85 and 0.94. The test-retest reliability of the inventory was 0.75 over one week. In terms of validity, Beck and Steer have provided evidence to support its content, concurrent, construct, discriminant, and factorial validity.

The Depression Anxiety Stress Scales (DASS; Lovibond & Lovibond, 1995a)

This forty-two-item self-report scale was designed to measure the states of depression, anxiety, and stress (fourteen items for each state) for individuals over 17 years of age. It was developed in Australia and is popular there and overseas (Antony, Bieling, Cox, Enns & Swinson, 1998; Brown, Chorpita, Korotitsch & Barlow, 1997; Crawford & Henry, 2003). The DASS is available in the public domain (website address: www.psy.unsw.edu.au/Groups/Dass/) and can be administered individually or in groups and takes only 10–15 mins to complete. Sample items for the three scales are as shown in Table 7.3.

Test takers are asked to use a four-point severity/frequency scale to rate the extent to which they have experienced the state referred to in each of the forty-two items of the DASS over the past week. The total scores for the three scales can be easily obtained by using a template and they can be compared to the mean total scores of a standardisation sample of 2914 non-clinical individuals (note that 1607 of these were university students) or to suggested cut-offs derived from this sample.

Based on this standardisation sample, the internal consistencies for the three scales of the DASS have been found to be high (Cronbach's alpha = 0.91, 0.84, and 0.90 respectively). Similar values of alpha have been obtained in a sample of clinically diagnosed individuals (Antony et al, 1998). Test-retest reliabilities (retest period = 2 weeks) for the three scales have also been found to be adequate (r = 0.71, 0.79, and 0.81 respectively; Brown et al, 1997). In terms of validity, the three-factor structure of the DASS has been supported by results of both exploratory and confirmatory factor analyses and its convergent and discriminant validity have been demonstrated by correlations with the BDI and the BAI (Crawford & Henry, 2003; Lovibond & Lovibond, 1995b). The DASS has been found to be sensitive in discriminating individuals with clinical problems from those not so diagnosed (Lovibond & Lovibond, 1995a).

TABLE 7.3 Sample items of the DASS

Scale	Items
Depression	I felt sad and depressed
	I felt that I had lost interest in just about everything
Anxiety	I experienced trembling (eg, in the hand)
	I felt I was close to panic
Stress	I found myself getting upset by quite trivial things
	I found it hard to wind down

PSYCHOLOGICAL REPORT

Once all relevant information about the client has been gathered using the particular tests chosen for the purpose, results need to be brought together to answer the referral question. This is usually done in the form of a written report that has a commonly agreed format (Tallent, 1993). (See Box 7.2 for a sample report.) A written report is important because it allows the referral agent and others to understand why and how the psychologist came to her particular conclusions and why particular suggestions are being made. A written report, compared to a verbal report, provides an enduring record.

The following headings and content are typically included in a psychological assessment report in the clinical and mental health setting:

1 Demographic data: Name, gender, address, age, date and place of birth, marital status, ethnic background (if applicable), name of psychologist, date of psychological assessment session.

2 Relevant background: A client's or patient's family, educational, vocational, psychological and medical history are usually included in this section. It is important to include only the information that is relevant to the current referral question.

3   Previous assessment: If the client or patient has been seen by another psychologist previously for a similar or related problem, it is necessary to briefly summarise the results of the previous psychological assessment. This will provide the reader of the report with an idea of what the functioning of the client or patient was like previously and allow the psychologist to compare the results of the two assessments (if similar techniques were used).

4   Assessment techniques and date and duration of assessment: In this section, the names and order of the psychological assessment techniques used should be listed chronologically. This will give the reader some idea about the length of the psychological assessment and the number and types of techniques used to answer the referral questions. For referral agents who might not be familiar with the names and purposes of the psychological assessment techniques, it is useful to provide a one-line description of the purpose of the tests used. For example, 'the MMPI–2 was administered on 25 Jan 2005. This test measures major patterns of personality and emotional disorders in adults 18 years and older'.

5   Results and interpretation: The results obtained using the various psychological assessment techniques are summarised and explained in this section. For tests that have a large number of scores and scales, it is easier to use a table to present the results. Score ranges rather than scores are sometimes used to indicate the margin of error (eg, plus or minus one or two SEM) associated with the estimate (see the reporting of the WAIS-III results in Box 7.2). Apart from describing the results obtained, the psychologist will also need to interpret what the results mean. In addition, these results should be interpreted within the context of the background information described earlier in the report. For example, it is easier to interpret why someone is showing a high score on the Beck Depression Inventory if it has been reported that there is a history of depression in the family and that a number of events (eg, losing a job or a relationship breakup) have recently happened in the client's or patient's life.

6   Recommendations: Based on the findings of assessment, recommendations for further action are usually offered. These may be in terms of what can be done to assist the person to deal with the problem, such as suggestions for a certain number of sessions of treatment or therapy. They could also be suggestions for psycho-education for both the client and his or her significant others. Sometimes the recommendations could be for further assessment or for reassessment after a given time.

7   Summary: This is the final section of a psychological assessment report and it is a precis of all the previous sections. Although this is the last section of the report, it is often the first section a referral agent reads. Therefore, it needs to be factually accurate, clearly written, and consistent with the information included and discussed in the other sections.

From the observations of Shellenberger (1982) and Brenner (2003) a good report is: individualised rather than general, answers the referral question directly, focuses on and describes behaviour, is written in a clear, precise, and straightforward manner without jargon, is written and delivered on time, emphasises strengths of clients, and provides explicit, specific, and implementable suggestions and recommendations.

It is good practice to seek an opportunity to explain and clarify the report rather than simply hand it to the client or the referral source. This can be accomplished in a face-to-face session or by a telephone call. Some follow-up may be needed to ensure that recommendations are implemented and that they are working well (Brenner, 2003; Wise, 1989). Sometimes the client initiates the follow-up because progress is not being made, but systematic follow-up helps ensure a positive outcome.

BOX 7.2

Example of a psychological assessment report

(This is a fictitious case developed to illustrate the content of a psychological report. As such, it is not meant to be comprehensive or in-depth.)

Client's Name:	John Smith	**File Number:**	135782
Date of Birth:	17/07/1965	**Age:**	39
Date of Initial Session:	03/01/2005	**Date of Final Session:**	10/01/2005
Number of Sessions:	2		

Referral information and presenting problem

John presented to the outpatient mental health clinic for psychological assessment. John works as an accountant for a large car company. He reported that he has always been very organised and efficient both at work and at home. However, he stated that, over the last six months, he has found it increasingly difficult to cope with work demands. He described having difficulty getting to work on time, meeting work deadlines, and making more mistakes with routine tasks. John reported being concerned by the level of difficulty he was having sustaining his attention and concentration at work. He stated that he found it difficult to remember names, addresses, and other information unless he wrote them down and found he was easily distracted at work. John also reported experiencing periods of insomnia, lack of appetite, and low energy and mood. He reported first experiencing these difficulties about six months ago; at about the same time, his wife Sally separated from him, and since this time he reported these symptoms had become worse. John stated that he felt that there was something wrong with his brain and wanted to have a cognitive assessment performed to ensure that he was not, as he put it, 'losing his mind'.

Sources of information

Clinical Interview: 03/01/05
Structured Clinical Interview for DSM–IV (SCID): 03/01/05
Beck Depression Inventory – Second Edition (BDI–II): 03/01/05
Beck Anxiety Inventory (BAI): 03/01/05
Depression Anxiety Stress Scales (DASS): 03/01/05
Wechsler Adult Intelligence Scale – Third Edition (WAIS–III): 10/01/05

Mental status examination

John is of medium height and slightly underweight. He was dressed in a dishevelled manner in a T-shirt and jeans. His nutritional condition appeared to be poor; his skin was pale and his hair was matted. He appeared to be very tired; he sat slumped back in his seat and gazed at the floor. However, he was cooperative throughout the interview. John's speech was mumbled and slow. His responses were non-spontaneous and minimal; he appeared to struggle to find the words to express himself. He described his mood as 'hopeless' which was consistent with his depressed affect. John reported that he had experienced thoughts about suicide, but did not have a specific plan to carry out this behaviour nor believe it would be likely for him to do so. John was oriented in time, place, and person. His concentration and memory recall appeared to be impaired.

History of presenting problem

When John was nine years of age his mother died. John lived with his father until he completed his university degree in Accounting in his mid twenties. It was at this time he married Sally. John and Sally have two children, a 15-year-old boy and a 12-year-old girl. John reported that he and Sally have had a difficult relationship, but in the last five years it had deteriorated considerably. Approximately six months ago, John's wife Sally separated from him taking the children. John is not aware of having any major medical or psychological problems during his childhood or currently and has not previously undertaken any psychological assessment or treatment. He reported that, prior to the last month, he has always been very organised at work and has been surprised by the level of difficulty he is currently experiencing with remembering things and with maintaining his concentration and attention. John also described the onset of his insomnia and low mood and energy levels as sudden and 'out of the blue'.

Assessment and results

The WAIS-III is a test used to assess general thinking and reasoning skills. The following scores show how well John performed compared to other people in his age group.

Indexes	Score range	Percentile	Classification
Full Scale IQ	111–19	84th	High Average
Verbal IQ	111–20	86th	High Average
Verbal Comprehension	112–23	88th	High Average
Working Memory	109–23	87th	High Average
Performance IQ	104–17	77th	High Average
Perceptual Organisation	110–24	88th	High Average
Processing Speed	85–103	32nd	Average

John's Full Scale IQ places him in the High Average range of intellectual functioning, achieving a score above that of approximately 84 per cent of his peers. The Verbal IQ score is a measure of acquired knowledge, verbal reasoning, and comprehension of verbal information. John's Verbal IQ score is in the High Average range; he performed better than approximately 86 per cent of his peers. The Verbal Comprehension Index (VCI) is similar to the Verbal IQ in that it provides a measure of acquired verbal knowledge and verbal reasoning. However, it does not include the measures of abilities related to working memory. John's VCI score is similar to his Verbal IQ score, exceeding that of 88 per cent of his peers and falling within a High Average range. The Working Memory Index assesses an individual's ability to attend to verbally presented information, to process information in memory, and then to formulate a response. John's performance on the subtests requiring working memory is in the High Average range; he performed better than 87 per cent of his age-mates.

The Performance IQ score provides an indication of an individual's non-verbal reasoning, spatial processing skills, attentiveness to detail, and visual-motor integration. John's non-verbal reasoning abilities as measured by the Performance IQ are in the High Average range and better than approximately 77 per cent of his same-aged peers. The Perceptual Organisation Index (POI) is a purer measure of non-verbal reasoning than the overall Performance IQ. The POI measures fluid reasoning, spatial processing, attention to detail, and visual-motor integration, but it does not rely on the individual's speed in processing information or performing tasks. John's POI score fell within the High Average range; he performed better than approximately 88 per cent of his same-aged peers.

The Processing Speed Index (PSI) provides a measure of an individual's ability to process simple or routine visual information quickly and efficiently and to quickly perform tasks based on that information. John's PSI score fell within the Average range, although towards the low end with his score better than approximately 32 per cent of his same-aged peers. John's relatively low performance on this index compared to his scores on the other indices could be interpreted as being the result of psychomotor slowing due to his depressive symptoms. Depression has been found to be associated with slowed mental processing and attentional deficits.

Self-report measures of depression and anxiety

John was administered the Structured Clinical Interview for DSM–IV (SCID) to assess whether his difficulties sustaining attention and concentration could be explained by a psychological condition. John's results on the SCID indicated that he met the diagnostic criteria for Major Depressive Disorder. John was also administered the Beck Depression Inventory (BDI), the Beck Anxiety Inventory (BAI) and the Depression Anxiety Stress Scale (DASS) in order to assess his level of depression and anxiety. John's results from these self-report measures are provided in Table 1. As can be seen in Table 1, John exhibited levels of depression, anxiety, and stress in the severe range.

Tests	Date Completed	Score	Norms Range
BDI	03/01/05 (Session 1)	32	Severe Depression
BAI	03/01/05 (Session 1)	41	Severe Anxiety
DASS	03/01/05 (Session 1)	Depression 40	Severe Depression
		Anxiety 17	Severe Anxiety
		Stress 34	Severe Stress

Diagnosis

Axis I	296.3	Major Depressive Disorder, Recurrent, Severe Without Psychotic Features
Axis II	V71.09	No diagnosis
Axis III		None
Axis IV		Recent separation
		Inadequate social support
		Threat of job loss
Axis V	GAF = 55	(at intake)

Summary and recommendations

- In summary, John is a 39-year-old male, who presented to the mental health outpatient clinic for the assessment of his cognitive and psychological functioning. During the intake session John described having difficulty sustaining his concentration and attention at work and reported dysphoric mood and insomnia.
- John's Full Scale IQ is in the High Average range (84th percentile). His index scores also fell in the High Average range except for his Processing Speed Index score, which is in the Average range (32nd percentile).
- On the SCID, John met diagnostic criteria for Major Depressive Disorder. John's BDI, BAI, and DASS scores indicated that at intake he was experiencing a severe level of depression, and anxiety symptoms and stress.
- My considered opinion is that John's presenting concerns—his difficulties with maintaining concentration and attention, insomnia, and dysphoric mood—are the result of depression and there is currently no evidence of cognitive impairment.
- I recommended that John receive psychotherapy for his depressive and anxiety symptoms. After receiving such treatment, John's difficulties with maintaining concentration and attention should abate. However, if this does not occur I recommended that John be referred for further psychological assessment.

Susan Brown
Psychologist

CONCLUDING REMARKS

The clinical and mental health setting is one of the main areas where psychologists conduct testing and assessment. In this chapter we have discussed the main techniques for assessing mental health problems. After clarifying a referral question with a client or a referral agent, psychologists in this area usually use the clinical interview and the Mental Status Examination to collect relevant information to assist them to develop hypotheses about the case. In addition, they have access to a large number of psychological tests to assess constructs such as intelligence, personality, psychopathology, depression, and anxiety. Testing and assessment usually conclude with the completion of a written report that has a commonly agreed format.

Questions for consideration

1   What are the main functions of a clinical interview?
2   What is the purpose of a Mental Status Examination? What are the main areas covered in this examination?
3   Briefly describe the purpose and content of the Wechsler Adult Intelligence Scale–III.
4   What evidence has been collected to support the validity of the WAIS–III?
5   Compare and contrast the MMPI–2 and the Rorschach.
6   Briefly describe the purpose and content of the DASS.
7   What are the characteristics of a 'good' psychological assessment report?

Further reading

Bagby, R M, Wild, N, & Turner, A (2003). Psychological assessment in adult mental health settings. In J R Graham, & J A Naglieri (Eds), *Handbook of Psychology: Vol 10, Assessment Psychology* (pp 213–34). Hoboken, NJ: John Wiley & Sons.

Goldstein, G, & Hersen, M (2000). *Handbook of psychological assessment* (3rd ed). New York: Pergamon.

Ownby, R L (1997). *Psychological reports: A guide to report writing in professional psychology* (3rd ed). New York: Wiley.

Wood, J, Garb, H N, Lilienfeld, M, & Nezworski, T (2002). Clinical assessment. *Annual Review of Psychology*, *53*, 519–43.

chapter eight

Organisational Testing
and Assessment

> ▶ A manager has a job vacancy to fill. What characteristics should she be looking for in someone applying for the position? Having determined these requirements, how can she select the best candidate for the position from those who have applied for it? Once she has made an appointment, how can she tell if her decision was a good one? Was the person appointed really suited to the job?
>
> ▶ A manager is responsible for a large department. How can he tell which members of his department are performing well from those who may need further training?
>
> ▶ A young university graduate has just been invited in for a job interview. What sort of things can he expect to be asked when he turns up?
>
> ▶ An experienced worker who has worked for the same organisation for many years was asked to sit some psychological tests. On the basis of his test scores the organisation has just retrenched him. Was this a fair and reasonable use of psychological tests?

INTRODUCTION

Industrial and organisational (I/O) psychology is one of the oldest fields of applied psychology. The importance of psychological issues in the workplace was recognised well over 100 years ago. Among the earliest published works in the area were Scott's analysis of advertising (Scott, 1908) and Hugo Munsterberg's general text for industry (Munsterberg, 1913). Indeed, as mentioned in Chapter 1, the application of psychology to military needs during World War I, a particular domain of work, provided the first great impetus to psychological testing in history. In Britain, the Industrial Fatigue Research Board was set up by 1918 and C S Myers established the Institute of Industrial Psychology in London shortly after. By 1919 the British Psychological Society had established an occupational section, also at Myers' behest. The Association of Consulting Psychologists was formed in the United States in 1930 and included a number of I/O psychologists among its members. Later the American Association of Applied Psychology (AAAP) was formed in 1937 which included a section dedicated to industrial and business psychology, Section D; and they eventually merged with a number of other groups to form the American Psychological Association (APA) in 1945. Division 14 of APA, the Society for Industrial and Organisational Psychology, is one of the largest groupings of I/O psychologists in the world. In Australia the organisational psychology division of the Australian Psychological Society was established in 1971. This became the Board of Organisational Psychology in 1981 and finally the College of Organisational Psychologists in 1993.

Although psychological testing and assessment are core components of I/O psychology, the field is concerned with all aspects of human behaviour in the workplace. I/O psychologists attempt to improve organisational productivity and worker performance as well as enhance the quality of working life. Major areas of application include work motivation, designing and redesigning jobs, recruitment and selection of new personnel, training and development of workers, managing individual and group performance, and facilitating organisational change processes. Psychological assessment and the evaluation of outcomes through tests and questionnaires figure strongly in all of these situations. Unlike other areas of applied psychology, which often deal with relatively small clinical populations, I/O psychologists deal with the vast majority of the normal population who go to work.

Although tests may be used to evaluate the effectiveness of any organisational intervention, there are two areas of application in which psychological assessment plays a central role: the assessment of workers' performance on the job, known as *performance appraisal*; and the prediction of that performance, usually prior to appointment, for *personnel selection* purposes. Reasons for the first are fairly obvious: the productivity of any organisation rests on the performance of each of its employees, hence managers are naturally interested in the effectiveness of individual workers. Reasons for the second are also clear: all attempts to improve the performance of workers once they join an organisation, through further training, incentive schemes, redesigning jobs, introducing new technology and the like, are dependent to some extent on starting out with good recruits. A highly skilled, high-quality workforce, identified by valid personnel selection programs, is likely to have positive repercussions throughout the organisation for many years. Indeed, a high-quality workforce is now widely recognised as one of the main ways of competing in the post-industrial age (Handy, 1994). New technology, plant and equipment can always be purchased but an organisation's workforce, its human capital, is unique and cannot be easily duplicated by the competition.

PERFORMANCE APPRAISAL

Given that performance of people at work is a form of human behaviour, the assessment of job performance involves the application of psychological assessment principles. For many years, it was assumed that good indicators of job performance were relatively easy to come by and this remains fairly true of jobs located at either end of the production and distribution process (see Table 8.1). At the manufacturing end, reasonably good indicators of job performance can be found 'laying around the shop floor' in the form of simple productivity counts like the number of widgets produced, or amount of scrap material or wastage, or the number of defects. At the distribution end, the number of products sold or the dollar value of sales can serve as useful indicators.

BOX 8.1

Team performance

Modern industry is increasingly organising groups of workers into teams. There are a number of benefits to this practice. First it provides a social context for work that does much to reduce the alienation felt by workers as a result of division of labour and job simplification that characterised much of the approach to job design for the past 200 years. Being a member of a team encourages communication and the exchange of ideas among workers. Workers organised as teams have a greater appreciation of the significance of their jobs to the broader organisation. This also facilitates motivation and innovation. Further, there is a social facilitation effect that results from working with colleagues. This is an increase in job motivation due to not wanting to let the team down. Finally, through teamwork, there is the opportunity to support each other. This can be especially important if one team member becomes ill. The ability of team members to perform each other's jobs leads to a degree of job enrichment that makes work more interesting and meaningful for individual workers.

The rise of teamwork presents a problem for performance appraisal specialists. Job performance is now as much a function of the team as it is of the individual worker. At what level should job performance be assessed; at the level of the individual worker or at the level of the group? Coming up with an adequate appraisal of team work performance has proven more difficult than assessing individual work performance. A number of crude approaches have been tried, such as viewing team performance as an aggregate of individual performance, but it is difficult to determine what form the aggregation should take. Should emphasis be given to the best workers on the assumption that the best workers will raise the standards of the team or should emphasis be given to the weakest workers on the assumption that they reduce the standard of the team? Alternatively, we could simply apply supervisor ratings or production counts to the team, but this still leaves the issue of handling team members, so the question posed in this box remains: How should we assess team performance?

One problem with productivity counts is that the rate of production is often outside workers' control. A good example of this is the assembly line where the rate of production is completely governed by the pace of the line. Another problem with simple productivity counts is their limited applicability to jobs not located at either end of the production and distribution chain. This includes growing numbers of jobs in mature service economies. For example, what could be counted in assessing the performance of a manager or supervisor? The number of meetings attended or the number of memos produced is not necessarily linked with effectiveness. Most professionals also would not view their performance in purely quantitative terms either. Is the best police officer the one who issues lots of speeding tickets? Should a good surgeon rush through a lot of operations? Or is a good psychologist one who administers lots of tests? For complex jobs, objects and events that can be counted often represent only a small fraction of what the job really entails and alternative methods of performance appraisal that combine multiple indicators of performance are required.

Even where productivity counts are applicable, it was soon realised that focusing on purely quantitative measures can have undesirable consequences. For example, sales people evaluated solely in terms of number of goods sold can become motivated to make sales to customers irrespective of their need and end up selling people things they don't want. As can be seen, quantitative measures of performance are notoriously deficient in terms of *quality* (see Chapter 5 on validity). Productivity counts say nothing about the quality of goods or services produced. As such, it was realised that job performance is a multidimensional construct having both qualitative as well as quantitative components. Measures of quality could be things like the number of products returned or the number of customer complaints; see Table 8.1 for other suggestions.

TABLE 8.1 Some performance indicators

Type of Indicator	Example
Quantitative Production Counts	Number of widgets produced Number of defects Number of products sold Dollar value of sales
Qualitative Production Measures	Number of defects or errors Amount of scrap material or wastage Number of products returned Number of customer complaints Number of dissatisfied customers Quality of work produced
Personnel Information	Absenteeism Turnover Length of service Length of downtime Number of accidents Number of grievances Rate of promotion
Training Proficiency	Scores on training exams Scores on performance tests Trainer ratings
Judgmental Data	Supervisor ratings of performance on the job or of samples of work Peer ratings Subordinate ratings Customer ratings

Another form of job performance information, often used to validate selection systems (see later) is personnel data. Personnel data are information about individual employees held in personnel files, such as length of service (tenure) or absenteeism. Length of service may be relevant to an organisation experiencing turnover problems. Focusing on absenteeism, on the other hand, is based on the idea that absences from work must be associated with lower levels of output. Although personnel data apparently are available for all workers, the main problem with measures of this sort is the rarity of the relevant event, such as resignation or absence. For many employees, the frequency of absenteeism or number of accidents will be zero. This leaves much personnel data highly skewed and difficult to analyse.

Ultimately it was realised that the many aspects of job performance have to be combined in some way to obtain a clear picture of someone's work performance and this aggregation invariably involves human judgment. For this reason, the most common form of job performance measure has become supervisor ratings. A judgment by an informed supervisor who appreciates all aspects of the job, in both quantitative and qualitative terms, and who has an adequate opportunity to observe a worker's performance in all relevant areas, is widely recognised as the most viable single measure of job performance.

Rating scales

A very simple method of capturing judgmental information is the graphic rating scale which typically involves marking a line representing the range of performance from lowest to highest, or circling a number on a Likert scale. Points along the scale can indicate variations in performance on a range of work-related dimensions. In spite of their apparent simplicity, users often complain about rating scales because of ambiguity about what the scale is trying to measure or the meaning of particular scale points. What, for example, is meant by 'average performance'? This difficulty led to much research into determining the best anchors for various points along rating scales. Although the one best-scale format was never discovered by such research, one of the most successful methods for determining scale anchors is that used in behaviourally anchored rating scales (BARS).

A BARS is a rating scale with explicit behavioural statements located along it. These statements provide an example of the kind of behaviour expected at that point along the scale. For an example, see Table 8.2. The advantage of BARS is that

TABLE 8.2 A behaviourally anchored rating scale for the role of customer service operator

Value	Behaviour
1	Does not attend to customers' needs. Argues with customer.
2	Attends to customers' needs but does not take responsibility for finding a solution to problems.
3	Attends closely to customers' needs but does not defuse the situation.
4	Defuses situation but customer may not be completely satisfied.
5	Takes responsibility and comes up with creative solutions to problems.

actual behaviours are identified with values on the scale. Besides clarifying the meaning of the scale, behavioural anchors can provide a degree of standardisation among raters; each rater is not left to his or her own devices in deciding what constitutes a score of 4 out of 5, say. The anchors also provide a basis for interpretation of the scale scores. Thus interrater reliability can be improved and greater agreement can be obtained about the meaning of particular scores.

The steps in developing a behaviourally anchored rating scale are as follows:

1   Critical incidents especially indicative of good and bad performance are obtained from interviews with job incumbents and supervisors.
2   These incidents are then content analysed and clustered into coherent behavioural themes or dimensions which will later form the basis of the individual questions.
3   Another group of incumbents and supervisors then rates the incidents within each theme on a 1 to 5, 1 to 7, or 1 to 9 point scale. The aim is to look for those incidents for which there is a high level of agreement. These will serve as the behavioural anchors on the scale.
4   A subset of anchors that survive step 3 is selected to represent scale points on the scale. The average rating across judges in step 3 provides a good indication of the appropriate scale points. It is important that anchors be developed for the entire range of the scale.

Ideally a different group of incumbents and supervisors is used for each step in the process so that each set of judgments is independent.

The main disadvantage of BARS is that raters can become overly focused on the anchors. Rather than viewing the anchors as indicative of a particular level of performance, some raters interpret them too literally. The anchors can trigger specific memories of atypical events. Thus, although the person being rated may generally perform well, if they had been involved in one unfortunate incident that was actually included as an anchor, the rater may give them the low rating for that reason alone. Care needs to be given to training raters when using BARS, or any other performance-rating instrument. Nevertheless, behaviourally anchored rating scales have proven a highly popular performance appraisal method. Further, the intensive development process which utilises many members from the organisation often generates considerable acceptance for the eventual system produced.

Behavioural observation scales

Latham and Wexley (1977) pointed out that raters may not have actually observed many of the behaviours used to anchor BARS. If this was the case then the anchors do not really serve to remove the ambiguity associated with the scales. To counter this, they proposed behavioural observation scales (BOS) where stems are composed of the kinds of behaviours that form the anchors of BARS but where the scale is based on the frequency with which the rater had observed the behaviour in question. The idea behind this is that desirable behaviours frequently observed are indicative of high performance whereas undesirable behaviours frequently observed suggest poor performance. Infrequently observed behaviour cannot be used to form an opinion either way. Identification of behavioural themes to include in the BOS format is arrived at via critical incident technique in the same way they were for BARS. Table 8.3 provides some examples of BOS.

TABLE 8.3 Some examples of behavioural observation scales

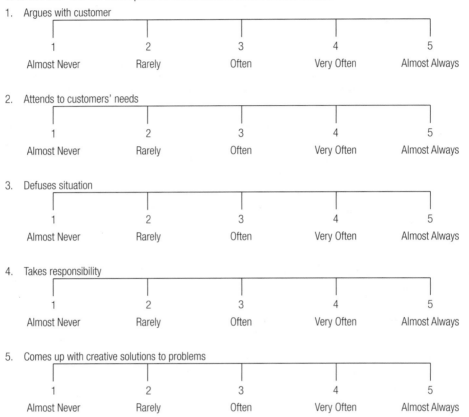

Assessments made using BARS or BOS are linked to typical workplace behaviours through a fairly rigorous design methodology. In spite of considerable research into scale formats, no clear winner has emerged and simple graphic rating scales appear to be about as good as the more sophisticated BARS and BOS (Landy & Farr, 1980).

Other methods

Although rating scales are the most common performance appraisal instrument, it is also possible to simply rank workers. In this case, supervisors list workers from best to worst. This is a straightforward task as long as the number of workers to rank is not too large. For larger numbers, it maybe easier to group workers into categories such as high, average, and low performers which is somewhat similar to ranking, although on a grosser scale, and provides much of the basic information obtained by ranking methods. No attempt is made to distinguish between people falling into a particular category, but at least the best and worst performers are identified. The category-based method may even be preferred in the case of fewer workers because it does not require fine discriminations to be made between each person ranked.

Another technique involves comparisons of each worker with every other worker. In this method, termed paired comparisons, each worker is paired with every other worker and the supervisor is asked to decide which member of each pair is better. Such methods can lead to a strong ordering of performance among workers, but becomes unwieldy as the number of pairs increases. The total number of comparisons to be made in a paired comparisons task equals $(n^2 - n) \div 2$ where n is the number of workers involved. Because the number of comparisons to be made increases with n^2, it starts to become laborious after about 10 workers.

BOX **8.2**

The role of technology

Technology, especially computer and automation technologies, greatly increases the productivity of workers, which is something all organisations want. However, for the purposes of assessing job performance, how do we partition the contribution of individual workers from the tools and technologies they use? What part of their performance is due to their own knowledge, skills, and abilities and what part is due to the contribution of the technology they are using? It has been suggested that technology in the workplace is analogous to performance-enhancing drugs in sport (Hesketh & Neal, 1999). In sport, we are interested in the unaided performance of individual athletes and performance enhancers are seen as cheating. In contrast, organisations have no such concerns. All organisations actively seek to enhance the performance of workers in every way possible. So are we to judge the operator-machine combination as a single unit? This makes sense at one level, but can exacerbate the assessment problem if worker performance is masked behind technology. Neal and Griffin (1999) have developed a model of individual work performance, which explicitly recognises the influence of technology, but the question remains: how should we assess worker performance in the context of performance-enhancing technology?

THEORIES OF PERFORMANCE

The fact that jobs differ in so many ways led to the realisation that, while we might talk abstractly about 'job performance', a single measure is not going to suffice to capture performance in all jobs. Job performance is multidimensional and contextually specific to a large extent. This realisation led researchers to begin focusing on specific aspects of performance and to develop theories of the components of job performance (Campbell, McCloy, Oppler & Sager, 1993). Two broad components have thus far been identified. The first emphasises the core technical aspects of the job and encompasses the basic tasks that comprise the job description. This is called 'task performance'. The second includes those behaviours directed more at successful continued performance of the work group or organisation such as helping out fellow workers or volunteering for committees and incidental activities. This second aspect of performance is called 'contextual performance' (Borman & Motowidlo, 1993). In many ways, contextual performance amounts to being a 'good citizen' at work. Neal and Griffin (1999) go even further to include non-observable factors such as planning, problem solving, and situational awareness within their model of performance and have included the impact of technology on task performance. Development of a viable theory of job performance in terms of the components, determinants, and antecedents of performance will provide a common language for the development of more effective human resource interventions in the areas of training, selection, and incentive practices.

PERSONNEL SELECTION

Personnel selection is the process of choosing from among a group of job applicants those to whom an offer of employment will be made. The aim, obviously, is to make the offer to the applicant or applicants with the greatest probability of performing well on the job. One way to do this would be to appoint everyone and monitor their performance over a period of time, say for 6 or 12 months, using the methods discussed above. At the end of the monitoring period, those with the best performance appraisal would be retained and the rest let go. This strategy is known as 'selecting on the criterion' and has the great advantage of allowing selection to be made on the basis of actual job performance, which, after all, is what the organisation is really interested in.

Unfortunately, selecting on the criterion has one major disadvantage; it is extremely costly for everyone involved. These days, no organisation can afford to appoint people it doesn't need, even temporarily. Further, the individuals who were ultimately unsuccessful would be highly inconvenienced by such a process. Most people would rather know the outcome of their application fairly quickly so they can get on with applying elsewhere.

Short of selecting on the criterion, what can an organisation do to select candidates? The next best thing is to make a *prediction* about future job performance based on information that *correlates* with success on the job; which is where psychological assessment comes in. From this point of view, personnel selection is the process of predicting from among a group of job applicants those with the greatest probability of success, based on measurements of personal characteristics that make them more suited or less suited to the position. Once the prediction has been made, candidates are rank ordered in terms of their predicted probability of success and selected top-down from that list. Performance measures discussed above serve as the dependent variable against which to validate these assessments.

It is important to remember that predictions are never perfect. There are too many extraneous factors that can influence job success. As such, the validities involved in selection are never close to a perfect predictive validity of 1.0. This means that selection errors will occur (see Chapter 5 on validity). Some people will be appointed whose performance ultimately does not measure up. Such cases are known as false positives. They are positives in the sense that a positive decision was made in their favour, but false in the sense that the decision was in error. Conversely, some people will miss out on a job offer even though they would have performed well if only given the chance. Such cases are known as false negatives. The only way to eliminate these errors is to use a predictor with a perfect validity of 1.0, and this will never occur. As we have seen in the previous section, even assessment of the criterion itself is far from perfect. So organisations and applicants must live with an imperfect process, hoping that, in the long run, it works reasonably well most of the time. Incidentally, realising that false negatives are not uncommon should allow you to cope with the inevitable rejection that accompanies any period of job hunting. Just because you weren't selected doesn't mean you're no good; you may well be a false negative and it's the organisation's loss as much as yours.

Organisations remain unaware of the impact of false negatives because the people involved are simply not around to make their effects known. From an organisation's point of view the worst thing that can happen to a false negative is that they join a competitor and contribute to its success. In contrast, false positives are something organisations do have to deal with and most organisations spend much time and effort trying to maintain the level of performance of all of their employees. A false positive can be very costly, especially if lengthy dismissal processes needs to be followed. For this reason many organisations try to get some of the benefit of selecting on the criterion, mentioned above, by instituting a *probationary period*. With this strategy even if their selection processes yield a few errors, organisations can fall back on performance appraisal to help eliminate any false positives that got through.

Viewed as an assessment and prediction problem, personnel selection is based on the assumption that applicants differ in the knowledge, skills, abilities, and other characteristics (KSAOs) needed for the job. The task is to identify those applicants whose KSAOs most closely match the job requirements. Personnel selection, therefore, is fundamentally the study of individual differences. For over 100 years, psychologists have been studying the dimensions along which people differ, primarily through psychological tests and other assessment devices. The main outcomes of this research effort are our current theories of cognitive abilities, personality, and interests. Other clusters of individual differences include preferences, personal style, and orientations, but they are not as well developed as those of abilities, personality, and interests. It is beyond the scope of this text to provide a comprehensive treatment of all theories of individual differences, but a few general remarks are in order.

Carroll's Three Stratum Theory

One of the best examples of current theorising in the area of cognitive abilities is Carroll's Three Stratum Theory (Carroll, 1993). This theory was based on extensive analysis of the patterns of relationships among scores on cognitive tests using the method of factor analysis. In fact, Carroll reanalysed all available data in the area, over

450 correlation matrices, during the formulation of his theory. The theory is an hierarchical one that posits a factor called general intelligence, general mental ability (GMA) or *g*, as the most abstract and general cognitive ability. Beneath *g* are the second stratum factors of fluid intelligence, crystallised intelligence, general memory and learning, broad visual perception, broad auditory perception, broad retrieval ability, broad cognitive speediness and processing speed. At the first stratum are the individual tests that measure the specific abilities. This theory is similar to Cattell's theory of fluid and crystallised intelligence (Cattell, 1971; Horn & Hofer, 1992; Horn & Noll, 1994), except that it posits a *g* factor at the third stratum. In some ways it is a combination of the British school of ability research, which began with Spearman and emphasised *g*, and the American school, exemplified by Thurstone and his students who emphasised what they referred to as 'primary mental abilities' at the second stratum.

Big Five theory of personality

In the personality domain, a great many theories have been proposed, but a degree of consensus has emerged over the past 10 to 15 years about personality description, largely through the impact of meta-analysis. A consensus has formed around the so-called Big Five personality factors, as shown in Table 8.4. As might be expected from the definitions provided, Conscientiousness has been found to be the most valid personality factor in predicting job performance.

TABLE 8.4 The Big Five theory of personality

Dimension	Description
Neuroticism vs Emotional Stability	The extent to which one is prone to dysfunctional emotional states like anxiety or depression
Extraversion vs Intraversion	The extent to which one is sociable and outgoing vs self contained and reserved
Openness to Experience	The extent to which one is open to new ideas and experiences vs traditional and conservative in one's outlook
Agreeableness	The extent to which one is easy to get along with socially and accommodating and considerate of other people
Conscientiousness	The extent to which one believes in a life of hard work, is dependable, and achievement striving

Meta-analysis

While on the topic of meta-analysis, it is worth spending a few moments explaining this method because it has been very influential in the area of personnel selection. Meta-analysis is the study of other research studies. That is, it attempts to distil the overall conclusion from a large number of other investigations. This is not unlike a literature review and meta-analysis can be thought of as a quantitative literature review, as opposed to the more traditional narrative literature review. The raw data for a meta-analysis are the effect sizes (eg, correlations between variables) reported in each primary study. As with any analysis, the first step in processing the raw data is to calculate its mean and standard deviation. The mean effect size gives the best estimate of the true effect size of the phenomenon being investigated by each study and the standard deviation of effect sizes tells us how much the studies disagreed in their estimation of this effect size. If there is a lot of variation between studies, this suggests the presence of moderator variables, ie, third variables which differed between the studies and on which the size of the effect in question may depend. If a moderator is suspected, the studies must be coded in terms of their study characteristics (eg, type of population sampled, context in which the data was obtained, etc) until the moderator is found. If there is no evidence of moderation, the mean effect size is taken as the best estimate of the effect that can be provided by the literature. Meta-analysis has been highly influential in the area of personnel selection through the process of meta-analysing validity coefficients. This particular application of meta-analysis is called validity generalisation (VG), because it has also shown that meta-analytically derived validities are also highly generalisable across different jobs, ie, type and level of job does not moderate the validities found.

At one time or another, virtually all types of tests of individual differences measures have been tried for personnel selection purposes and a picture has slowly emerged of the most valid and useful devices. This literature has been summarised in the VG League Table (Schmidt & Hunter, 1998; see Table 8.5). The first thing evident in the League Table is that GMA sits at the top as the best single predictor of performance in virtually all jobs. This is moderated, to some extent, by job complexity, the only moderator evident in the table. GMA is more valid for more complex jobs. Schmidt and Hunter (1998) hypothesised that the reason GMA is so successful is that it predicts learning, both prior learning and learning on the job, which translates into job knowledge and thence into successful performance. Apart from its high validity, another advantage of GMA is its low cost. Over the decades psychologists have developed a large number of very good intelligence tests that measure GMA. We will review a number of these tests later in this chapter, but they can also be found in other chapters of this book.

Given the range of assessment devices evident in the table, an important question to ask is how to choose between them? The answer to this question is 'job analysis'. Job analysis is the process of gathering detailed information about a particular job, including the main tasks carried out, and the main requirements for performing the job. Methods of job analysis include questionnaires and tests, interviewing and questioning workers and supervisors involved in the job. Job analysis is a specialised field within I/O psychology and is largely beyond the scope of this text. Suffice it to say, a selection system cannot be constructed without a detailed understanding of the job in question and the process of developing that understanding is job analysis. Indeed all applications within industrial and organisational psychology begin with developing an understanding of the job through job analysis. Standard texts on I/O psychology provide details on how to carry this out.

TABLE 8.5 The VG League Table

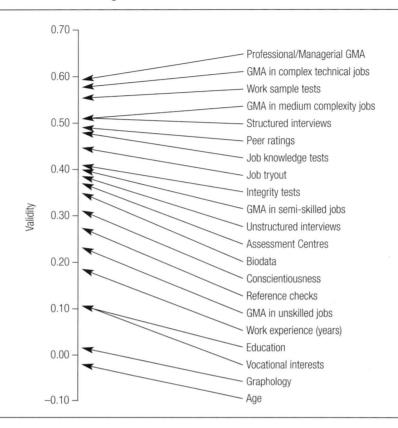

Adapted from Schmidt, FL, & Hunter, J E (1998). The validity and utility of selection methods in personnel psychology: Practical and theoretical implications of 85 years of research findings. *Psychological Bulletin, 124,* 262–74.

Returning to the League Table; close behind GMA are work sample tests. These are specifically designed hands-on simulations of the main work tasks to be performed in a particular job. For example, an applicant for the position of an electrical technician might be asked to repair a series of defective electric motors. Not surprisingly, the ability to demonstrate good performance on actual job tasks is indicative of high potential for performing the job. In contrast to GMA tests, the biggest disadvantage of work sample tests is their expense. Although a number of off-the-shelf tests are available for a few occupations, new work sample tests usually need to be developed for each job, thus making them very expensive in practice. The expense can be justified if the job is important enough and sufficient use can be made of the tests once they are developed. Tasks selected for inclusion in a work sample test should be central to the job as indicated through job analysis.

Interviews are ubiquitous in personnel selection because few organisations are prepared to appoint someone they haven't met. Unstructured interviews have been found to have some validity, but extensive research shows that providing structure is the best way to increase the validity of interviews. By structure is meant the degree of discretion the interviewer is given to deviate from a predetermined set of questions and format. A structured interview using questions based on job analysis information, asked in a fixed format to each applicant, is the best way to maximise the validity of interviews. Ideally the same interviewers and location should be used. In other words, interviews become more valid when they look like standardised tests, even to the extent of developing procedures for scoring each interviewee's answers. This usually amounts to trying to think of the most likely answers to each question and categorising them as good or bad prior to conducting the interview. Formally scoring an applicant's answers has the advantage of decreasing human judgment and increasing the objectivity of the process. The same principles of standardisation that apply to psychological tests should apply to interviews. In some ways an interview can be thought of as a test or questionnaire administered verbally (just like some psychological tests such as the Wechsler intelligence scales, see Chapters 7 and 11, can be thought of as structured interviews). Selection interviews should not resemble the type of celebrity interview carried out by journalists on television which try to unearth a few interesting titbits from someone's life history. Such chat can be good for building rapport, but should be moved through fairly quickly in order to get to the structured interview proper.

Not surprisingly, peer ratings, ie, evaluations of one's performance by coworkers and colleagues, provide a good indicator of job performance. After all, your peers have had a lot of opportunity to see you in action and maybe have even had the good fortune of working closely with you. The main problem with peer ratings is that they are virtually impossible to obtain for applicants from outside the organisation. Nevertheless, appointing from within is always a good strategy because it allows someone's actual job performance, rather than predictions of it, to form the basis of selection. Another disadvantage of peer ratings is that they can be strongly influenced by interpersonal skills and perceived friendliness, reducing selection to little more than a popularity contest. In the worst-case scenario, collusion may occur to render peer ratings completely useless.

Job knowledge tests ask questions about specific aspects of the job. If job knowledge translates into 'know-how' that in turn translates into performance, as suggested above, it is not surprising that job knowledge is a good predictor of performance. The main disadvantage of job knowledge tests is that they are only relevant for experienced workers. New entrants into a field cannot be expected to have developed much job knowledge, unless formal qualifications are a prerequisite for entry, in which case the assessment underpinning the qualification constitutes the job knowledge test.

Job tryout is the case of selecting on the criterion discussed earlier and involves hiring someone for a few months and seeing how well they fare. As mentioned, it can be expensive and requires great commitment on the part of the organisation. In any case, many supervisors are reluctant to fire people once they are appointed, thus reducing the advantages of job tryout. Probationary periods are a good way of implementing job tryout, but it is not uncommon to see performance drop after the probationary period is over.

A great deal has been written about integrity tests in recent years. Integrity tests attempt to gauge someone's honesty or good character. They have also been found to assess dependability and conscientiousness. Indeed, one theory of integrity is that it is a superordinate personality factor comprised of conscientiousness, agreeableness, and emotional stability from the Big Five. Integrity tests became very popular in the USA after the use of the polygraph method of lie detection was discredited in the early 1990s and seem relevant to jobs for which a high degree of trust is required, such as security guards and cash handlers. Two broad classes of integrity test exist: those that are overt and make no attempt to disguise their intent and those that are less obvious or covert. Overt tests are made up of items like: 'How much money have you stolen from your employer during the past twelve months?' It does not take much of an inference to doubt the integrity of an applicant who freely admits to stealing large sums of money, although it seems odd that such questions are not rendered useless by the effects of social desirability. After all, who would admit to such offences? Nevertheless, the validity associated with integrity tests shows that they do work and theories have been proffered as to why they don't lead to blatant distortion. Covert tests are more like personality or biodata tests (see below) and do not openly tap honesty behaviours. The inference about integrity from such tests is much less direct and it is thought that they are more likely tapping into broad tendencies towards delinquency or anti-social behaviour that may be precursors of specific bouts of dishonesty.

An assessment centre sounds like a place you go to be assessed, but it is a method rather than a place. An assessment centre is similar to a large test battery comprised of many different assessment activities that are applied to groups of around ten to twenty people at a time. Any of the assessments discussed here could be included as an assessment centre exercise along with various group activities, such as management simulation games, group discussions, and oral presentations. Trained observers monitor the performance of each participant and compare their scores and ratings at the end of the assessment centre to identify the most promising candidates. It goes without saying that all exercises used in an assessment centre should have some relevance for the job in question. Assessment centres have been particularly popular for identifying managerial potential.

Biodata is short for 'biographical data', which is information about one's past experience and life history. Some life experiences have been found to be highly predictive of performance for some jobs. For example, the most famous biodata item was a question used to select pilots during World War II. This single question was almost as predictive of pilot performance as an extensive selection process which included a whole battery of knowledge tests and simulation exercises. The question referred to applicants' childhood hobbies and was, 'Did you ever build a model aeroplane that flew?' Traditionally biodata questionnaires were constructed on a purely empirical basis by trying out different items and seeing how well they correlated with performance. Information supplied in application forms provided a good starting point for such empirically keyed biodata questionnaires. More recently, empirical keying has been criticised as being too atheoretical and modern biodata items are chosen on more rational grounds. A good collection of biodata items can be found in Glennon, Albright and Owens (1965).

Conscientiousness is one of the Big Five personality factors and has already been discussed. The definition shown in Table 8.4 makes it fairly clear why conscientiousness is likely to be related to job performance. Interestingly, conscientiousness is the only personality factor that appears in the League Table. In spite of its popularity and apparent relevance, personality does not have a great deal of relevance for many jobs. All kinds of people can be successful in most jobs so long as they have the requisite KSAOs. Personality factors are more likely to be relevant to contextual performance than task performance.

Reference checks are letters of recommendation from previous employers and knowledgeable others who can vouch for you. These are potentially a very useful source of information, although recent experience suggests that many referees are reluctant to relay negative information. Possibly the best approach to reference checking is to conduct a telephone interview, thus avoiding a written statement, and ask whether or not they would be prepared to rehire the candidate.

Work experience is the number of years a person has been employed in the line of work in question. This counts to some degree, because experience also translates into practice of job relevant tasks, learning and 'know how', which are all important for high performance. However, the benefit of experience and learning seems to be better captured by GMA than by time on the job per se.

Education refers to the amount of formal schooling completed. It is somewhat surprising to see education faring so poorly, especially given that educational qualifications are often mandatory for entering many careers. Does this result mean that unqualified people would perform just as well as qualified people? Probably not. The low validity associated with education is probably due to the inevitable restriction of range produced by the need for formal entry qualifications. In many jobs, everyone has been selected for education. If they did not complete their training they would not even be considered. Although meta-analysis corrects for restriction of range, the restriction of range produced by minimal educational qualifications is slightly different and cannot be corrected for. Meta-analysis corrects for restriction of range when restriction of range is an artefact, a methodological deficiency, in the validation study. Clearly, minimal educational qualifications are not artefactual in this sense so restriction of range due to education operates legitimately in the world of work and has the result that once educational standards are achieved, education provides little additional information about expected performance.

Vocational interests, discussed in Chapter 11, have little to do with one's ability to perform well in one's chosen occupation. Just because you are interested in a particular line of work doesn't mean that you will be good at it, although there is interplay between interests and ability to the effect that most people are interested in things they are good at.

SELECTION AS A SOCIAL PROCESS

Up to now, we have been considering selection purely from the organisation's point of view. From this perspective, personnel selection is the prerogative of the organisation and assumes that all applicants will gratefully accept a job offer if it is made. However, a more general framework exists. In reality, applicants can turn offers down. The more general framework views selection as a social process and incorporates the views of the job applicant into the equation as well as those of the organisation (Herriott, 1988, 1989, 2002). While the organisation is appraising the applicant, the applicant is also appraising the organisation and may eventually decide to go elsewhere. From this perspective, selection is more akin to a process of negotiation whereby each party, the organisation and the applicant, is trying to find reasons to continue the relationship. Either party can break off at any point and discontinue the selection process. Finally, when an offer is made, the applicant must decide whether to accept it or not. Even after employment begins, both parties continue to appraise each other.

The social process perspective explains why not all job offers are accepted and why some selection practices persist in spite of their lower validity. In particular, social process theorists argue that unstructured interviews remain popular because this is where the negotiation takes place. Much current research in selection has attempted to gauge applicant reactions to the selection process and the findings broadly support the social process view. This research primarily conceptualises applicant reactions in terms of justice perceptions which are used to predict whether applicants are likely to be predisposed to accept a job offer if one is made (Gilliland, 1993, 1994). Not all applicant reaction research is framed within the social process perspective, however, because many organisations now realise that all dealings with the public, including job applicants who may not join their organisation, play a role in determining the organisation's public image.

In a recent survey of selection practices in New Zealand, Taylor, Keelty and McDonnell (2002) noted the increased level of research into personnel selection over the past decade or so. Further, they noted that this research is finding its way into practice in the form of increased use of more valid methods. The authors suggest that this is primarily due to increasing numbers of graduates with advanced training in I/O psychology and a growing number of specialist firms and consultancies offering psychological testing services. The main deficiency reported by the authors was a tendency to avoid using job analysis as a way of determining job requirements.

BOX 8.3

Equal employment opportunity

Psychological assessment in organisations exists within an extensive legal framework. Laws that directly apply to personnel selection involve principles of equal employment opportunity (EEO); that is, the basic idea that all members of society should have equal access to employment and that employment decisions should be based on merit rather than characteristics that are irrelevant to the job. It may seem odd that anti-discrimination legislation exists in a context of selection. Isn't the whole point of selection to discriminate among a group of job applicants to find the most suitable person? Nevertheless, society seeks to eliminate discrimination on certain dimensions deemed irrelevant and/or likely to be the cause of significant social tension.

EEO principles were first introduced to Australia with the ratification of the International Labour Organisation Convention No 111, Discrimination (Employment and Occupation), in 1973. Since that time they have been enacted through seven federal and numerous state acts, such as the *Human Rights and Equal Opportunity Commission Act* of 1986 and the *Workplace Relations Act* of 1996.

To summarise this legislation, it is unlawful to discriminate against someone in employment decisions on the basis of:

- Race (including racial vilification)
- Gender (including sexual harassment)
- Sexuality, eg, heterosexual, homosexual
- Age
- Marital status
- Pregnancy
- Parenthood
- Breastfeeding
- Status as a carer
- Family responsibilities
- Political beliefs/activities
- Trade union or employer association activity
- Medical record
- Physical impairment
- Intellectual impairment
- Physical features
- Religion
- Criminal record

Information about any of the above issues should not be collected unless it can be clearly demonstrated to be job relevant. The types of employment situation covered by EEO legislation include: job advertisements, contents of application forms, interviews, job offers, conditions of employment, opportunities for promotion, access to training, retrenchment, and retirement.

Indirect Discrimination

When adhering to EEO principles, it is important to realise that discrimination can sometimes be inadvertent. For example, height requirements for police officers or fire fighters, which might at first seem relevant to physically demanding jobs, can discriminate against women because females are, on average, about 13 cm shorter than males. Another example is requesting a photograph as part of a job application. This might at first seem useful for administrative purposes such as remembering dealings with a particular applicant but a photograph clearly provides information that falls under the Acts, eg, information about race, gender, and age. For this reason, photographs should, as a rule, not be requested.

SOME TESTS USED IN SELECTION

Wonderlic Personnel Test

A popular test of GMA for personnel selection purposes is the Wonderlic Personnel Test (Wonderlic Personnel Test Inc, 1992). The test comprises fifty items of varying item types, including vocabulary items, which ask for the definition of words and tap verbal abilities; knowledge items which ask about everyday concepts like days of the week and months of the year and tap crystallised abilities; arithmetical items which require some degree of calculation and tap numerical abilities; and figural items which require different shapes to be imagined or compared and tap spatial abilities. The heterogeneous nature of the items allows the total score on the test to tap GMA. Recall that most definitions of general intelligence emphasise a broad and diverse battery of tasks. It is as if the Wonderlic was made up of a few items taken from many different second stratum tests. One reason for the popularity of the Wonderlic is that it can be administered and scored in only 20 minutes—12 minutes for completion of the test itself. Further, the Wonderlic can be administered in groups. These factors make the test very efficient and cost effective. With over 60 years of use, the Wonderlic comes with extensive norms for almost 150 occupations and educational groups. Australian norms, however, are not available. The manual reports test-retest reliabilities ranging between 0.82 and 0.94 and validities with the WAIS and WAIS – R in the 0.80s and 0.90s.

ACER Advanced Tests

A set of ability tests widely used in Australia are the ACER Advanced Tests (ACER, 1982). These tests comprise a verbal or language test with alternative forms, AL and BL; and a numerical or quantitative test with alternative forms, AQ and BQ. The two language tests are made up of 29 items tapping language abilities, including verbal reasoning, similarities, vocabulary, and verbal analogies. Verbal reasoning items involve short paragraphs in which examinees are asked to evaluate an argument or derive a logical conclusion; similarities items ask examinees to identify a pair of words of similar meaning; vocabulary items ask about the explicit meaning of words and verbal analogies items are of the form A is to B as C is to… The quantitative tests are also comprised of 29 items tapping numerical abilities, including number series, matrices, and numerical reasoning. Number series items are of the form: 1, 2, 3, 4, 5… which number comes next? Matrix reasoning items have been described in Chapter 7. Numerical reasoning problems are short paragraphs posing problems with an arithmetic solution, such as: 'I started out with 20 cents and spent 10 cents. How much money do I have left?' There is a 15 minute time limit for the language test and a 20 minute time limit for the quantitative test. Each test can be presented individually or in groups.

The manual claims that each test also taps GMA, and this is especially true of the sum of the language and quantitative scores. Australian norms are available for school students aged 15½ to 17½, including years 11 and 12, and for first year TAFE and tertiary students. Internal consistency reliabilities (KR20) range between 0.91 in a group of 15 year olds to 0.84 in a tertiary sample. Given that alternative forms exist for each of the tests, alternative form reliabilities were also reported. These range from 0.73 for the language test in a group of 15 year olds to 0.84 for the combined test score in a group of Year 11 students.

ACER Speed and Accuracy Tests

A very common form of assessment, long used in the selection of clerical and administrative personnel, are speed and accuracy tests in which examinees are required to rapidly scan lists of names or numbers for errors. A good example is the ACER Speed and Accuracy Test (ACER, 1962). This test consists of 160 pairs of random numbers, between three and twelve digits in length, followed by 160 pairs of names of people and fictitious companies (see Table 8.6). Participants have 6 minutes to work through each list and indicate whether the members of each pair are the same or different. The total score is the number of pairs correctly identified minus the number wrong. Separate gender norms are supplied for children aged 13½ to 15½, university students, and adults in a range of occupations such as military service, sales people, clerks, mechanics, and farmers. Test-retest reliabilities reported are 0.69 for young boys, 0.81 for young girls and 0.81 in a sample of young women.

TABLE 8.6 Typical speed and accuracy test items

Number Checking			
95068	95088	Same	Different
305	305	Same	Different
58903	58923	Same	Different
9436	9436	Same	Different
2961	2861	Same	Different
Name Checking			
T.G. Smith Pty. Ltd.	T.B. Smith Pty. Ltd.	Same	Different
James Cook	James Cook	Same	Different
All Hours Computer Rentals	All Hours Computor Rentals	Same	Different
Dave's Glass Ltd.	Daves Glass Ltd.	Same	Different
Joe & Sons	Joe & Son	Same	Different

The tests surveyed here represent only a small fraction of ability tests used in personnel selection. Other tests discussed elsewhere in this book are also used. Although individually administered tests are usually deemed too expensive for use in personnel selection, group administered tests such as Raven's Progressive Matrices, discussed in Chapter 11, are commonly used.

CONCLUDING REMARKS

Performance appraisal involves the assessment of workers' performance on the job. Quantitative indicators exist for some jobs, but should always be supplemented by assessments of quality. The vast majority of jobs require the subjective judgment of performance by a relevant observer such as a manager or supervisor. A number of rating and ranking formats have been devised for this purpose. However, apart from straight ranking, simple graphic rating scales have been found adequate for most purposes. These can be supplemented by behaviourally anchored rating scales or behaviour observation scales if a clearer indication of the behaviours involved is required.

Personnel selection involves the psychological assessment of individual differences among job applicants with a view to identifying the knowledge, skills, abilities, and other characteristics that are predictive of future job performance. A great many predictors have been investigated over the years and the outcome of many validation studies has been summarised in the Validity Generalisation League Table. Particular sets of predictors should be chosen on the basis of job analysis, but the League Table provides a good indication of validities that can be expected.

Questions for consideration

1   Comment on the advantages and disadvantages of quantitative vs qualitative performance measures.
2   What is the difference between BARS and BOS?
3   What are the steps involved in constructing a BARS?
4   Why is general mental ability the best single predictor of job performance?
5   Think of a particular job and suggest some potential methods of selecting someone for that position.

Further reading

Cascio, W F, & Aguinis, H (2005). *Applied psychology in human resource management* (6th edn). Upper Saddle River, NJ: Pearson Prentice Hall.

Gatewood, R D, & Feild, H S (2001). *Human resource selection* (5th edn). Fort Worth, TX: Harcourt College Publishers.

Herriot, P (2001). *The employment relationship: a psychological perspective.* Philadelphia: Taylor & Francis.

Murphy, K R, & Cleveland, J N (1995). *Understanding performance appraisal: Social, organizational, and goal-based perspectives.* Thousand Oaks, CA: Sage Publications.

Neuropsychological Testing and Assessment

9

> ▶ The relatives of a 75-year-old war veteran noticed that he seemed to be more forgetful and less able to handle routine tasks than before. He was referred to a neuropsychologist to determine if he was suffering from dementia.
>
> ▶ The disability officer of a university referred a first-year university student who had failed a number of courses to a neuropsychology clinic to find out if she had a learning disability.
>
> ▶ A 10-year-old boy was diagnosed with a brain tumour. After chemotherapy and radiation therapy, he was referred to a neuropsychologist to evaluate the effect of the tumour and treatment on his cognitive functions.
>
> ▶ A young female was involved in a car accident 12 months earlier. She was referred by a rehabilitation specialist for a neuropsychological assessment to determine which of her cognitive processes were affected by the injury and whether or not she could return to her former job.

INTRODUCTION

In the twenty-first century, it is well known that the human brain is responsible for producing, controlling, and mediating our behaviour (Box 9.1 provides a brief description of the structures and functions of the human brain). Damage to the brain caused by external or internal factors, as illustrated by the above examples, can lead to significant changes in functions such as sensation, attention, memory, problem solving, language, visuo–spatial processing, and movement, and as a consequence, to problems in living. The branch of psychology that specialises in the assessment and treatment of brain injury is clinical neuropsychology. In this chapter, we provide an introduction to neuropsychological assessment by addressing the following questions: What is clinical neuropsychology? When and how did clinical neuropsychology develop as a specialty area of psychology? What is neuropsychological assessment? What are the purposes and procedures of neuropsychological assessment? What are the commonly used neuropsychological tests?

BOX 9.1

Structures and functions of the human brain

Although the human brain is on average only 1500 g in weight and 1.4 l in volume, it is the most complex organ of our body. The brain is made up of 100 billion **neurons** or brain cells and 10 times the number of **glia** (meaning *glue*) or **glial cells**. The neurons are the basic functional units of the brain. The three main types are **sensory neurons**, **motor neurons**, and **interneurons**. The complex networks formed between the neurons via **synapses** (*connections*) and the electrical and chemical communications of this network enable us to encode and process information and to produce behaviour. As their names suggest, the glial cells hold the neurons together and provide supporting functions.

Structurally, and to a certain extent functionally, the brain can be divided into four main areas, namely, the **hindbrain**, the **midbrain**, the **between brain**, and the **forebrain**. Continuing from the spinal cord, the hindbrain includes the **cerebellum** (meaning *little brain*) and the **brain stem**. The cerebellum consists of two highly wrinkled structures attached to the brain stem (see Figure 9.1) and their functions include motor learning, coordination of complex motor movements, and coordination of some mental processes. The brain stem is made up of three structures: the **medulla oblongata** (meaning *oblong marrow*), the **pons**

FIGURE 9.1 Midsagittal section of the human brain showing structures and locations of the brain stem and midbrain

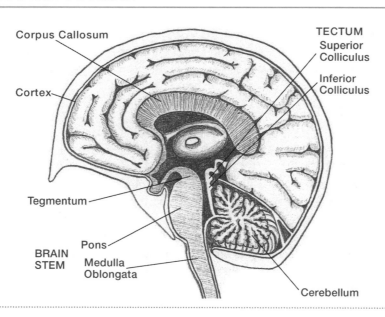

(meaning *bridge*), and the **reticular formation** (meaning *net-like formation*) (see Figure 9.1). The medulla oblongata is situated just above the spinal cord and it has several nuclei that control vital life functions such as the regulation of breathing, swallowing, and heartbeat. The pons is a key connection between the cerebellum and the rest of the brain and it is involved in functions such as eye movements and balance. The reticular formation is located inside the brain stem. It consists of both nerve cell bodies (grey in colour) and nerve fibres (white in colour) and has a net-like appearance, hence its name. The reticular formation is involved in the regulation of sleep-wake cycles and in maintaining arousal.

The two structures in the midbrain include the **tectum** (meaning *roof*) and the **tegmentum** (meaning *floor*). The tectum comprises the superior and inferior **colliculi** (meaning *little hills*) (see Figure 9.1). While the superior colliculus receives information from the visual pathways, the inferior colliculus receives information from the auditory pathways. These two structures are involved in the production of movements relating to sensory inputs, for example, orienting behaviour to sound or light. The tegmentum is not a single structure but is composed of a number of nuclei. The better-known and more important nuclei include the **substantia nigra** (meaning *black substance*), which is involved in movement initiation, and the **red nucleus**, which is involved in limb movement.

The two principal structures of the between brain are the **thalamus** (meaning *inner chamber*) and **hypothalamus** (meaning *under thalamus*) (see Figure 9.2). Despite its small size, the hypothalamus is made up of a large number of nuclei (viz, twenty-two) and is involved in many important life functions such as eating, sexual behaviour, sleeping, temperature regulation, hormone function, emotional behaviour, and movement. Similar to the hypothalamus, the thalamus is made up of a large number of nuclei, but these are much larger in size than those in the hypothalamus. The thalamus locates strategically between the forebrain and the brain stem. As such it acts as a gateway or relay station between all the sensory information (with the exception of olfactory information) travelling to and from the brain.

FIGURE 9.2 Structures and location of the between brain (inside view)

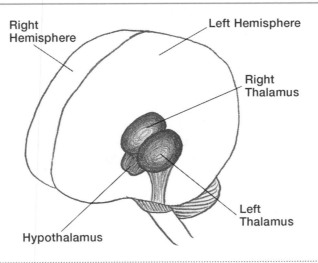

The forebrain or the **cerebrum** is the largest part of the human brain. It is divided into two **cerebral hemispheres** (viz, left and right) that are joined by a structure called the **corpus callosum** (meaning *hard body*). The corpus callosum consists of 200 million nerve fibres and it allows the left cerebral hemisphere to communicate with its right counterpart. The outer layer of the forebrain is the **cortex** (meaning *bark*) and it consists mainly of nerve cell bodies or **grey matter**. The inside of the forebrain comprises mainly nerve cell fibres or **white matter**. Like the cerebellum, the forebrain is wrinkled. This is because the large area of cortex in humans needs to be crinkled up and pushed together in order to fit within the confines of the skull. The bumps on the surface of the forebrain are called **gyri** and the grooves are known as the **sulci**. The deep, prominent sulci are called **fissures**. There are no clear anatomical demarcations for the cortex of the forebrain but traditionally it is divided into four lobes (see Figure 9.3). The **frontal, temporal, parietal**, and **occipital** lobes are named after the skull bones above the four areas. Such divisions are, therefore, arbitrary and should not be used as a strict functional guide.

FIGURE 9.3 The four lobes of the human brain

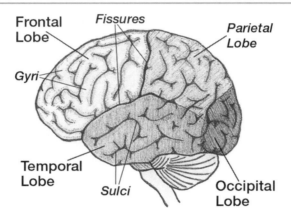

The occipital lobe is situated at the back of the forebrain and its function is to register, process, and interpret visual stimuli. As its name suggests, the frontal lobe is situated at the front of the forebrain and its function is to initiate, plan, and produce motor behaviours. In addition, the frontal lobe is involved in a group of loosely related processes (viz, planning, problem solving, working memory, regulation) called the executive functions. In recent years, the prefrontal lobe has also been found to be involved in some memory functions. The parietal lobe is located immediately behind the frontal lobe and its function is to register, process, and interpret somatosensory stimuli and to control visual actions. In addition, because the parietal lobe shares boundaries with the other three lobes, it is involved in the integration of various sensory stimuli. The temporal lobe is located underneath the temple area of the human head and its function is to register, process, and interpret auditory stimuli. Other functions mediated by the temporal lobe include memory and learning, regulation of emotional behaviour, and identification of visual objects. Although the four lobes in the two cerebral hemispheres share similar functions for the left and right sides of the body, during the evolutionary process the two hemispheres developed to mediate different functions. Whereas the left hemisphere has become the specialised area for the comprehension and production of language, the right hemisphere has become the specialised area for processing visuo-spatial relationships.

The forebrain also contains two other important functional structures that are located beneath the cortex (see Figures 9.4 and 9.5). They are called the **basal ganglia** and the **limbic system**. The basal ganglia are a collection of nuclei that include the caudate nucleus (meaning *tailed nucleus)*, the putamen *(*meaning *husk* or *shell)*, and the globus pallidus (meaning *pale globe*). These nuclei are responsible for controlling and coordinating voluntary motor movement. The limbic system also comprises a large number of substructures and they include the amygdala (meaning *almond*), the hippocampus (meaning *seahorse*), and the cingulate cortex. The limbic system has been found to be involved in memory, motivation, and regulation of human emotion.

FIGURE 9.4 Structures and location of the basal ganglia (inside view)

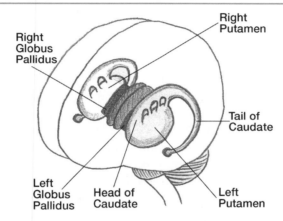

FIGURE 9.5 Structures and location of the limbic system (inside view)

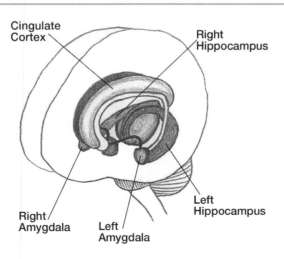

> In this section, we have provided a brief and general description of the structures and functions of the human brain. Interested readers who desire a more comprehensive and in-depth treatment of these topics can consult advanced texts and references such as Afifi and Bergman (1998), Kolb and Whishaw (2001), Nauta and Feirtag (1986), and Darby and Walsh (2005).

WHAT IS CLINICAL NEUROPSYCHOLOGY?

Donald Hebb was the first person to formally used the term 'neuropsychology', in his 1949 book *Organization of Behavior: A Neuropsychological Theory* to describe the scientific study of the relationships between the brain and behaviour (Oliveira-Souza, Moll & Eslinger, 2004). In 1967, a group of psychologists formed the International Neuropsychological Society (INS) to promote this newly emerged discipline. Today, the INS has more than 4500 members throughout the world. Within the discipline of neuropsychology, there are a number of sub-branches, including experimental neuropsychology, comparative neuropsychology, cognitive neuropsychology, and clinical neuropsychology. Experimental neuropsychology aims to understand the behavioural organisation of the human brain by studying normal individuals in the laboratory. Comparative neuropsychology tries to achieve the same aim by studying animals such as primates and rats in the laboratory (Beaumont, 1988; Milner, 1998). Cognitive neuropsychologists and clinical neuropsychologists both have an interest in patients with brain injury. Whereas the cognitive neuro-psychologist studies these patients to identify and clarify the underlying processes of human cognition, the clinical neuropsychologist specialises in their assessment and treatment (Ellis & Young, 1996; Heilman & Valenstein, 2003).

Clinical neuropsychology is one of the fastest growing applied disciplines of psychology and is recognised as a specialty area of psychology in many countries (Cullum, 1998; Hebben & Milberg, 2002). In 1975, the National Academy of Neuropsychology was founded in the USA to represent and promote the interests of clinical neuropsychologists. The division of clinical neuropsychology (Division 40) was officially recognised by the American Psychological Association as a specialty area in 1996, the Special Group in Clinical Neuropsychology of the British Psychological Society was redesignated the Division of Neuropsychology in 1999, and the Board of Clinical Neuropsychology (later changed to the College of Clinical Neuro-psychology in 1993) of the Australian Psychological Society was set up in 1983.

Typically, the job of a clinical neuropsychologist includes:

(a) conducting neuropsychological assessment on individuals with or suspected to have a brain injury;
(b) providing psycho-education, counselling or psychotherapy for individuals with brain injury (and in some cases, their immediate family members or partners);
(c) planning, conducting, and evaluating neuropsychological rehabilitation for individuals with brain injury based on the results of neuropsychological assessment; and
(d) conducting clinical research.

While some clinical neuropsychologists perform these functions in a multi-disciplinary team with other health professionals (eg, neurologists, neurosurgeons, physiotherapists, occupational therapists, speech pathologists, social workers) in a hospital or a rehabilitation centre, some clinical neuropsychologists undertake these tasks independently in private practice. In most countries, the training of clinical neuropsychologists is reserved for postgraduate programs. For example, in the USA, clinical neuropsychologists usually have PhD or DPsych training and are certified by the American Board of Clinical Neuropsychology or the American Board of Professional Neuropsychology (Meier, 1997). In Australia, Masters level training is the minimum academic training for membership of the College of Clinical Neuropsychology.

A BRIEF HISTORY OF NEUROPSYCHOLOGICAL ASSESSMENT

The field of neuropsychological assessment began in the 1940s and 1950s when psychologists were approached by other health professionals to assist in deciding if the behaviour of their patients was due to brain injury or other causes (Box 9.2 provides a brief description of the major types of brain injuries). Neurologists and neurosurgeons were interested in whether their patients showed signs of behavioural deficits or excesses caused by damage to the brain; psychiatrists were concerned about whether the behavioural dysfunction of their patients was due to 'functional' (ie, non-organic) causes. Before the development of imaging techniques such as computer tomography (CT) and magnetic resonance imaging (MRI), psychologists used what they called a 'test for brain damage' or 'test of organicity' to assist them to diagnose damage to the brain. Although some of these tests were rather simple, they were shown to be quite sensitive to the effects of injury to the brain (Lezak, 1995).

BOX 9.2

Major neuropathological conditions

Injuries to the brain are usually acquired after birth and they can be caused by either internal (eg, burst of a cerebral artery) or external (eg, introduction of neurotoxins to the brain) factors. The causes and effects of some common neuropathological conditions are summarised below:

Alzheimer's disease

This insidious degenerative disease accounts for 50–70 per cent of all dementias. It was named after the German neurologist, Alois Alzheimer, who in 1906 observed abnormal changes (viz, accumulation of amyloid plaques and neurofibrillary tangles) in the brain of a 51-year-old female patient with symptoms of dementia. In Australia, it is estimated that people over the age of 65 have a 1 in 15 chance of developing this disease. For people over the age of 85, the chance is 1 in 4. The total number of individuals suffering from this disease in Australia is about 162 000 and this number is expected to increase dramatically as the population ages. The symptoms of Alzheimer's disease include: memory and learning problems, problem with abstract thinking, word-finding difficulty, loss of judgment, disorientation (loss of sense of time, place, and people), and personality change. To date, there is no direct clinical test for Alzheimer's disease and diagnosis is by exclusion (ie, making diagnosis by excluding as many other causes as possible). The effect of this disease is progressive and irreversible and the course from diagnosis to death usually takes about 7 to 10 years.

Traumatic brain injury

There are two types of traumatic brain injury, namely, open and closed head injury. The former is caused by fast-moving projectiles, such as a bullet, or sharp objects, such as a knife. Closed head injury, on the other hand, is caused by the impact of blunt external forces (eg, in an assault) or by the sudden acceleration/deceleration of the moving brain (eg, in a fall or in a motor vehicle accident). In open head injury, the skull is usually perforated, the effect of the injury is confined to the area of the brain damaged by the external object, and loss of consciousness is uncommon. In contrast, in closed head injury, the skull may be fractured but not perforated, the effect of the injury is more widespread, and loss of consciousness is common. In Australia and other countries, closed head injuries are more common than open head injuries and the incidence of closed head injury is estimated to be about 200 per 100 000 head of population. The highest number of closed head injuries occurs in the 15–35 age group and the ratio of males to females is about 3 to 1. The severity of closed head injury is usually assessed using the Glasgow Coma Scale (GCS), an index of the depth of coma or the duration of Post-Traumatic Amnesia (PTA), that is, the duration between injury and the regaining of day-to-day memory and orientation. Although the effect of closed head injury depends very much on the severity of injury, common symptoms include: slowing in speed of information processing, attentional and memory problems, personality change, impulsivity, emotional problems, and speech problems.

Stroke

The initial symptoms of a stroke usually occur suddenly and they can include numbness, weakness or paralysis of the face, arm, or leg on one side of the body, loss of speech, blurred or decreased vision, dizziness or loss of balance, headache, and confusion. A stroke occurs when the blood supply to one part of the brain is interrupted or severely reduced. There are two main types of stroke, ischaemic and haemorrhagic. The former type occurs when blood clots or other particles block one of the arteries that supplies oxygen and nutrients to the brain and lead to death of brain cells to one or more parts of the brain. About 80 per cent of all strokes are ischaemic in nature. The latter type occurs when a blood vessel in the brain leaks or ruptures because of hypertension or weak spots in the blood vessel walls called **aneurysms**. In Australia, stroke is the largest single cause of disability of all neurological disorders. According to the Australian Bureau of Statistics 2.2 per cent of the population have had a stroke. Among sufferers, 30 per cent will die in the first year after the stroke, 35 per cent will remain permanently disabled, 25 per cent will have non-disabling impairments, and 10 per cent will fully recover.

Brain tumour

A brain tumour is an abnormal growth of cells in the brain. There are two main types, primary and secondary. Primary brain tumours originate in the cells in the brain and they can be either benign (non-cancerous) or malignant (cancerous). Secondary brain tumours are metastases (migrating cancerous cells) that originate from other parts of the body. The former is usually less common than the latter (ratio about 1:3). Brain tumours are most common in people older than 65 years and in children under 8 years old, and they are the second leading cause of cancer death in people under the age of 20 years. A brain tumour can cause different symptoms and these may develop gradually or appear suddenly. The nature and number of symptoms depend on the size, location, and rate of growth of a particular brain tumour. Some of the more commonly reported symptoms include headaches, nausea, vomiting, vision problems, loss of sensation or movement in limbs, difficulty with balance, speech problems, personality or behavioural changes, epileptic seizures, hearing problems, and hormonal disorders. A brain tumour can cause temporary or permanent damage to the brain depending on whether it is diagnosed or treated early.

Epilepsy

Epilepsy is a condition in which a person suffers from a seizure or temporary disruption of brain function due to periodic disturbance of the brain's electrical activity. Epileptic seizures can be classified as symptomatic or idiopathic. In the former, the cause of the seizure can be identified and in the latter, the cause of the seizure is spontaneous and cannot be traced. Epileptic seizures can also be classified according to the origin of the abnormal electrical activity in the brain. Focal seizures are those that originate in a specific area of the brain and then spread to the other parts. Simple partial seizures and complex partial seizures are subtypes of focal seizures. Generalised seizures are those that involve the whole brain without focal onset. Absence (petit mal seizures) and generalised tonic-clonic (grand mal seizures) are examples of generalised seizures. It is estimated that about 1 in 80 people in Australia have epilepsy. The symptoms of epilepsy depend on the type of epilepsy but they usually include disruption of sensory function, loss of consciousness, and motor problems.

Infection

Because the brain is one of the most important organs of the body, it is well protected by the skull, the meninges (covering of the brain), and the blood-brain barrier (a thin barrier that limits the types of substances that can pass from the blood into the brain). Occasionally, however, the brain can be invaded by bacteria, viruses, fungi, protozoa, or parasites and be infected. The consequences of these infections can be very serious if they are not treated in time. Meningitis is a general term that describes the infection of the meninges and it can be caused by bacteria or viruses. Encephalitis is the inflammation of the brain usually caused by a virus. Primary encephalitis occurs when a virus directly invades the brain and secondary encephalitis occurs when a virus first infects another part of the body and enters the brain subsequently. Some common symptoms of infection of the brain include headache, drowsiness, seizure, stiff neck, confusion and disorientation, fever, nausea, and vomiting. More long-term effects can be generalised and affect the whole brain but can also be specific. For example some viruses have an affinity for a certain area of the brain and the behavioural effects depend on the area of infection.

The early successes were encouraging to both the psychologists and the referring health professionals and led to the rapid development of the field of neuropsychological assessment and the proliferation of tests designed to assess brain damage. In the late 1960s and early 1970s, however, the future of neuropsychological assessment seemed to be in doubt when more sensitive neuroimaging techniques were developed to detect structural damage to the brain. Contrary to expectation, neuropsychological assessment continued to flourish in the 1980s and continues to the present day, because both the psychologists and the referring health professionals realised that, apart from diagnosis, psychological tests can be used to provide a comprehensive assessment of the strengths and weaknesses of a person who has suffered a brain injury (Lezak, 1995). Results of neuropsychological assessment can be used to provide feedback to the client, monitor recovery, plan treatment, and evaluate its effect. For a more comprehensive review of the history of neuropsychological assessment, readers are advised to consult Goldstein (1992) and Meier (1997).

WHAT IS NEUROPSYCHOLOGICAL ASSESSMENT?

Neuropsychological assessment is defined as the application of neuropsychological tests and other data-collection techniques to answer referral questions or solve problems for individuals with known or suspected brain injury. Because neuropsychological tests are sensitive to brain function, they are sometimes considered to be different from the other psychological tests. Although the use to which they are put is different, these tests still retain all the basic characteristics of a psychological test and they still have to fulfil all the required psychometric properties before they can be considered useful.

PURPOSES AND PROCEDURES OF NEUROPSYCHOLOGICAL ASSESSMENT

A neuropsychological assessment is usually conducted for a number of purposes. These include:

(a) diagnosis
(b) description of neuropsychological functions
(c) prognosis
(d) treatment planning
(e) monitoring the rate of recovery; and
(f) evaluating the effects of treatment.

As mentioned earlier in this chapter, clinical neuropsychologists are now less involved in the diagnosis of suspected brain injury because of advances in neuro-imaging techniques such as CT scans and MRI. These techniques, however, are not 100 per cent reliable and they are not suitable for detecting all types of changes in the brain (eg, early dementia, Attention Deficit Hyperactivity Disorder). Neuropsychological assessment is still required for diagnostic purposes in ambiguous cases. According to Lezak, Howieson and Loring (2004), a comprehensive description of neuropsychological function has become the most important purpose of a neuropsychological assessment, enabling a clinical neuropsychologist to document the functions that are impaired and those that are spared in an individual after a brain injury. Using this information, the clinical neuropsychologist can explain problems experienced by the individual in everyday living, provide psycho-education, and make predictions about the person's return to the community and to work.

The process of neuropsychological assessment generally comprises five steps:

(a) interviewing
(b) gathering other relevant information
(c) neuropsychological testing
(d) interpreting test results and integrating information
(e) report writing and providing feedback.

Similar to psychological assessment in other areas, neuropsychological assessment typically starts with an interview. During the interview, the client is asked to provide information about the nature and duration of the referral problem, the effect of this problem on his or her everyday functioning, and their medical, educational, vocational, social, and psychological history. Because brain injury can affect a person's ability to provide accurate information during an interview, information collected is usually checked for accuracy with family members or partners and official records. In addition, reports from the hospital and from other professionals are collected to understand the nature and severity of the injury and to assist in the interpretation of tests results.

Neuropsychological testing is usually the most time-consuming step in neuropsychological assessment. During this step, a client is administered instruments designed to measure a number of important neuropsychological functions. After the tests are administered, a clinical neuropsychologist scores and interprets the results, in the context of the test taker's background. For example, an average level of performance on a test can be a good or bad sign depending on the person's previous educational and academic achievements. Finally, a report is written and feedback is provided to the person, and where appropriate to family members and partners.

NEUROPSYCHOLOGICAL FUNCTIONS COMMONLY ASSESSED

The functions commonly included in a neuropsychological assessment are sensory function, attention, memory and learning, language, visuo-spatial function, executive functions, motor function, and premorbid functioning (Lezak et al, 2004; Mapou, 1995;

Reitan & Wolfson, 1993). Both fixed and flexible batteries have been used to assess these functions. As the name suggests, the fixed battery uses the same subtests for all clients referred for neuropsychological assessment. The Halstead–Reitan Neuropsychological Battery is an example of a fixed battery (see Box 9.3). The flexible battery approach, on the other hand, uses a number of core subtests for all clients but uses different subtests depending on the referral question or the results of the other tests. Although both approaches are used in the USA, the flexible battery is more commonly used by clinical neuropsychologists in Australia. In this section, we will briefly consider some of the neuropsychological tests commonly used to assess these functions. Because of space limitations, what follows is not meant to be a comprehensive or definitive list of tests for neuropsychological assessment. Readers interested in finding out more about neuropsychological tests of different functions can consult excellent references in the area (eg, Lezak et al, 2004; Mitrushina, Boone & D'Elia, 1999; Spreen & Strauss, 1998).

BOX 9.3

Halstead-Reitan Neuropsychological Battery (HRNB)

This battery was originally developed in the 1940s by Halstead to provide a comprehensive measurement of neuropsychological functions. It was last updated in 1993 (Reitan & Wolfson, 1993). The HRNB is an individually administered test and completion of the whole battery takes about 6 to 8 hours. The subtests of the battery and the functions they measure are summarised below:

Category test

In this subtest, test takers are required to determine the rules for categorising pictures of geometric figures by using feedback based on whether they got the last item correct or incorrect. It measures abstract reasoning and complex concept formation.

Tactual performance test

For this subtest, test takers are blindfolded and required to place large wooden blocks of different shapes on the correct cutout positions of an upright board using their dominant hand, nondominant hand, and both hands. After the form board and the blindfold are removed, test takers are also required to draw the outline of the form board from memory. The subtest measures sensorimotor and kinaesthetic abilities and incidental spatial memory.

Speech sounds perception test

Sixty nonsense syllables are presented using a tape recorder in this subtest and test takers are required to pick out the presented sound from four written choices. The functions measured are perception of auditory verbal stimuli, auditory-visual synthesis, and sustained attention.

Seashore rhythm test

This subtest is presented using a tape recorder. Test takers are required to indicate if thirty pairs of rhythmic sounds are the same or different. The functions measured by the subtest include auditory perception and sustained attention.

Finger tapping test

In this subtest, test takers are required to tap as rapidly as possible on a telegraph-type key fitted with a mechanical counter. It measures gross motor speed.

Trail making test

This subtest has two parts, A and B. In the first part, test takers are asked to use a pencil to connect 25 numbered circles on a piece of paper as quickly as possible. In the second part, the task is to connect numbered and lettered circles alternately (1-A-2-B etc). The functions measured by this test are simple and complex information-processing speed and cognitive flexibility.

Aphasia screening test

Test takers are required to undertake tasks such as repeating short phrases, naming pictures, following instructions, and copying pictures. It is used to screen receptive and expressive language problems.

Sensory-perceptual examination

In this subtest, test takers are required to respond to a series of simple auditory, tactile, and visual stimuli, unilaterally and bilaterally. It measures a person's sensory-perceptual abilities.

The HRNB is one of the tests most commonly used by clinical neuropsychologists in the USA (Camara et al, 2000) but it is not commonly used in Australia and New Zealand (Knight & Godfrey, 1984; Sharpley & Pain, 1988). The main strength of this test battery is the use of a standard set of measures on which patients' performances can be compared. However, it has been criticised because of its inflexibility and the amount of time it takes to complete the battery (Hebben & Milberg, 2002).

Sensory functions

These functions comprise the ability to encode and perceive sensory stimuli in the visual, auditory, and somatosensory domains reliably and accurately. Impairments in these functions are important because they limit the amount of stimulus information that can be taken in by the individual. According to Lezak et al (2004), special care should be taken in assessing individuals with basic sensory impairments and in interpreting their results. This is because failure to do so may to lead to misinterpretations and incorrect conclusions. The Sensory-Perceptual Examination from the HRNB (see Box 9.3) can be used to assess sensory function. Sometimes information about these functions can be obtained from sources other than neuropsychological testing (eg, neurological, audiological, and ophthalmological examinations and assessment by occupational therapists and physiotherapists).

Attention

Difficulties with attention are commonly reported by individuals with brain injury. It is now widely acknowledged that attention is not a unitary construct. Models of attention (eg, Mirsky, Anthony, Duncan, Ahearn & Kellam, 1991; Posner & Petersen, 1990; Shum, McFarland & Bain, 1990) suggest that there are at least three components of attention: namely, attention span, focused attention, and selective attention, each with a different neuroanatomical basis. The attention span component refers to the ability to encode and reproduce, in correct order, the stimuli presented and it is mediated by the inferior parietal lobule (McCarthy & Warrington, 1990). Focused attention is the ability to scan stimuli for a specific target and respond to it. The superior temporal and inferior parietal cortices and structures of the corpus striatum have been found to be associated with this component (Mirsky, Fantie & Tatman, 1995). Selective attention refers to the ability to maintain cognitive or response sets in the presence of distracting stimuli and the cingulate cortex has been found to mediate this ability (Pardo, Pardo, Janer & Raichle, 1990).

The Digit Span subtest of the Wechsler Intelligence Scales is commonly used to assess attention span. In this subtest, number sequences of varying length are presented aurally to the test taker. The Forward condition of the subtest requires the test taker to repeat the number sequence in the order presented and the Backward condition requires repetition of the sequence in the reverse order. The reliability of the subtest has been found to be excellent (split-half reliability = 0.90, test–retest reliability = 0.83; Kaufman & Lichtenberger, 1999). Performance on the Digits Forward and Digits Backward subtests has been found to be sensitive to damage to the left temporal area of the brain. Performance on the Digits Backward subtest has been found to be sensitive to right frontal-lobe injuries (Golden, Espe-Pfeifer & Wachsler-Felder, 2000). Visual attention span can be assessed using the Spatial Span subtest from the Wechsler Memory Scale Third Edition (WMS-III; Wechsler, 1997b).

The Trail Making Test (see Box 9.3) and the Digit Symbol subtest from the WAIS are commonly used tests of focused attention. On the Digit Symbol, a test taker is given a key that pairs a different geometric shape with the numbers 1 to 9, and asked to draw the shape appropriate to each number in a random sequence of the numbers 1 to 9. The subtest has a time limit of 120 seconds. It has been found to have a test–retest reliability of 0.86 and has been found to be very sensitive to the effect of brain injury (Kaufman & Lichtenberger, 1999).

Stroop (1935) found in a series of experiments that the names of colours were difficult to read if the colour in which the name was printed did not correspond to the name of the colour. Thus 'green' printed in red took more time to read than when it was printed in green. Golden and his colleagues (1978, 2002) developed a commercially available test based on these findings, the Stroop Color-Word Interference Test. There are three trials in the test. Each trial uses a different card on which five columns of twenty items are printed. In the first trial the test taker is asked to read, as quickly as possible, rows of colour names (viz, red, green, and blue) printed in black ink. In the second trial the test taker is asked to name as quickly as possible the colour of four Xs printed on a card. Finally, in the third trial, the test taker is required to name the colour of the ink in which words are printed. All words are printed in a colour conflicting with the name indicated (eg, the word 'red' printed in green or the word 'blue' printed in red). Each trial has a time limit of 45 seconds and the key measure obtained for this test is an interference score derived from the three trials. The psychometric properties of this test are good. For instance, the Stroop has good test–retest reliability (0.75 to 0.90; Uttl & Graf, 1997); is moderately related to the Perceptual Organisation and Freedom from Distractibility factors of the WAIS; and loads in factor analyses on a component of attention called sustained mental processing (Shum et al, 1990). Further, the Stroop interference score has been found to be sensitive in distinguishing those with brain injuries from their noninjured peers (Hanes, Andrewes, Smith & Pantelis, 1996).

Memory and learning

According to Squire (1987), 'Learning is the *process* of acquiring new information, while memory refers to the persistence of learning in a state that can be revealed at a later time' (p 3). Similar to attention, memory is not a unitary construct. Figure 9.6 is a model of memory adapted from Squire (1992). It can be seen from the model that there are two types of memory, declarative and nondeclarative memory. Most clinical tests focus on declarative rather than nondeclarative memory. This may be because deficits in nondeclarative memory are not commonly found after brain injury (Shum, Sweeper & Murray, 1996). Declarative memory can be further divided into episodic and semantic memory (Tulving, 1972). Semantic memory represents a person's knowledge of the world (eg, date of major events, details of historical events). Episodic memory, on the other hand, is the memory for personal events (eg, the name of one's primary school, what one did last Christmas). Most tests of memory and learning are involved in the assessment of episodic memory.

FIGURE 9.6 A neuropsychological model of human memory

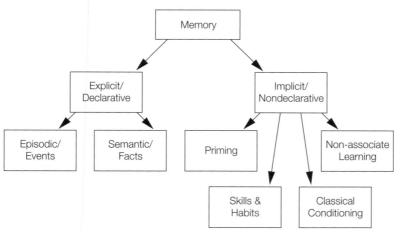

Source: Adapted from Squire, 1992

Episodic memory can be subdivided into short and long-term memory. Because of the lateralisation of brain function, it is also necessary to assess memory for both visual and verbal materials.

One of the most commonly used batteries for memory and learning is the Wechsler Memory Test – Third Edition (WMS–III; Wechsler, 1997b). It was developed to provide a comprehensive assessment of memory functioning that is clinically relevant. It is an individually administered test designed for individuals aged 16 to 89 years. The administration time of the core subtests is estimated to be between 30 to 60 mins. There is a software package that provides for computer scoring and interpretation. The WMS–III consists of six primary and five optional subtests (see Table 9.1). In addition, six of these eleven subtests have an immediate as well as a delayed condition, making a total of seventeen subtests altogether.

TABLE 9.1 Primary and secondary subtests of the WMS–III

Subtests	Description
Primary	
Logical Memory I & II	Recall of details of short stories read to the test taker
Verbal Paired Associates I & II	Learn, over a number of trials, a list of eight word pairs (eg, table-flower).
Faces I & II	Learn twenty-four target faces and then pick them from forty-eight faces (half of them target and half of them new)
Family Pictures I & II	Learn details of four family pictures and then recall the locations and activities of persons in the pictures
Letter Number Sequencing	Test taker presented aurally with random number and letter sequences in increasing length and then asked to repeat the stimuli in order (numbers first and then letters)
Spatial Span	Shown sequence of tapping (with increasing length) on a three-dimensional board with ten blocks and required to repeat the order of tapping, first in the same order and then backwards
Secondary Subtest (Optional)	
Information and Orientation	Answer historical, autobiographical, and information questions
Word List I & II	Learn, recall, and recognise a list of twelve words over a number of trials
Mental Control	Recall over-learned information (eg, alphabet, days of the week etc)
Visual Reproduction I & II	Learn, recall, and recognise a number of geometric figures
Digit Span	Recall a series of numbers presented orally forward and backward

The norms of the WMS–III comprise a sample of 1250 individuals from thirteen age groups (viz, 16–17, 18–19, 20–24, 25–29, 30–34, 34–44, 45–54, 55–64, 65–69, 70–74, 75–79, 80–84, 85–89 years of age). The performance of a test taker on the WMS–III can be summarised in terms of eight primary memory indices, namely, Auditory Immediate, Auditory Delayed, Visual Immediate, Visual Delayed, Immediate Memory, Auditory Recognition Delayed, General Memory, and Working Memory. Similar to the WAIS–III, these indices have a mean of 100 and a SD of 15. The average internal consistency of the WMS–III primary index scores was found to range from 0.74 to 0.94 and the test-retest reliability (one month) to range from 0.62 to 0.82 across subtests. The manual provides evidence to support the validity of the test. Basically the WMS–III has been found to be sensitive to damage caused by brain injury. For example, patients with traumatic brain injury and Alzheimer's disease have been found to perform significantly more poorly than normals on the WMS–III. In addition, results of factor analyses support the memory indices used in the test battery.

The Rey Auditory Verbal Learning Test (RAVLT) and the Rey-Osterreith Complex Figure Test (Rey Figure; Rey, 1964) are popular and are commonly used by clinical neuropsychologists in Australia and other parts of the world to assess verbal and visual memory. In the RAVLT, the test taker is read a list of fifteen words five times and asked to recall as many words as possible after each trial. After that, the test taker is read a second list of 15 words and asked to recall as many words as possible from this list. This is followed by an immediate, a 20-min delayed recall, and a recognition trial of the first list of words. A number of indices can be obtained from test performance (eg, number of words recalled for each of the eight trials, number of words recognised, total number of words recalled for the first five trials of the first word list, learning, and retroactive and proactive interference). Using a sample of 51 normal volunteers and a test-retest interval that ranged from 6 to 14 days, Geffen, Butterworth and Geffen (1994) found the test-retest reliability of the RAVLT to be modest (median r = 0.60). In terms of validity, the RAVLT has been found to be sensitive to verbal memory deficits in those with Alzheimer's disease or those with closed head injury (Bigler, Rosa, Schultz, Hall & Harris, 1989). Geffen, Moar, O'Hanlon, Clark and Geffen (1990) have collected normative data for this test in Australia. In the Rey Figure, a test taker is first asked to copy a two-dimensional drawing made up of lines and shapes. The test taker's visual memory ability is assessed by an incidental recall of the figure and delayed recall 20 to 30 min after initial presentation. The Rey Figure showed a high interrater reliability (ie, >0.95) when strict scoring criteria are observed (Spreen & Strauss, 1998). Further this test has been shown to produce consistently different response patterns in those with posterior and frontal lobe lesions (Lezak, 1983).

Language

For most right-handers, the function of language is mediated by the left cerebral hemisphere. Assessment of the language function of an individual with known or suspected brain injury, therefore, enables a clinical neuropsychologist to draw some conclusions about the functioning of the left cerebral hemisphere of that individual. Because of the significance and utility of language in our society, language problems resulting from brain injury can have important implications for the recovery and rehabilitation of individuals with such injury. Clinical neuropsychologists, as well as speech pathologists/therapists, are interested in the assessment of language. A comprehensive assessment typically includes both spoken and written language (Mapou, 1995), and input (understanding written and spoken words) and output (speech production and writing) functions within each.

Screening tests (eg, the Aphasia Screening Test of the Halstead-Reitan Neuropsychological Battery) allow a brief assessment of a person's language functioning.

However, other tests are needed to provide a more comprehensive assessment of the various areas of language functioning. The Western Aphasia Battery (WAB; Kertesz, 1982) and the Boston Diagnostic Aphasia Examination (BDAE; Goodglass, Kaplan & Barresi, 2000) are two examples of comprehensive language assessment batteries. According to Lezak et al (2004), the WAB has satisfactory reliability and validity and is sensitive in distinguishing the language abilities of those who have suffered stroke in the left versus the right hemisphere and those with mild Alzheimer's disease. The BDAE has interrater agreement that is typically above 0.75 (Lezak et al, 2004), and Davis (1993) found that BDAE scores predicted performance on other aphasia tests better than patient functioning in everyday circumstances.

Visuo-spatial function

In contrast to language, visuo-spatial function in humans is generally mediated by the right cerebral hemisphere of most right-handers. Damage to the right cerebral hemisphere has been found to affect a person's ability to perceive and understand visuo-spatial relationships and undertake three-dimensional constructional tasks.

Although a person's visuo-spatial ability can be gauged from performance on other neuropsychological tests (eg, performance subtests of the WAIS–III), specific tests of visuo-spatial functions have been developed. The Hooper Visual Organisation Test (HVOT; Hooper, 1983) and the Rey-Osterreith Complex Figure Test (Rey, 1964) are two examples. In the HVOT, a test taker is asked to identify thirty pictures of 'cut-up' objects (see Figure 9.7 for an example). As indicated previously, the task for a test taker on the Rey Figure is to copy a two-dimensional drawing made up of lines and shapes. Based on a sample of 166 college students and a sample of 73 psychiatric inpatients with mixed diagnosis, the split-half reliabilities of the HVOT were found to be 0.82 and 0.78 respectively (Hooper, 1948, 1958). Lezak et al (2004) reported that the test-retest reliability for the HVOT varies from 0.68 to 0.86 across samples tested to date. Further, tests of its construct validity showed that a perceptual organisation factor on the WAIS accounted for 45 per cent of the HVOT variance, suggesting that the HVOT is a valid test of perceptual organisation.

To assess a person's spatial awareness ability, the Standardised Road-Map Test of Direction Sense (Money, 1976) can be used. In this test, the examiner traces a dotted

FIGURE 9.7 A simulated example of a Hooper Visual Organisation Test item

pathway on a road map with a pencil and asks the test taker to tell the direction (right or left) taken at each turn. Lezak et al (2004) reported that the road map test is able to distinguish those with parietal-lobe injuries from those with Huntington's or Alzheimer's disease.

Executive functions

Although there are disagreements among clinical neuropsychologists about the definition, nature, and number of executive functions, it is widely accepted that these functions are mediated by the prefrontal cortex. In addition, it is agreed executive functions are responsible for goal-directed behaviours in humans and that impairments in these functions are debilitating and difficult to rehabilitate. Working memory, concept formation, problem solving, and planning are commonly considered executive functions. Because of space limitations, a comprehensive description of tests used to assess executive function is not included in this section. Instead a discussion of a recently developed battery of executive functions, namely, the Delis-Kaplan Executive Function System (D-KEFS; Delis, Kaplan & Kramer, 2001) will be used to illustrate the functions and tasks commonly included in the assessment.

The D-KEFS consists of nine subtests, namely, Trail Making Test, Verbal Fluency, Design Fluency, Color-Word Interference Test, Sorting Test, Twenty Questions Test, Tower Test, Proverb Test, and the Word Context Test. Table 9.2 summarises the descriptions of these tests and the functions they measure. One of the strengths of this test is its comprehensiveness. The nine tests of the battery allow an examiner to assess all the executive functions at the same time, using the same normative data. The size of the standardisation sample was 1750 and included age groups from 8 to 89 years. Although the reliability of the principal scores for the nine subtests is acceptable, some of the additional scores are not as high, and more research is needed to support the validity of the test (Ramsden, 2003).

TABLE 9.2 Descriptions of tasks and functions measured by the nine subtests of the D-KEFS

Subtest	Description	Function Measured
Trail Making Test	This is a modified version of the test from the Halstead-Reitan Neuropsychological Battery. Test taker is required to join circles on a piece of paper	Flexibility of thinking
Verbal Fluency	Test taker is required to generate words in a phonemic format from over-learned concepts	Fluent productivity (verbal)
Design Fluency	Test taker is required to generate as many figures as possible by connecting rows of dots	Fluent productivity (spatial)
Color-Word Interference Test	This is a modification of the Stroop Color-Word Interference Test. Test taker is required to inhibit an automatic verbal response and generate a conflicting response	Verbal inhibition
Sorting Test	Test taker is required to sort objects into sixteen different sorting concepts on two sets of cards	Concept formation, cognitive flexibility, and problem solving

TABLE 9.2 (cont.)

Subtest	Description	Function Measured
Twenty Questions Test	Test taker is required to identify various categories and subcategories represented in 30 objects and formulate abstract, yes/no questions	Hypothesis testing, abstract thinking, and impulsivity
Tower Test	Test taker is required to move disks across three pegs to build a tower in the fewest number of moves	Planning, reasoning, and impulsivity
Proverb Test	Test taker is required to provide a correct abstract interpretation of a proverb	Ability to generate and comprehend abstract thought and metaphorical thinking
Word Context Test	Test taker is required to discover the meaning of made-up or mystery words based on clues given	Deductive reasoning and abstract thinking (verbal)

Motor functions

A comprehensive assessment of motor functions usually includes lateral dominance, strength, fine motor skills (speed and dexterity), sensorimotor integration and praxis (Mapou, 1995). A person might be able to encode, process, retrieve stimulus information, and plan actions but be prevented from achieving a behavioural goal because of problems with motor functions. As with sensory functions, information about a test taker's motor functions can be obtained from other sources (eg, neurological, occupational therapy, and physiotherapy examinations). The following tests illustrate how motor functions are assessed.

The hand dynamometer (see Figure 9.8) is commonly used to assess motor strength. To obtain reliable scores, the test taker is asked to grasp the handle of the mechanical hand dynamometer as hard as possible three times, alternating between the dominant and non-dominant hand. Average motor strength (in kilograms) for each hand is obtained based on scores of these trials. To measure motor speed, the Finger Tapping Test of the HRNB (see Box 9.3) is commonly used. In this test, the test taker is asked to tap as quickly as possible for 10 seconds on a mechanical device similar to a telegraph key. A counter is fitted to the device for recording the number of taps. To obtain reliable measures, five trials are administered, alternating between the dominant and non-dominant hands and the average number of taps per trial for each hand is obtained. Reliability data for the Finger Tapping Test are variable, with Lezak et al (2004) reporting test-retest correlations of between 0.64 and 0.94 for those with brain disorders. Even those with diseases that involve the spinal cord, such as multiple sclerosis, show significant slowing effects on the Finger Tapping Test (Lezak et al, 2004).

The Purdue Pegboard (Purdue Research Foundation, 1948) is usually used to assess motor dexterity. This test was originally developed to select assembly line workers. In this test, the test taker is required to place metal pins in two rows of holes with the dominant hand, non-dominant hand, and both hands, within a 30-second time limit. An assembly trial (time limit = 1 minute) that requires more complex visual–motor coordination can also be administered. This trial requires the

FIGURE 9.8 The hand dynamometer

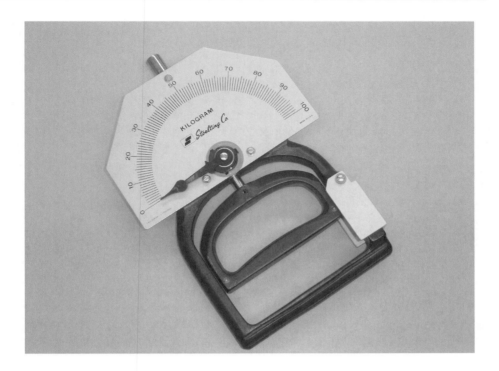

test taker to build an 'assembly', that is, by placing a pin, a washer, a collar, and a washer sequentially for each hole. The test taker alternates between the dominant and non-dominant hand. Lezak et al (2004) again reported variability in test-retest reliability, with correlations from between 0.35 to 0.93 noted. In terms of its ability to predict a lateralised lesion, the test scores on the Purdue Pegboard represent a significant predictive gain over patient's base rate scores. By using appropriate normative data for these tests of motor function, an examiner can determine if the reductions of a test taker in motor strength, speed, and dexterity are due to injury on the right, left, or both sides of the brain.

CONCLUDING REMARKS

Injury to the human brain can lead to long-term and significant disability for an individual. Neuropsychological assessment is an essential step for the management and treatment of individuals suspected or found to have brain injury. In this chapter we have talked about the purposes of and the steps in neuropsychological assessment. We have also discussed the functions commonly examined during a neuropsychological assessment and described some of the commonly used psychological tests that measure these functions. In so doing, we have introduced you to one of the fastest growing subbranches of psychology.

Questions for consideration

1 Psychological tests are different from neuropsychological tests. Do you agree?
2 Discuss the function(s) of the following brain structures:
   (a) cerebellum
   (b) thalamus
   (c) temporal lobes
   (d) basal ganglia
3 What does a clinical neuropsychologist do?
4 What is neuropsychological assessment and what are the steps of neuropsychological assessment?
5 What functions are measured by the following tests?
   (a) Halstead-Reitan Neuropsychological Battery
   (b) Stroop Color Word Interference Test
   (c) Rey-Osterreith Complex Figure Test
   (d) Purdue Pegboard

Further reading

Hebben, N, & Milberg, W (2002). *Essentials of neuropsychological assessment*. New York: Wiley.

Kolb, B, & Whishaw, I Q. (2003). *Fundamentals of human neuropsychology* (5th edn). New York: Worth.

Lezak, M D, Howieson, D B, & Loring, D W (2004). *Neuropsychological assessment* (4th edn). New York: Oxford University Press.

Oliveira-Souza, R, Moll, J, & Eslinger, P (2004). Neuropsychological assessment. In M Rizzo & P J Eslinger (Eds), *Principles and practice of behavioral neurology and neuropsychology* (pp 47–64). Philadelphia: W B Saunders.

Snyder, P J, & Nussbaum, P D (Eds) (1998). *Clinical neuropsychology: A pocket handbook for assessment*. Washington, DC: American Psychological Association.

chapter ten

Forensic
Psychological Testing
and Assessment

▶ While shopping at a supermarket, a young man slipped, fell, and injured himself. His solicitor referred him to a psychologist for an assessment to determine the extent of damage caused by the injury for the purposes of compensation.

▶ A psychologist employed by corrective services was asked to assess a new inmate. Specifically, she was asked to determine if this person was suffering from a mental disorder.

▶ A judge at the family court ordered the parents of a young girl to be assessed by a psychologist. Results of the assessment were used to assist the resolution of the custody dispute.

▶ A young woman who was involved in a car accident complained that her ability to remember had dramatically decreased since the accident. Because the extent of her complaint was at variance with the severity of the accident and neurological findings, the possibility of her exaggerating her problem was raised.

INTRODUCTION

The origin of the word 'forensic' can be traced to the Latin word 'forensis', which means 'of the forum' where the law court of ancient Rome was held. The *Australian Oxford Dictionary* defines the word 'forensic' as 'of or used in connection with courts of law'. Forensic psychology is a recently emerged branch of psychology that specialises in applying psychological knowledge and skills to the working of the legal and criminal justice systems. As illustrated by the above examples, forensic psychologists typically provide assessment services to clients of the legal and criminal justice systems to answer referral questions relating to diagnosis, decision making, and prediction. In this chapter, we provide an introduction to forensic psychological testing and assessment by addressing the following questions: What is forensic psychology, what do forensic psychologists do, and what are the main settings of forensic assessment? What are the similarities and differences between forensic and other types of psychological assessment? What are the common psychological tests and assessment techniques used by forensic psychologists? What are some of the issues and limitations relating to forensic assessment?

FORENSIC PSYCHOLOGY AND FORENSIC PSYCHOLOGICAL TESTING AND ASSESSMENT

As a branch of applied psychology, forensic psychology is relatively young. In the UK, the term 'forensic psychology' was introduced by Haward in 1953 to address the County Durham Psychology Group (Gudjonsson & Haward, 1998). In the USA, although experimental psychologists have been asked to appear in courts as expert witnesses since the 1900s, forensic psychology was not formally recognised as a specialty area of psychology by the American Psychological Association until August 2001 (Heilbrun, Bank, Follingstad & Fredrick, 2000; Ogloff & Douglas, 2003). In Australia, the College of Forensic Psychologists was established by the Australian Psychological Society in 1993.

Broadly speaking, forensic psychology can be defined as the application of psychology to the legal system (Ogloff & Douglas, 2003). Heilbrun et al (2000) put forward a more specific definition: 'Forensic psychology will be defined as the professional practice by psychologists within the areas of clinical psychology, counselling psychology, neuropsychology, and school psychology, when they are engaged regularly as experts and represent themselves as such, in an activity primarily intended to provide professional psychological expertise to the legal system'.

Testifying in court as expert witnesses (see Box 10.1), providing psychological treatment to offenders and victims of crime, and conducting research on the accuracy of testimony of witnesses are some of the domains of forensic psychology. However, one of the major contributions of forensic psychology is the provision of forensic assessment (Ackerman, 1999). (For ease of expression, the term forensic psychological testing and assessment will be shortened to forensic assessment for this chapter.) The primary purpose of forensic assessment is the collection of relevant and useful information with psychological tests and other assessment techniques to assist decision makers in the legal and criminal justice systems in making decisions about offenders or those suspected of an offence (Ogloff & Douglas, 2003). Psychologists in other specialty areas are sometimes engaged in this work, but they can be considered to be conducting forensic assessment, and need to follow the guidelines and ethics for practise in this specialty. Furthermore, to practice in this area, they are required to have training and experience in the law that is relevant to the particular area of practice, be it clinical, neuropsychological or educational.

BOX 10.1

Forensic assessment and psychologists as expert witnesses

Before the results of forensic assessment are actually presented in a court of law as evidence provided by an expert witness, it has to be decided: (a) whether this evidence is really necessary and (b) whether the evidence is admissible under the requirements of the court. The practical and legal criteria relating to these decisions can differ between countries and between states in the same country. According to Ogloff and Douglas (2003), the results of forensic assessment are needed if they are found by the court to be relevant and related to one or more legal standards raised by the case. In addition, the court needs to weigh up the relevance and utility of the evidence being presented (its probative value) against its potential to bias the jury (its prejudicial value). In deciding whether the evidence is admissible, three requirements must be satisfied: (a) the evidence is required by the judge or the jury to assist in decision making; (b) the person who provides the evidence must be suitably qualified; and (c) if the expert witness uses scientific facts or data, they must be widely accepted by other experts in the area (Ogloff & Douglas, 2003). While other witnesses in a court case are required to provide factual information, expert witnesses may provide factual information as well as offer an opinion. In the USA, some specific criteria (known as the Daubert Criteria) have been developed based on the *Daubert v Merrl Dow Pharmaceutical* case (Ackerman & Kane, 1998). These require the psychologist to: (a) use psychological tests or assessment techniques that are theoretically and psychometrically sound; (b) draw conclusions based on scientifically validated theory; (c) weigh and qualify testimony based on theory and empirical research; (d) know how to defend the scientific basis of the procedure used. To assist the selection of psychological tests to fulfil these criteria, Heilbrun (1992) suggested the following specific guidelines:

1   Use commercially available tests that are adequately documented in at least two sources (viz, a test manual and the *Mental Measurements Year Book*).
2   Unless there are justifiable reasons or explanations, use tests with reliability coefficients of at least 0.80.
3   Use tests that are directly relevant to the legal issue involved or at least use tests that assess psychological constructs that are relevant to the legal issue.
4   Make sure that tests are administered based on standardised instructions using materials or stimuli provided by the test publisher in an optimal testing environment (eg, quiet, well lit, free of distraction).
5   Make sure that tests chosen are applicable or suitable (in terms of age, gender, ethnic and educational background) to the person being assessed.
6   If possible, select tests that provide formulae for making objective, actuarial conclusions or predictions.
7   If possible, assess the response style of the person and interpret the psychological test results of that person in light of this finding.

As applies to other fields of professional psychology mentioned in the earlier chapters of this book, training of forensic psychologists is usually reserved for the postgraduate level. In Australia, a minimum of 6 years of full-time university training, including 2 years of specialised postgraduate study and supervision, is the minimum requirement for membership of the College of Forensic Psychologists of the Australian Psychological Society. Most of the forensic psychology training programs in the USA are typically at the doctoral level (viz, PsyD or PhD).

SETTINGS OF FORENSIC ASSESSMENT

In Australia and other Commonwealth countries, three jurisdictions are recognised: criminal, civil, and family. Criminal law is concerned with crimes against the public or the Crown, civil law with the resolution of conflicts between individuals or organisations, and family law with conflicts within families or between partners in married or de facto relationships. Apart from being employed to support courts in these jurisdictions, psychologists are employed in other settings such as police departments, correction centres, corrective and forensic mental health services, private practice, and research organisations.

Within these settings, forensic assessment is conducted for a number of purposes. For example, in the criminal law area, results of forensic assessment have been used by the defence, the prosecution, or the court for pretrial, presentencing, and sentencing purposes. In some countries, results of forensic assessment have also been used to assist criminal law courts to determine the mental state of the defendant at the time of the offence or to decide if a defendant is competent to stand trial. In the civil law area, forensic assessment has been requested to establish the extent of personal injury (eg, cognitive impairment as a result of a car accident or emotional harm as a result of a traumatic event such as a bank robbery), to determine the effect of an unfair dismissal, and to determine the capacity of individuals in making financial decisions or changing the content of a will. In the family law area, results of forensic assessment have been used to assist in deciding custody of and access to children and removing children from parents.

The results of forensic assessment can have significant and long-term impacts on the lives of the persons who are assessed and on the lives of those around them (Martin, Allan & Allan, 2001). This underscores the importance of training and experience for psychologists working in the forensic area and highlights the responsibilities that come with conducting forensic assessment.

DIFFERENCES BETWEEN FORENSIC AND THERAPEUTIC ASSESSMENT

Forensic assessment is considered by some (eg, Melton, Petrila, Poythress & Slobogin, 1997) as specialised clinical psychological assessment because it requires the training and advanced knowledge and skills similar to that received by clinical psychologists. Others (eg, Greenberg & Shuman, 1997; Heilbrun, 2001), however, contend that, unlike other branches of psychology (eg, clinical, counselling, and neuropsychological)

TABLE 10.1 Differences between forensic and therapeutic assessment

	Therapeutic	Forensic
Purpose of assessment	Diagnosis and treatment of psychological problem	Assist decision makers in legal/criminal justice system
Psychologist–client relationship	Helper and client or patient	Objective or quasi-objective professional stance
Who is being served?	The individual client	Variable, may include the individual client, the attorney and the court
Notification of purpose of assessment	Psychologist and client are assumed to share a similar purpose. Formal, explicit notification not necessary	Formal, explicit notification of purpose is necessary because psychologist and client do not necessarily share similar purpose
Nature of standard being considered	Medical, psychiatric, and psychological	Medical, psychiatric, psychological but also legal
Source of data	Self-report, psychological tests, behavioural assessment, and medical	Self-report, psychological tests, behavioural assessment, and medical but also other information (files, observations)
Response style of client	Assumed to be reliable	Not assumed to be reliable
Clarification of reasoning and limits of knowledge	Assumed and optional	Important
Written report	Comparatively brief and focused on conclusions	Lengthy and detailed. Need to document findings, reasoning, and conclusions
Court testimony	Not expected	Expected

that are therapeutic in nature, forensic assessment is different from these disciplines in a number of aspects (see Table 10.1).

The primary purpose of forensic assessment is to assist decision makers in the legal or criminal justice systems to address specific legal issues, such as whether a defendant is competent to stand trial or the risk of managing an inmate in a certain way. The primary purpose of therapeutic assessment, in contrast, is to diagnose and treat clients with psychological or mental problems. The referral question for therapeutic assessment arises out of the needs of a client, but the referral question for forensic assessment is based on legal criteria for decision making. While the process of therapeutic assessment is usually (but not always) a means to an end (ie, treatment), the process of forensic assessment is commonly an end to itself. Typically, the process of forensic assessment terminates after relevant information or data are collected to prepare a report that addresses a specific legal issue.

In terms of relationships between the psychologist and client, therapeutic assessment is similar to that between a doctor and a patient (ie, between a helper and someone who seeks help). As such, it is assumed that in this relationship the psychologist will act with the best interests of the client in mind and that the client will voluntarily and truthfully provide the information required by the psychologist in order to be helped. In contrast, forensic assessment is different from its therapeutic counterpart in that the psychologist does not assume the role of a helper for a client. Instead, she adopts a more objective stance during the assessment and will neither accept nor reject the information or data provided by the person she assesses until they can be checked and validated.

For therapeutic assessment, the 'client' is the person who seeks help from the psychologist. The 'client' for forensic assessment, on the other hand, may be more than one person. Usually the 'client' is the decision maker or the person (eg, a judge or a lawyer) in the legal or criminal justice system who referred the person to be assessed. Because of this difference, the purpose of assessment is usually formally or explicitly explained to the person who is being assessed before the assessment is done. Formal or explicit explanation of the purpose is not usually necessary for a therapeutic assessment because of an implicit understanding between the client and the psychologist (ie, diagnosis and treatment of a problem).

The two types of assessment also differ in terms of the nature of the standards used. For therapeutic assessment, a psychologist is guided by scientific and professional standards. While these two standards are relevant for forensic assessment, legal standards need to be taken into consideration as well. The selection of assessment procedures can be used to illustrate this point. In therapeutic assessment, a psychologist can decide what psychological tests or assessment techniques to use for a client based on the referral question. In forensic assessment, the choice of an assessment technique needs to be considered in the light of relevant legal standards to ensure that the constructs being measured bear on the legal standards.

Self-report during an interview, psychological test results, and medical histories are usually used as data in both therapeutic and forensic assessment. Additional data commonly used in forensic assessment includes information recorded on legal files and observations made by personnel who work in legal or corrective settings. This additional information may be more directly related to the legal issue involved. Furthermore, this information is important for double-checking the accuracy of the other data collected. This is because in forensic assessment a psychologist does not automatically assume that the responses of the individual referred for assessment are accurate. The individual may want to exaggerate or minimise the extent of his problems or symptoms in order to gain a favourable outcome in his case.

The findings, reasoning, and conclusions of a therapeutic assessment are not usually subjected to strict clarification or challenge because of an implicit acceptance of the professional expertise of the psychologist who conducted the assessment. Moreover, psychological reports written for therapeutic assessment are normally not expected to be brought to a court of law. In contrast, reasoning and findings of forensic psychological reports are expected to be scrutinised and challenged because of the adversarial nature of the legal system. As such, forensic psychological reports are comparatively longer and more detailed than is the case with therapeutic reports.

PSYCHOLOGICAL TESTS AND ASSESSMENT TECHNIQUES COMMONLY USED IN FORENSIC ASSESSMENT

According to Heilbrun, Roger, and Otto (2002), three types of assessment techniques can be used in forensic assessment: (a) forensic assessment instruments, (b) forensically relevant instruments, and (c) clinical instruments. The first type is specifically designed for forensic assessment and these instruments are directly relevant to a specific legal standard. For example, the MacArthur Competence Assessment Tool – Criminal Adjudication (Poythress, Monahan, Bonnie & Hoge, 1999) was specifically developed to assess the American legal standards for competence to stand trial. The second type is not designed based on any specific legal standards but the constructs measured by these instruments are related to a legal standard. Examples of this type of assessment technique include tests that measure constructs such as psychopathy, violence risk, or malingering. The third type includes psychological tests or techniques that are not developed specifically for the purpose of forensic assessment but have been adopted by forensic psychologists to answer legal questions. Examples of these instruments include the WAIS, MMPI, and the BDI. In previous chapters of this book, we have discussed quite a number of the third type of assessment techniques. Therefore, in this chapter we will focus on the first two types of techniques for legal areas such as competency to standard trial, risk assessment, custody evaluation and malingering.

Competency to stand trial

In the area of criminal law, the issue of whether a defendant is competent to stand trial is an important but difficult one. This issue is based on the assumption that it is unfair to put someone on trial if he does not have the ability or capacity to understand the matters brought against him. This reduced ability or capacity could be due to intellectual handicap, mental illness, or cognitive decline. Compared to other requests for assessment of competency (eg, competency to change a will or consent to medical treatment), the number of requests for competency to stand trial is comparatively high. Although this kind of assessment is likely to be conducted by forensic psychologists or forensic psychiatrists in the USA, it is considered the domain for forensic psychiatrists in Australia (Freckelton, 1993). In the literature, a number of tests and techniques have been developed to assess a person's capacity to stand trial. In this section, we will review the Competency Screening Test (CST; Lipsitt, Lelos & McGarry, 1971) and the MacArthur Competence Assessment Tool – Criminal Adjudication (MacCAT – CA; Poythress et al, 1999).

As the name suggests, the CST is a screening device used to decide if a more comprehensive assessment is necessary for defendants who may be unfit to stand trial. It comprises 22 unfinished sentences (relating to legal/judicial processes) that the test taker has to complete and administration usually takes about 25 minutes. The responses of the test taker on the items are scored using a three-point scale (0, 1, and 2) depending on their appropriateness. Randolph, Hicks, Mason, and Cuneo (1982) reported a high level (0.92) of interrater reliability for the CST. The same study found significant correlations between scores on the CST and opinions of court psychiatrists. Despite these results, the CST has been criticised on the grounds that the sentence completion procedure is based on questionable assumptions and scoring methods and the construct being assessed may not be directly related to the legal standard of competency to stand trial (Ackerman, 1999).

The MacCAT – CA was developed based on Bonnie's (1992, 1993) theory of legal compentency and is an update of the MacSAC – CD (MacArthur Structured Assessment of Competencies of Criminal Defendants). It is an individually administered instrument intended for use with criminal defendants and takes about 25 to 55 minutes to administer. It comprises 22 items that are related to the formal functional abilities associated with the legal construct of competency to stand trial. These items include three discrete competence scales: understanding (eight items), reasoning (eight items), and appreciation (six items). The first scale covers the ability to understand general information related to the law and adjudicatory proceedings. The second scale covers the ability to discern the potential legal relevance of information and capacity to reason about specific choices that confront a defendant in the course of adjudication. The third scale covers the rational awareness of the meaning and consequences of the proceeding in the defendant's own case. Each item is rated on a three-point scale (0, 1, and 2) and a high score indicates a high level of capacity.

The MacCAT – CA was standardised on a sample of 729 pretrial felony defendants (90 per cent males) in the USA. Norms are not available for individuals with IQs under 60. In terms of reliability, the internal consistencies of the three scales for the standardisation sample were 0.81, 0.85, and 0.88. Interrater reliability for the three scales was reported as 0.75, 0.85, and 0.90. In terms of validity, the construct validity of the MacCAT – CA has been supported by expected patterns of correlations with measures of cognitive ability, psychopathology, and ratings of experienced clinicians. Despite these results, Rogers, Sewell, Grandjean, and Vitacco (2002) cautioned that the MacCAT – CA items are vulnerable to faking by the test taker.

Risk assessment/prediction of aggression or dangerousness

Within the criminal justice systems, forensic assessments are commonly requested to determine how risky or dangerous certain inmates are. The results of the assessment are typically used for making decisions such as sentencing, parole, and classification.

The Psychopathy Checklist – Revised (PCL – R; Hare, 1991) was developed by Canadian forensic psychologist Robert Hare to assess psychopathic (antisocial) personality disorders in forensic populations. This individually administered rating scale comprises twenty items that cover a wide range of psychopathic traits and behaviours. To rate these items, a semi-structured interview (of about 1.5 to 2 hours) and a review of collateral information (of about 1 hour) needs to be conducted. Ratings on the twenty items using a three-point scale (0 = absent, 1 = possible or to some degree, and 2 = present) produce a total score that ranges from 0 to 40. This score provides an overall assessment of psychopathy or the degree of match to the prototypical psychopath (cut-off score of 30). Two factor scores can also be derived from the ratings: the callous, selfish, remorseless use of others and a chronically unstable and antisocial life style. Norms are available (for male offenders, female offenders, and male forensic patients).

The PCL – R has gained popularity in the forensic area and much research has been conducted to support its utility. The PCL – R is considered the 'gold standard' in predicting violence and recidivism because it has been found to have very good psychometric properties (Martin, Allan & Allan, 2001). Its internal consistency has been found to be high based on data obtained from male offenders, with 0.85 for the total score and 0.64 to 0.71 for the factor scores. Interrater reliabilities have been found to range from 0.84 to 0.93 for data obtained from male offenders and range from 0.93 to 0.97 for female offenders. In terms of validity, the PCL – R has been found to be a very good predictor of many problem behaviours. However, it is rather time-consuming to administer, score, and interpret and, according to its developer, competent use of the instrument requires a high level of training.

Custody evaluation

In the area of family law, one of the most difficult decisions for a judge is to determine with cases of divorce, abuse or neglect, or guardianship, who should have custody of a child and what provisions, if any, should apply to the custody. Forensic assessment is frequently requested by decision makers in family courts in Australia and other parts of the world to assist in making decisions about child custody (Ackerman & Ackerman, 1997; Powell & Lancaster, 2003). According to the guidelines provided by the American Psychological Association (1994), during the assessment, providers of forensic assessment need to keep reminding themselves that the child's interest and well-being are paramount. Although specific referral question(s) may be requested by the court or others, the primary purpose of the evaluation is to assess factors (individual or family) that affect the best psychological interests of the child. These factors include the psychological and developmental needs of the child and the parenting capacity of the prospective custodians.

One of the most obvious psychological assessment techniques for use in child custody cases arising out of parental divorce is the interview (Ackerman, 1999). Usually the child or the children involved are interviewed separately from the adults and different sets of questions are used for these two groups. During an interview with adults, the areas typically covered include demographics, place of residence, marital history, place of employment, employment history, educational history, names and ages of children, history of medical and psychiatric problems, alcohol use, problems with the law (including sexual abuse or sexual assault), current life circumstances and functioning. During an interview with children, questions can be used to explore areas such as the child's reaction to a court decision, the child's desire to see more or less of a parent, who disciplines the child at home and how it is done, and the level of involvement of each parent in the family and in family activities.

Apart from the interviews, a number of psychological tests and assessment instruments may be used to assess the general cognitive ability and personality of the parents and the children involved in a custody evaluation. Because most of these tests (eg, the WAIS, MMPI, NEO-PI, etc) have been reviewed before, the reviews will not be repeated here. In the remaining part of this section, we focus on an assessment instrument specifically developed for child custody.

One of the commonly used instruments in the USA and Canada is the Ackerman-Schoendorf Scales of Parent Evaluation of Custody (ASPECT; Ackerman and Schoendorf, 1992). This instrument was designed to directly evaluate the suitability of a parent for custody based on characteristics identified in the literature. Basically, the ASPECT requires the assessor to respond to 56 questions using a Yes–No format. The assessor's responses are based on information collected from: a parent questionnaire, interview and observation of each parent with and without the child, scores obtained from tests routinely used for child custody evaluation, and the results of an IQ assessment of the child. Responses are collated and an overall index called the Parental Custody Index (PCI; T score with a mean of 50 and SD of 10) is obtained for each parent. Recommendations can be made by comparing the index for each parent. T-score difference of 10 points or more are considered significant and interpretable. The PCI of the ASPECT has been found to have adequate internal consistency (0.76 based on 200 subjects) and high interrater reliability (0.96). There are also some data that support its validity.

Malingering

It is assumed in psychological testing and assessment that when a test taker fills in a self-report measure or completes an objective test, the result is a true reflection of their thoughts and feelings or their ability. In some cases this assumption may be false. Clients might want to present themselves in a negative or positive manner. For example, a person who is given a personality test might want to endorse items that are contrary to his behaviour or belief because he wants to present himself in a positive light to the psychologist or the referral agents. This problem has been found to be more common in the forensic assessment area. This is because many clients in the legal and criminal justice systems may not actually want to undertake the assessment, or they know that the results of the assessment may have serious implications for their lives. On some personality tests (eg, the MMPI or the 16 PF) items have been added in an attempt to detect the tendency to fake good or bad. In this section, we discuss two psychological tests that have been developed specifically to detect malingering, the attempt to exaggerate symptoms or claim symptoms one does not have.

The Structured Interview of Reported Symptoms (SIRS; Rogers, Bagby & Dickens, 1992) was designed to 'detect malingering and other forms of feigning of psychological symptoms' in adults 18 years and older. Specifically, it focuses on deliberate distortions in self-presentation. The SIRS is an individually administered instrument that comprises 172 items. These items cover a wide range of psycho-pathology, including symptoms that are unlikely to be true. Thirty-two of the items are repeated to detect inconsistency in responding (eg, providing different answers to the same question). The SIRS uses a structured interview method and takes from 45 minutes to 1 hour to complete. Ratings on the items are categorised into eight primary scales (rare symptoms, symptom combinations, improbable or absurd symptoms, subtle symptoms, blatant symptoms, severity of symptoms, selectivity of symptoms, and reported versus observed symptoms), and five supplementary scales (direct appraisal of honesty, defensive symptoms, symptom onset and resolution, overly specified symptoms, and inconsistency of symptoms). Scores on each of these scales are classified as being 'honest', 'indeterminate', 'probably feigning', or 'definite feigning' based on research findings collected with psychiatric patients, normals, simulators, and malingerers.

The internal consistency for the SIRS primary and supplementary scales has been found to range from 0.66 to 0.92. Its interrater reliability has been found to range from 0.89 to 1.00. In terms of validity, the SIRS has been found to be effective in discriminating between individuals instructed to feign mental illness (viz, simulators), honest responders, and suspected malingerers. Construct validity of the SIRS is supported by results of factor analyses. Finally, its construct validity has been supported by correlations with the validity scales of the MMPI.

One of the most common symptoms associated with malingering is memory impairment (Rogers, 1997; Shum, O'Gorman & Alpar, 2004). This is because problems with forgetting and remembering are frequently associated with the effect of compensable brain injury (eg, motor vehicle accident, assaults, falls, etc). This fact is also reinforced in the community by popular books, movies, and TV programs. To 'assist neuropsychologists in discriminating between bona fide memory-impaired patients and malingerers' Tombaugh developed the Test of Memory Malingering (TOMM; 1996). The TOMM is an individually administered test that is suitable for adults 16 to 84 years old and takes only 15 minutes to complete. Basically, it aims to detect response bias, intentional faking, and exaggeration of symptoms by showing a test taker fifty line-drawings of ordinary objects and then asking her, after a delay, to recognise the target among a choice of two drawings. The TOMM was developed based on the assumption that on a two-choice recognition test for fifty target items, a person's performance should not be lower than the chance level (ie, less than 25 items). According to Vitelli (2001) the TOMM has been found to have high coefficients of internal consistency (0.94 to 0.95) but no information on test-retest or interrater reliability has been included in the test manual. Furthermore, validation studies found that simulators and suspected malingerers performed significantly more poorly on the TOMM than normals, and individuals with TBI and other organic problems. In one particular study, the sensitivity (proportion of simulators correctly classified) was found to be 93 per cent and specificity (proportion of non-simulators correctly classified) 100 per cent. (See pp 91–2 for comments on sensitivity and specificity.) Finally, test performance on the TOMM was not found to be sensitive to age, education, and cognitive impairment.

LIMITATIONS OF FORENSIC ASSESSMENT

It has to be acknowledged that the practice of forensic assessment is not without its critics. Faust and Ziskin in 1988 in the prestigious journal *Science* questioned the contribution of psychologists and psychiatrists as expert witnesses in courts. They argued that the evidence provided by psychologists and psychiatrists in court is of low reliability and validity and does not assist decision making by the court. Faust and Ziskin expanded their arguments in a number of books that provided lawyers with a resource for challenging psychological evidence in court (Faust, Ziskin & Hiers, 1991; Ziskin & Faust, 1988). In response to the original article, a number of psychologists (eg, Fowler & Matarazzo, 1988; Heilbrun, 1992; Matarazzo, 1990) argued that Faust and Ziskin were selective in reviewing evidence relating to the utility of forensic assessment and had overstated the case.

The controversy has, however, alerted psychologists who work in the legal area to the limitations of forensic assessment. These limitations include: self-report instruments are prone to malingering, actuarial formulae have not been developed for many assessment instruments to interpret and predict behaviours, and small sample size in some of the validation studies conducted. The controversy has also prompted professional psychological societies to develop clear guidelines to improve the practice of forensic assessment.

CONCLUDING REMARKS

To recapitulate, the purpose of forensic assessment is to collect relevant data using psychological tests and other assessment techniques to assist decision makers in the legal and criminal justice systems to make decisions. Compared to therapeutic and other types of assessment, forensic assessment has to follow not just scientific and professional standards and guidelines but also legal standards and requirements. Results and reports of forensic psychological assessment are more likely to be subjected to scrutiny, clarification, and challenge because of the adversarial nature of the legal and criminal justice systems. This further highlights the importance for psychologists of writing psychological reports that are empirically sound and based on research findings and for them to be familiar with ethical and professional guidelines (eg, confidentiality, informed consent, duty to warn and protect, record keeping) that relate to psychological assessment. In reviewing some of the more commonly used tests and techniques used for forensic assessment, we hope we have made you more aware of the typical referral questions raised in the legal and criminal justice systems and how they are answered by these assessment instruments. Finally, given the relatively short history of forensic psychology, it is important to be aware of the limitations of forensic assessment and some of the latest developments in the area.

Questions for consideration

1 What is forensic assessment?
2 Can a clinical psychologist conduct forensic assessment?
3 What are some of the common settings where forensic assessment is conducted?

4   Describe a psychological test designed for forensic assessment and evaluate its psychometric properties.
5   What are some of the issues that one needs to take into consideration when assessing a person's competency to stand trial?
6   What is malingering? Why does it happen? What techniques have been developed to assess malingering?
7   Forensic assessment does not assist decision making in the legal and criminal justice systems. Do you agree with this statement? Why and why not?

Further reading

Martin, M, Allan, A, & Allan, M M (2001). The use of psychological tests by Australian psychologists who do assessments for the courts. *Australian Journal of Psychology, 53,* 77–82.

Ogloff, J R P, & Douglas, K S (2003). Psychological assessment in forensic settings. In J R Graham, & J A Naglieri (Eds), *Handbook of Psychology: Vol. 10 Assessment Psychology* (pp. 345–63). Hoboken, NJ: John Wiley & Sons.

Otto, R K, & Heilbrun, K (2002). The practice of forensic psychology. *American Psychologist, 57,* 5–18.

van Dorsten, B (2002). *Forensic psychology: From classroom to courtroom.* New York: Kluwer Academic.

chapter eleven

Educational Testing
and Assessment

> ▸ A school teacher wants to know her class's standing on the three R's so she gives her students a reading test, a writing test, and a test of arithmetic.
>
> ▸ A child is being very disruptive in class. In order to help diagnose his behaviour problems he is referred to an educational psychologist for assessment.
>
> ▸ A mother believes that her child is gifted. Wanting to provide her child with the best opportunities at an early age, she has his intelligence assessed in order to determine how well he will cope with an accelerated curriculum.
>
> ▸ A young teenager is trying to decide which subjects to take at school. In order to help clarify the things she is interested in, she completes a vocational interests test.
>
> ▸ A teenager is starting to think about leaving school. To get some information about his career options he visits a vocational counsellor who asks him to complete a vocational interests test prior to the counselling session.

INTRODUCTION

Along with preparation and delivery of the material to be taught, assessment and evaluation is one of the core competencies of any teacher, trainer, or educator. The origins of educational psychology can be traced back to the ancient Greek teacher/philosophers (Charles, 1976). Socrates (470–399 BC) invented a method of teaching by prolonged questioning that still bears his name; Democritus (460–370 BC) extolled the virtues of education and pointed to the home environment as exerting as great an impact on a person's intellectual development as formal study; and Aristotle (384–322 BC) wrote the first treatise on learning and memory. In *De Memoria et Reminiscentia (On Memory and Reminiscence*, 350 BC), Aristotle emphasised the importance of context and the method of presentation of the material to be learned (Weinstein & Way, 2003). Aristotle also drew attention to individual differences among students and how teachers should attempt to tailor their instruction to each learner.

Through the millennia, many scholars have addressed educational issues. German educators have been particularly influential. Educationists such as Johann Herbart (1776–1841) emphasised the importance of psychology to education and developed a five-step teaching process as early as 1824 that still makes sense today: motivate the subject matter, present the material, integrate it with what is already known, emphasise general principles, and facilitate practice. Another German, Friedrich Froebel (1782–1852) was the founder of the kindergarten movement.

Modern psychology's application to educational concerns can be traced to William James and a series of lectures published in 1899 entitled *Talks to Teachers on Psychology*. At around the same time, in 1901 E L Thorndike, with Woodworth, propounded his theory of identical elements as the basis for the transfer of learning to new situations. Shortly after, Thorndike published an essay entitled *The Contribution of Psychology to Education* in the inaugural issue of the *Journal of Educational Psychology* in 1910. Among other things, Thorndike emphasised the importance of measurement, particularly through the emerging field of psychological testing. Since Thorndike's day, psychological testing and assessment has remained a cornerstone of educational psychology and the provision of psychological services to children (Kamphaus, Petoskey & Rowe, 2000).

Educational psychology emerged as a distinct branch of psychology during the first half of the twentieth century. The British Psychological Society had established an educational psychology section by 1919 and Division 15 of the American Psychological Association, the Division of Educational Psychology, was founded in 1945. In Australia the educational psychology division of the Australian Psychological Society was established in 1967. This became the Board of Educational and Developmental Psychology in 1983 and finally the College of Educational and Developmental Psychologists in 1993.

ROLE OF ASSESSMENT IN EDUCATION

Broadly speaking, tests used within educational settings can be classified into two main classes: *achievement tests* or *aptitude tests*. Achievement tests assess past learning, ie, learning that has already been achieved, whereas aptitude tests assess future learning potential. Probably no other form of assessment is more common than the teacher-constructed achievement test designed to assess learning at the end of a specific course of study. We are all familiar with this type of class test or exam at school. The need to constantly develop new achievement tests each year means that their validity is mainly determined by content: most items in teacher-constructed achievement tests are derived from what was just taught. Although the vast majority of achievement tests are specific in nature, it is possible to develop general achievement tests aimed at assessing basic skills developed during any mode of instruction.

Like achievement tests, aptitude tests may be general or specific, although, unlike achievement tests, general aptitude tests are more common. General aptitude tests are virtually indistinguishable from ability or intelligence tests described later in this chapter and elsewhere in this book. Well constructed general aptitude tests correlate with academic performance about 0.4. Specific aptitude tests can be constructed for particular skills and abilities if a more focused assessment is required.

Besides these two broad classes of test, educationists have also identified two roles for testing within education and training settings. These are formative and summative modes of assessment (Scriven, 1967). Summative assessment refers to the familiar kind of evaluative function served by the tests discussed above and most of the other tests described in this book. The main summative purposes of tests in education and training include: evaluating learning at the end of a course for purposes of accreditation or evaluation of the teaching process, selection decisions for admitting students into highly sought-after courses, and diagnosing learning difficulties, students with special needs, or giftedness.

In addition to summative mode, the field of education is unique in finding a functional role for assessment. Formative assessment is assessment designed to serve an educative as well as an evaluative purpose. That is, formative assessment is as much about facilitating learning as it is about evaluating learning. The familiar take-home exam is a good example of formative assessment. From a summative point of view, take-home exams make little sense because there is no way of knowing how much help the student got from parents or friends. They may even have looked up the answer in a textbook or encyclopaedia. From a summative point of view, such activities would be seen as cheating. Formatively speaking, however, take-home exams can easily be justified: even if the student gets help, so long as learning occurs, the assessment piece has done its job. Formative assessment might be better conceived as a problem or learning task dressed up to look like a test. It is hoped that this format will increase the student's motivation to complete the task and thus learn something.

Finally, another important form of assessment in education, one that merges into the area of work and organisational psychology, is the assessment of vocational interests—helping someone choose a career that interests them and the courses of study that lead to it.

BOX 11.1

Local norms

Local norms are norms developed for specific geographical regions. Applying North American norms to test scores obtained in Australia or New Zealand is an example of not using local norms. Local norms have the advantage of more precisely focusing test interpretation on the local population. This can be important in areas where there are strong cultural differences or where the local population differs significantly in some way from the original population used for norming. The usefulness of local norms depends on how well they were constructed. If they are built up over time from a convenience sample of available test scores then they may not actually be representative of the local population at all. In this case the local norms may actually be worse than the original test norms. If the local population does not differ from the original population used for norming, then there is little advantage in developing local norms. Nevertheless, local norms are vital in some applications of psychological assessment (Levin et al, 1987). As much care and effort needs to be put into developing local norms as in developing any set of norms. Indeed, the value of a psychological test is as much a function of the quality of its norms as it is of the relevance of the construct or the content of the items.

An excellent example of the development of local norms is the Macquarie University Neuropsychological Normative Study (MUNNS) (Carstairs & Shores, 2000) in which 399 healthy young adults from the Sydney metropolitan area were tested on a battery of neuropsychological tests used for rehabilitation and medico-legal assessments. The test battery comprised eleven tests, including the Wechsler Memory Scale – Revised (Wechsler, 1987); Rey Auditory Verbal Learning Test (Lezak, 1995); Wechsler Adult Intelligence Test – Revised (Wechsler, 1981); and the Depression, Anxiety and Stress Scales (Lovibond & Lovibond, 1995a). A stratified random sampling plan ensured the representativeness of the sample in terms of age, gender, language background, socio-economic status and level of education. Participants were screened for prior head injury resulting in loss of consciousness, use of certain therapeutic or recreational drugs, inability to understand English, and physical or intellectual disability which interfered with performance on the tests. Over 10,000 people were contacted in order to find sufficient numbers in scope to participate in the study, giving some idea of the effort required to produce a set of good quality norms.

APTITUDE TESTS

Wechsler Intelligence Scale for Children—Fourth Edition (WISC–IV; Wechsler, 2003)

One of the most frequently used general aptitude tests designed for school-aged children is the WISC–IV (Kamphaus et al, 2000). The WISC–IV is an individually administered test of cognitive ability for children aged between 6 and 16, inclusive. As an assessment of general cognitive functioning, the WISC–IV can be used to identify a child's intellectual strengths and weaknesses as well as diagnose giftedness and mental retardation. It can provide guidance for planning treatments and making placement decisions in clinical and educational settings and assist in neuropsychological evaluation. Further, tests like the WISC–IV have always figured strongly in educational, developmental, clinical, and neuropsychological research.

The WISC–IV is similar in structure to Wechsler's other ability tests, such as the WAIS–III used for testing adults and described in detail in Chapter 7. Indeed, many of the subtests of both tests are identical, albeit with different levels of difficulty (see Table 11.1). The WISC–IV is the latest adaptation of a long line of Wechsler tests for children, beginning with the WISC, first published in 1949 (Wechsler, 1949), in which Wechsler adapted subtests from his original Wechsler-Bellevue Intelligence

Scale for use with children. The original WISC had twelve subtests: Information, Arithmetic, Similarities, Vocabulary, Digit Span, Comprehension, Picture Completion, Picture Arrangement★, Block Design, Object Assembly★, Coding, and Mazes★ (★ = not retained in WISC–IV). The subtests are organised in terms of Verbal and Performance scales. These scales provided the familiar Verbal, Performance and Full Scale IQ scores (VIQ, PIQ, and FSIQ) that became synonymous with the Wechsler tests. Originally designed for use with children aged between 5 and 15, the age range was advanced one year in the next edition published 25 years later (WISC–R; Wechsler, 1974) although the same twelve subtests were retained. The third edition (WISC–III; Wechsler, 1991) introduced one new subtest, Symbol Search, and four new index scores.

TABLE 11.1 Subtests of the WISC–IV

Subtest	Description	Abilities Measured
1. Block Design	Same as the WAIS–III but with easier items, see Table 7.1	
2. Similarities	Same as the WAIS–III but with easier items, see Table 7.1	
3. Digit Span	Same as the WAIS–III but with easier items, see Table 7.1	
4. Picture Concepts	The child is presented with two or three rows of pictures of common objects and is required to choose one object from each row that share a common characteristic	Concept formation
5. Coding	The Coding subtest is made up of two parts. Coding B is the same as the WAIS–III Digit Symbol – Coding described in Table 7.1. In Coding A the symbols are paired with geometric shapes instead of numbers	Attention and visuo-motor coordination
6. Vocabulary	Same as the WAIS–III but with easier items, see Table 7.1	
7. Letter-Number Sequencing	Same as the WAIS–III but with easier items, see Table 7.1	
8. Matrix Reasoning	Same as the WAIS–III but with easier items, see Table 7.1	
9. Comprehension	Same as the WAIS–III but with easier items, see Table 7.1	
10. Symbol Search	Same as the WAIS–III but with easier items, see Table 7.1	
11. Picture Completion	Same as the WAIS–III but with easier items, see Table 7.1	
12. Cancellation	The child is presented with a page cluttered with 320 small pictures of animals and common objects and asked to cross out all the animals as quickly as possible within 45 seconds	Perceptual speed
13. Information	Same as the WAIS–III but with easier items, see Table 7.1	
14. Arithmetic	Same as the WAIS–III but with easier items, see Table 7.1	
15. Word Reasoning	The child is asked to identify the concept being described by a series of clues	Verbal comprehension and reasoning

Five new subtests were introduced with the WISC–IV in order to boost the validity of the test: Picture Concepts, Letter-Number Sequencing, Matrix Reasoning, Cancellation, and Word Reasoning. The four index scores were an attempt to reflect developments in understanding of the structure of human cognitive abilities which emphasised more discrete aspects of intellectual functioning. Highly content-valid and plausible though they seemed for many years, Wechsler's organisation of his tests in terms of basic verbal and performance dimensions did not seem to be borne out by factor analytic research (Carroll, 1993; Horn & Noll, 1994). Instead, the factors reflected fundamental structures of problem solving and knowledge, such as fluid and crystallised intelligence, and clusters of cognitive and perceptual processes such as memory, processing speed, visual and auditory perception. To bring the structure of the WISC more into line with current thinking, the Verbal and Performance scales were dropped from the WISC–IV and emphasis was given to the various indices introduced with the WISC–III and WAIS–III. Thus the third editions of the WISC and the WAIS can be seen as transition points between Wechsler's original organisation and newer theories of the structure of human cognitive abilities established in the literature. We might expect other tests in this series, like the WAIS–IV, to follow suit.

The first ten subtests shown in Table 11.1 are deemed 'core' and the remaining five are 'supplemental', ie, optional. The purpose of including supplemental tests is to extend the range of abilities sampled by the test and to provide additional information. If necessary, a supplemental test can be used as a substitute for a core test if a problem arises with the administration of the core test, such as when a child refuses or is unable to complete it. For example, the Picture Completion subtest requires much less fine motor control than the Block Design subtest and is very useful when testing a child with motor difficulties. As such it can be used as a substitution for the Block Design subtest in the calculation of the Perceptual Reasoning Index and the Full Scale IQ. Only one substitution is allowed per index, however. In calculating the Full Scale IQ, only two substitutions from different indices are allowed. Administration of the ten core subtests takes about 65 to 80 minutes.

Scoring proceeds in a similar way to the WAIS–III described in Chapter 7. First, total raw scores are obtained from each subtest. Usually raw scores are simply the total number of items answered correctly; however, many WISC–IV subtests give extra credit for quicker responses and some give partial credit for acceptable, though not perfect, answers. Total raw scores are then converted to scaled scores which are further summed. Finally, each sum of scaled score is converted to its appropriate index or IQ. All IQ and Index Scores have a mean of 100 and a standard deviation of 15.

The WISC–IV was normed on a stratified sample of 2200 children, divided evenly into the 11 age groupings. Stratification was performed with respect to age, gender, ethnic group, parents' education, and geographical region, according to the US census of 2000. Table 11.2 shows the split-half and test-retest reliabilities of the WISC–IV. Test-retest reliabilities were obtained on a subgroup of 243 children from the main standardisation sample retested after an interval of 2 to 9 weeks (average = 32 days). Interscorer agreement was assessed for a number of subtests that required human judgment. Agreement ranged between 0.95 for Comprehension and 0.98 for Similarities and Vocabulary. These coefficients, together with the information summarised in Table 11.2, indicate that the WISC–IV has high reliability.

TABLE 11.2 Reliability of the WISC–IV

Score	Reliability	
	Split-Half	Test-Retest
Full Scale IQ	0.97	0.93
Verbal Comprehension Index	0.94	0.93
Perceptual Reasoning Index	0.92	0.89
Working Memory Index	0.92	0.89
Processing Speed Index	0.88	0.86
Subtests		
Block Design	0.86	0.82
Similarities	0.86	0.86
Digit Span	0.87	0.83
Picture Concepts	0.82	0.76
Coding	–	0.84
Vocabulary	0.89	0.92
Letter-Number Sequencing	0.90	0.83
Matrix Reasoning	0.89	0.85
Comprehension	0.81	0.82
Symbol Search	–	0.80
Picture Completion	0.84	0.84
Cancellation	–	0.79
Information	0.86	0.89
Arithmetic	0.88	0.79
Word Reasoning	0.80	0.82

Note: split-half reliability could not be calculated for Coding, Symbol Search, and Cancellation because of the speeded nature of these subtests.

FIGURE 11.1 Structure of the WISC–IV, supplemental subtests shown in italics

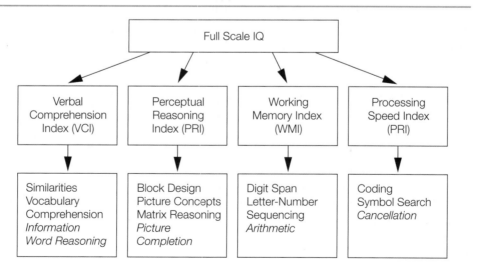

Building as it does on its predecessor and sharing similar subtests with the other Wechsler tests, the WISC–IV brings with it considerable content, factorial, and construct validity (Prifitera & Saklofske, 1998). As expected, corresponding subtests from the WISC–IV and other Wechsler tests are highly correlated. Both exploratory and confirmatory factor analysis revealed the factor structure illustrated in Figure 11.1. Finally, in a series of 11 special group studies, the WISC–IV was shown to differentiate between children independently diagnosed with learning disorders, language disorders, attention-deficit/hyperactivity disorder, and children suffering from traumatic brain injury, as well as children identified as gifted.

Raven's Progressive Matrices

Matrix Reasoning was a new subtest introduced in the WISC–IV (it had already appeared in the WAIS–III), but the effectiveness of matrix items was recognised soon after their invention in the 1930s by J C Raven (Penrose & Raven, 1936; Raven, 1938). Seeking a pure measure of Spearman's *g*, Raven hit upon the idea of a non-verbal reasoning test made up of two-dimensional figural analogies. Examples of matrix items can be found in Chapter 7. Indeed, the progressive matrices are widely recognised as probably the best single measure of general intelligence (Carpenter, Just & Shell, 1990) and are often used as a marker for fluid intelligence.

The progressive matrices come in three forms: a set of Coloured Progressive Matrices for children, first introduced in 1947 and revised in 1956; a Standard set for children aged six to adult, revised in 1948 and again in 1956; and an Advanced set for higher ability populations such as university students and professionals, also introduced in 1947 and revised in 1962. The Standard Progressive Matrices are composed of sixty items arranged in five sets of increasing difficulty, beginning with very easy items designed to be self-evident and progressing through items drawing on various perceptual relations until reasoning by analogy in one and two dimensions is required. The progressive nature of the items means that working through them is also supposed to provide training in the thought processes required for their solution. Administration can be timed, twenty minutes, or untimed and can be individual or in groups, yielding a very flexible set of uses for this test. Its excellent psychometric properties and ease of administration have led to its extensive use in education, industrial, and military settings. Its non-verbal nature has also led to the suggestion that it is not subject to the same cultural influences as other tests (Jensen, 1980). As such it has been used extensively in cross-cultural research and settings involving examinees from non-English speaking backgrounds.

Australian norms for the Standard Progressive Matrices were developed in 1986 (de Lemos, 1989), separately for timed and untimed conditions. A nationally representative sample of just over 4000 school students from Years 3 to 11 was used to construct the norms. Internal consistency and test-retest reliabilities are shown in Table 11.3. Clearly the reliability of this test is very good across the age range sampled. The progressive matrices have been extensively studied. Specific validation research includes correlating it with other measures and teacher assessments of student performance. Correlations range between 0.4 for teacher ratings to 0.76 for the relationship with the Jenkins Non-Verbal Test. For an accurate indication of high-level mental functioning, few tests have achieved the popularity of Raven's progressive matrices.

TABLE 11.3 Reliability of standard progressive matrices: Australian edition

Year	KR-21 Timed Version	KR-21 Untimed Version	Test-Retest
3	0.88	0.88	0.83
4	0.85	0.86	0.85
5	0.80	0.85	0.76
6	0.78	0.83	0.82
7	0.79	0.82	0.71
8	0.80	0.79	0.76
9	0.77	0.82	0.73
10	0.79	0.82	0.80
11	0.81	0.83	0.81

Note: Test-retest reliability is correlation between timed and untimed versions.

GENERAL ACHIEVEMENT TESTS

If general aptitude tests provide good measures of fluid abilities, problem solving and reasoning, then general achievement tests provide good measures of crystallised abilities, those associated with acquired knowledge and learning. An excellent example of a general achievement test is the Wechsler Individual Achievement Test – Second Edition (WIAT–II; The Psychological Corporation, 2002). Achievement tests are a fairly recent addition to the Wechsler suite, with the first version of the WIAT being published in 1992, 11 years after Wechsler's death. The WIAT–II assesses the basic academic skills of literacy and numeracy, including reading, comprehension, and written and oral expression. It is designed to be used with children from as young as four to adults all the way up to 85 years of age and takes between 45 minutes and two hours to administer. Teenagers and adults tend to take longer because the tasks they are set are longer and more involved. For example, the last Written Expression item for adults is a 15 minute essay. The WIAT–II can be used to assist diagnosis of learning difficulties, eligibility for placement in special education programs, and other intervention decisions. Note that it is not designed to assess giftedness.

The WIAT–II is composed of nine subtests divided into four areas or composites, see Table 11.4. Content and item type are more varied within each subtest than in the ability measures, partly due to the extremely wide age range that the test is designed to cover and partly due to the variety in learning achievement that occurs at different ages. For example the Word Reading subtest begins by asking infants to point to a single letter and ends by asking examinees to read rare polysyllabic words out loud. To manage this variety, some subtests have up to nine different starting points, depending on the age of the examinee. Adult examinees skip most of the

TABLE 11.4 WIAT–II Composites and Subtests

Composite	Subtest	Achievements	Types of Task
Reading	Word Reading	Phonological awareness, decoding and reading skills	Naming letters, generating rhymes, identifying beginnings and endings of words, matching sounds, reading aloud
	Reading Comprehension	Reading comprehension	Reading aloud, matching words with pictures, answering questions, demonstrating comprehension
	Pseudoword Decoding	Phonetic decoding	Appropriate pronunciation of non-words
Mathematics	Numerical Operations	Ability to identify and write numbers	Counting, solving arithmetical and algebraic problems
	Math Reasoning	Mathematical reasoning	Counting, identifying geometric shapes, solving arithmetic word problems, interpreting graphs, identifying mathematical patterns, statistics and probability
Written Language	Spelling	Spelling	Writing dictated letters, sounds and words
	Written Expression	Writing skills, written word fluency	Writing the alphabet, generating sentences, writing a paragraph or short essay
Oral Language	Listening Comprehension	Listening carefully	Matching a picture with a word or sentence, finding a word to match a picture or verbal description
	Oral Expression	Language skills, verbal fluency	Repeating sentences, telling stories, generating directions

items designed for children. Detailed scoring protocols are supplied, particularly for the Written and Oral Expression subtests which require human judgment of examinees' written or verbal responses. In these subtests, examinees construct sentences, write an essay, tell stories, and give directions. Two scoring protocols are given for these items: an older 'holistic' protocol that was used in the original WIAT and requires a larger degree of subjective judgment; and a more mechanical protocol that describes the content of the ideal answer and enumerates many features of the response such as number of spelling or pronunciation errors, structure, logic, and organisation. Raw scores from each subtest are converted into standard scores, summed and converted into the relevant composite standard score, as in Table 11.4. A total score is also provided, based on the sum of the standard scores of all subtests.

The WIAT–II was normed on 5586 people, almost 1000 more than the WISC–IV and WAIS–III combined. The main reason for this is the extremely large age range that the test can cover; about the same as the WISC–IV and WAIS–III combined. Table 11.5 shows the split-half and test-retest reliabilities. Test-retest reliabilities were calculated in a separate study of 291 examinees who were tested twice. The test-retest interval ranged between 7 and 45 days. A second study looked at interscorer agreement for the two subtests requiring the greatest degree of subjective judgment and found them to be 0.85 and 0.96 for Written and Oral

TABLE 11.5 Reliability of the WIAT–II

Score	Split-Half	Test-Retest
Reading Composite	0.98	0.97
Word Reading	0.97	0.98
Reading Comprehension	0.95	0.93
Pseudoword Decoding	0.97	0.95
Mathematics Composite	0.95	0.95
Numerical Operations	0.91	0.92
Math Reasoning	0.92	0.94
Written Language Composite	0.94	0.94
Spelling	0.94	0.96
Written Expression	0.86	0.85
Oral Language Composite	0.89	0.92
Listening Comprehension	0.80	0.91
Oral Expression	0.86	0.86
Total Composite	0.98	0.98

Expression respectively. This, together with the coefficients summarised in Table 11.5, indicates that the WIAT–II has strong reliability. Three sources of validity evidence are supplied with the test: a discussion of content validity, an analysis of factor structure, and experiments with special populations. In general, the test behaved as expected.

The most serious limitation with the WIAT–II is that it represents only one particular way of operationalising academic achievement. Good items for various aptitudes have become fairly clear, due to the emerging picture of the structure of cognitive abilities. The same could not be said for achievement items. In many ways, there are as many valid achievement tests as there are ways of teaching.

The demand for brief assessment tools has grown enormously in recent years (Kamphaus et al, 2000). To meet this demand, many test publishers have developed shortened versions of some of their measures. A brief form of the WIAT–II is available, known as the WIAT–II–A (Wechsler Individual Achievement Test – Second Edition – Abbreviated; The Psychological Corporation, 2001). The WIAT–II–A uses only three of the subtests from the full WIAT–II: Word Reading, Numerical Operations, and Spelling, and each has fewer items.

APPLICATIONS OF ACHIEVEMENT AND APTITUDE TESTS

Special needs

At primary and secondary school levels, interest is usually in recognising students with special needs. The sooner such needs can be identified, the sooner remedial work can begin. Achievement tests can be used to assess a student's progress through the standard curriculum, whereas aptitude tests can be used to diagnose deeper problems with their learning and reasoning abilities. A growing number of behaviour rating scales and checklists with which parents or teachers record the frequency and occurrence of certain behaviours are also available (Kamphaus et al, 2000). Assessment of special needs lies at the boundary of educational and clinical psychology.

Giftedness

More recently interest has also developed in the other end of the ability continuum, namely identifying gifted students who may benefit from a more enriched or accelerated curriculum. Giftedness is invariably assessed using intelligence or aptitude tests, although peer ratings and teacher nominations have also been used. The needs of gifted students have been especially identified since it is believed that, if not catered for, these students may lose motivation and fail to reach their full potential, becoming bored and frustrated with the slow pace of education around them. In extreme cases boredom may lead to misbehaviour in the classroom. Although it sounds highly desirable, growing up gifted presents its own difficulties, such as loneliness and isolation through difficulties in fitting in with one's peer group (Clark, 1988). As such it is important to identify gifted children to ensure that they remain stimulated and able to develop their talents to the fullest.

Admissions decisions

At the organisational level, another application of testing in schools is the assessment of potential candidates for places within programs. Admissions decisions involve deciding who gets into a course or program of study. This is analogous to personnel selection described in Chapter 8 and can be an extremely difficult decision for administrators to make. Many see the value in an objective, third-party, standardised assessment as providing a common benchmark along which to compare applicants. A good example of this is applying to go to university. Universities must decide who will be admitted into particular degree programs. In an era of funding constraints, universities are keen to offer places to those most likely to succeed in higher education. When students drop out or fail, neither party has benefited fully from the experience. On the principle that the best predictor of future performance is past performance, previous educational achievement figures strongly in admissions decisions in Australia: how well you performed at school determines your marks for getting into university. Thus performance on achievement tests like the NSW Higher School Certificate or the Victorian Certificate of Education figure strongly in admissions decisions. Research suggests, however, that additional sources of information can improve this decision, thus allowing universities to make even more accurate admissions decisions. The main additional source of information is aptitude tests.

General aptitude tests have been criticised as being biased in favour of majority middle-class white children, and so have figured less strongly in admissions decisions in Australia in recent decades. However, in the past, they were also used to identify students from disadvantaged backgrounds who had the potential for further study. Research consistently shows that aptitude tests reliably do what they were designed to do, namely identify those students who are most likely to succeed at academic pursuits. It would be easy to combine achievement and aptitude tests in admissions decisions, by means of a regression equation, that would yield more accurate decisions than using achievement or aptitude alone, but the majority of admissions decisions in Australia rely mainly on achievement. Exceptions appear to be in admission to some programs such as in medicine or business, for which specific aptitude tests have been developed like the GMAT (Graduate Management Admissions Test) and the UMAT (Undergraduate Medicine and Health Sciences Admission Test).

BOX 11.2

Should all children be routinely tested?

This has been an ongoing source of debate in educational circles. The answer really depends on what you are trying to achieve through testing. Critics of tests point to their shortcomings, less than perfect reliability and validity, and argue that they place children under undue pressure. Intelligence and aptitude tests come in for particularly heavy criticism since it is claimed that they may serve to stigmatise low scorers who must then carry the burden around with them for many years. Low test scores can even become a self-fulfilling prophecy if the person becomes sufficiently demotivated and stops trying.

Oxford don Charles Ludwig Dodgson, better known as Lewis Carroll and author of the children's classic *Alice in Wonderland*, argued 150 years ago that instead of testing young people to find out how much they remember, we should be testing old people to see how much they've forgotten! This is a somewhat specious argument from a man who specialised in nonsense and flawed logic, and deliberately ignores the instrumental role that testing plays within our society. It's a bit late testing someone after they've retired.

Advocates of testing point out that intelligence and aptitude tests remain the best predictors of many salient life outcomes, including success at school and performance in the workplace (Gottfredson, 2002). This should come as no surprise because these tests were deliberately designed from the outset to assess the abilities conducive to success in our complex technological society.

Validities for predicting academic success can be of the order of 0.4 and, even higher in the workplace (see Chapter 8). While significant, this only explains 20 per cent to 30 per cent of the variance in outcome, leaving plenty of scope for outside influences to play a part in someone's success in life. Indeed, our society is constantly inventing new ways of being successful. Such is the nature of a dynamic economy.

While tests have a place and can provide much useful information, particularly in diagnosing educational difficulties and special needs, a case can be made for remaining ignorant. If a child appears to be developing normally, is there really any reason to assess his or her IQ? Wanting to do so is a bit like wanting to jump ahead and read the last page of a good story. It's very tempting, but the story is a lot more enjoyable when you don't know how everything will turn out, and the same could be said for someone's life story. Unless there is something in the child's development to suggest abnormality, is anything really lost in letting them discover their own potential without trying to pre-empt it with a test score? After all, did you really want to know that Alice eventually woke up and it was all a dream?

VOCATIONAL INTERESTS

The assessment of vocational interests has developed into another major category of testing. These tests try to determine what line of work, career, or course of study someone might be interested in pursuing. Vocational interest tests employ a range of techniques to identify an individual's preferences. The oldest and perhaps most face-valid approach was to present examinees with a list of occupations, such as police officer, fire fighter, farmer or accountant, and ask them to rate their level of interest in that line of work. Given that examinees will probably not have had any experience in most of the occupations listed, such an approach to assessment relies on widely held stereotypical beliefs about what constitutes particular types of jobs. The lists need to be carefully prepared in terms of easily recognisable, prototypical occupations. The aim is to represent as much of the world of work as possible using only a few dozen of the many thousands of occupations on offer. Once the broad direction of someone's interests is identified the next stage of vocational counselling involves considering a more detailed list of possible jobs within a particular job family or theme. An accurate picture of preferred occupations, one not based on stereotypes, can be achieved in the next stage of counselling through reading material, the Internet, videos, work experience or observation, and discussion with actual job holders.

It soon became clear that just presenting a list of occupations was not completely satisfactory. After all, if one truly knew the nature of all the occupations listed, what was the point in sitting the test? Other lines of questioning about likes and dislikes, hobbies, and leisure activities were also found to be very useful.

By far the most popular vocational interests instrument is John Holland's Self Directed Search (SDS) (Tinsley, 1992). The SDS was first developed by Holland in the early 1970s and is now used in more than twenty-five countries around the world. Holland began working in the vocational interests field in the 1950s and developed an occupational list of the form described above called the Vocational Preference Inventory (Holland, 1958). Using this instrument he first identified the so-called 'hexagonal model' of interests, see below, which developed into the theory on which the SDS is now based (Holland, 1992). The SDS consists of five sections: *Occupational Daydreams*, in which participants are asked to simply make a list of occupations that they might find interesting, prior to any priming by other sections of the test; *Activities*, in which participants are asked to specify whether or not they like or dislike the type of activity indicated; *Competencies*, in which participants are asked to specify how competent they think they are at performing certain activities or in using a range of tools; *Occupations*, in which participants are asked to indicate their liking for the occupations listed, as described above; and *Self-Estimates*, in which participants are asked to rate their abilities in various areas (Shears & Harvey-Beavis, 2001). The Daydream section is meant to provide a pure indication of participants' occupational aspirations. Alternatives within the Activities section include items like: repair cars, play chess, draw pictures, go dancing, and sell things; alternatives in the Competencies section include items like: use an electric saw, perform a scientific experiment, sing, teach children, and make a speech; and options in the Self-Estimates section include items like: mechanical ability, scientific ability, and artistic ability.

Clearly there is a strong element of self-reported competencies and abilities in this test in addition to the ratings of interest for certain activities and occupations. This is based on the idea that most people like doing what they're good at, although how interests develop is still a topic of debate among vocational interests theorists. Nevertheless, the assessment of interests as well as self-efficacy is a hallmark of modern interest instruments. Bear in mind that self-rated ability is not the same thing as ability and there is no necessary correspondence between interests and actual abilities. That is to say, just because a person may be interested in something doesn't mean they will be good at it. There is no guarantee of finding a job at which one will excel via vocational assessment.

Holland believes that interests are more an expression of personality than ability and his theory centres around six ideal personality types labelled Realistic (R), Investigative (I), Artistic (A), Social (S), Enterprising (E), and Conventional (C). These types are so important to the theory that RIASEC has become a common acronym for it. An important distinguishing feature of the theory, and one which probably explains much of its popularity, is that it classifies work environments according to the same basic scheme as well. Thus there are also supposed to be six distinctly Realistic, Investigative, Artistic, Social, Enterprising, and Conventional groups of occupation. As such, the activities, competencies, occupations and self-estimates in the SDS are organised around these themes.

The theory can probably be best understood in terms of the ideal types. Thus, according to the theory, realistic people like directly interacting with the physical world in a way which involves much practical knowledge but little need for abstract thought, social interaction, or self-expression. In line with their 'down-to-earth' attitudes, Realistic people tend to be fairly materialistic and value tangible personal characteristics such as money, power, and status (Holland, 1992, p 19). Occupations that permit expression of these personality characteristics include farming, mining, construction, and transport occupations. Small business operations in any of these areas such as electrician, motor mechanic, smash repairer, hairdresser, or corner store owner also give expression to the practical and materialistic values of this type. Currently, over half the available jobs in the economy are Realistic in nature, although, with the rise of automation and new technology, this may be on the decline.

Similarly, Investigative people like analysing and solving problems, theorising and dealing with abstract concepts. In particular, they have little interest in business activities. Typical Investigative occupations include science and engineering and other occupations requiring high degrees of technical and theoretical knowledge such as computer programming and financial analysis. Artistic people tend to be value creativity and have a need to express themselves in creative or artistic ways. The theory embraces the stereotype of Artistic people as being somewhat nonconformist and emotional with an abhorrence of routine. Besides the fine arts and music, some commercial occupations in the fashion and media industries would be considered Artistic. On the whole, artistic occupations are relatively rare in the economy. Social people enjoy high degrees of interaction with others, especially in an educational or welfare role, and have a heightened sense of ethics and social responsibility. They are also supposed to be somewhat impractical and uninterested in manual work. Typical social occupations include teaching, counselling and the helping professions.

Enterprising people have a strong business orientation, especially with regard to sales and management, and leadership positions in government and industry. A key source of satisfaction lies in their ability to organise and persuade others to certain courses of action and they particularly value political and economic power. Consequently they tend to dislike dealing with abstract concepts and intangibles especially if they are difficult to explain to others or do not lead to an immediately perceived benefit. Conventional types are also fairly business oriented but more inclined toward administrative rather than leadership positions. They do not mind routine procedures or structured activities and especially dislike ambiguity and vague task requirements. As such, they tend to be fairly conservative. Typical Conventional occupations include accounting, secretarial, administrative, and clerical occupations. Evidence broadly in favour of the theory continues to accumulate and its basic principles have not changed appreciably in recent years (Prediger & Vansickle, 1992).

Finding a satisfying job involves essentially looking for a good person–environment fit (P-E fit). For example, a good match occurs for a Realistic person in a Realistic job or an Investigative person in an Investigative job and so on. Although these descriptions are highly stereotypical, the theory is rescued from pure cliché by its emphasis on profiles rather than types per se when it comes to real people and real work environments. Thus a person's personality is not to be understood simply in terms of one of the six types, but via his or her profile on all six types. The descriptions above are of *ideal types* which would rarely, if ever, be encountered in reality. Holland (1992), however, does take the familiarity of these stereotypes as a major source of evidence for their existence. Many other 'typologies' exist within personality theory, but Holland's theory is distinctive in its emphasis on occupational characteristics.

Although he concedes that all six scores could be meaningfully taken into account, Holland prefers to assign three letter codes to each profile according to the three highest scores. Thus a person whose profile scores were $R = 6, I = 5, A = 4,$ $S = 3, E = 2,$ and $C = 1,$ say, would be given the code RIA; an environment whose profile was $R = 1, I = 2, A = 3, S = 4, E = 5,$ and $C = 6$ would be given a code of CES; and so on. Clearly, then, the personality theory which Holland has in mind embraces $6 \times 5 \times 4 = 120,$ rather than six, different types. The full profile would define $6! = 720$ different types. Environments are given one of the 120 codes according to the profiles of the people living or working in them. This formulation has the advantage of allowing the same interest inventory to be used to assess both people and environments and many studies have been carried out to classify occupations according to these terms (Gottfredson, Holland & Ogawa, 1982).

As may be evident from the descriptions above, the types are not independent. The 'hexagonal model', shown in Figure 11.2, illustrates the hypothesised relations among the types. According to Holland, 'the distances between the types and environments [on the hexagon] are inversely proportional to the theoretical relationships between them' (Holland, 1992, p 5). Thus Realistic types are fairly similar to Investigative and Conventional types, but very dissimilar to Social types; Artistic types are fairly similar to Investigative and Social types and very dissimilar to Conventional types and so on. Distance or similarity is determined from proximity matrices such as the correlation matrix between scores on scales measuring the six

FIGURE 11.2 The hexagonal model

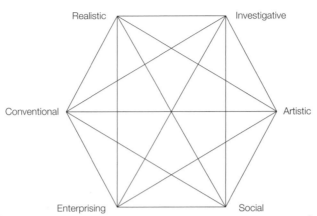

Source: From Holland, 1992, p 29

types. Understandably, the hexagonal model has been a major source of construct validity evidence for the theory and many studies have sought to verify the hypothesised hexagonal structure among scales measuring the Holland types.

The SDS is scored by summing the number of votes in favour of each code. The process is very simple and self-scoring is encouraged. Holland believes reflections during self-scoring lead to a greater understanding of the types and yield additional personal insight (Shears & Harvey-Beavis, 2001, p 39). Internal consistency reliability for the SDS ranges from 0.83 for the Realistic scale among school-age females to 0.91 for the Investigative scale among tertiary students. Validating interest inventories can be difficult because there is not necessarily an external criterion on which to base a prediction. Interest theorists are quick to claim that interests do not necessarily indicate success or suitability for a particular career so the external criterion of career success may not be a good choice of criterion. Much further information-gathering needs to follow administration of an interest inventory like the SDS. The SDS has been validated by comparing agreement between the letter belonging to the highest score and the first letter of the codes belonging to the occupations indicated in the Occupational Daydreams section. The agreement is usually around 50 per cent. This does not appear to be an overwhelming endorsement of validity, but is of the order typically found for other interest inventories (Holland & Rayman, 1986). Perhaps a more acceptable validation method would be to correlate interest scores with indices of job satisfaction among incumbents with several years of experience in a particular occupation.

STRONG VOCATIONAL INTEREST INVENTORY

The grandfather of all interest inventories is the Strong Vocational Interest Inventory (SVII), first developed by E K Strong in the 1920s (Strong, 1927). The inventory is composed of 325 items that ask about an examinee's interest in occupations, activities, hobbies, school subjects, and types of people. Unlike the SDS, the SVII uses extensive norms and each examinee's pattern of scores is compared to patterns obtained by satisfied incumbents in over 200 occupations. This is the unique strength of the SVII, but means that it must be computer scored in order to tap into its extensive occupational database. Output is divided into three levels of abstraction. At the most abstract level are scores on six RIASEC themes, followed by 25 Basic Interests, followed by, at the lowest level, scores on 211 Occupational Scales. Rounds, Davidson and Dawis (1979) have suggested that the SVII is the best measure of the RIASEC types available.

Strong followed a highly empirical route in developing the SVII. He did not start with a theory of vocational interests, but began work gathering statements of interest from many different people in many different occupations. These were later refined into scales and later the hexagonal model introduced as an organising principle.

The instrument has been studied extensively during 80 years of use. Test–retest reliabilities are reported for three samples and are generally in the high 0.80s and low 0.90s. Even three year stability is of the order of 0.80. In terms of validity, the scores have been shown to differentiate between people working in different occupations.

Just when you thought the six RIASEC types encapsulated the domain of vocational interests, Tracey and Rounds (1995) have argued that the space of vocational interests is actually circular in nature (see Figure 11.3). If the pie is cut

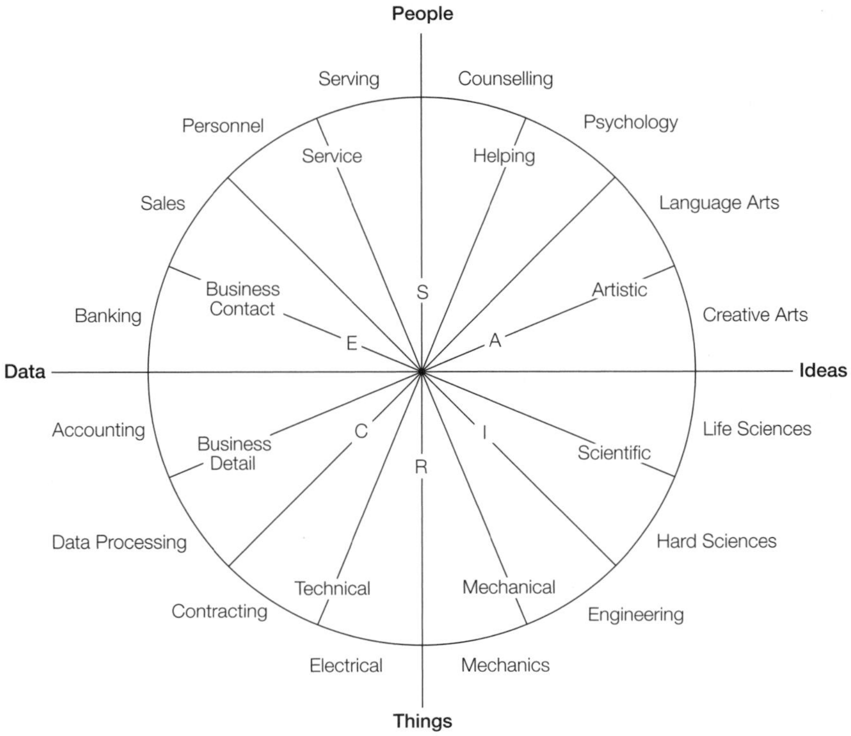

FIGURE 11.3 The circumplex structure of vocational interests

into six slices it yields Holland's hexagonal model, but one could just as legitimately use eight slices or even 16, as shown in Figure 11.3. The two dimensions of the circumplex have been labelled the contrast between an interest in 'people' versus an interest in 'things', and an interest in 'data' versus an interest in 'ideas' (Prediger, 1976).

CONCLUDING REMARKS

Testing and assessment have figured strongly in education for over 100 years. Achievement tests are used extensively to assess the level of learning achieved by each student in a course or achievement in education more generally. Aptitude tests are used to assess giftedness or special needs. In this chapter we have closely examined the structure of a number of popular general aptitude and achievement tests. We have also considered the assessment of vocational interests, information that can be used to help young people choose courses that may interest them and formulate a plan of study leading to a particular vocation later in life.

Questions for consideration

1   What is the difference between an achievement test and an aptitude test?
2   Justify the use of take-home exams.
3   Think of an example item for each of the subtests that make up the WISC–IV.
4   Define the six interest types in Holland's theory of vocational interests.
5   What are some of the instrumental uses of testing in our society?

Further reading

Holland, J L (1992). *Making vocational choices: A theory of vocational personalities and work environments* (2nd edn). Odessa, FL: Psychological Assement Resources.

Kubiszyn, T, & Borich, G (2003). *Educational testing and measurement: Classroom application and practice* (7th edn). New York: Wiley.

Nitko, A J (2004). *Educational assessment of students* (4th edn). Upper Saddle River, NJ: Merrill.

Osipow, S H & Fitzgerald, L F (1996). *Theories of career development* (4th edn). Boston: Allyn & Bacon.

Overton, T (2000). *Assessment in special education: An applied approach* (3rd edn). Upper Saddle River, NJ: Merrill.

Reynolds, C R, & Kamphaus, R W (2003). (Eds). *Handbook of psychological and educational assessment of children: Intelligence, aptitude, and achievement*. New York: Guildford.

part four

4

Prospects
and Issues

chapter twelve

The Future of Testing and Assessment

INTRODUCTION

Discussion of the future of any field necessarily involves an element of speculation. One can discern trends that are imminent in the literature, or seem to be on the horizon, but there is always the possibility of some unforeseen development. Our discussion of the future of testing and assessment will be organised into three sections: content developments, technical and methodological developments, and contextual changes.

CONTENT DEVELOPMENTS

Content developments refer to advances in psychological theory, ie, new constructs emerging from the literature, for which psychological tests may be developed in the future. These are potential sources of ideas for new approaches to testing. Already we can discern new approaches to cognitive abilities and personality theory.

Criticisms of traditional formulations of intelligence are well known. Several authors have sought to expand the concept of intelligence over the past decade or so, and research along these lines is likely to continue. The two most prominent theorists in this regard are Gardner (1983) and Sternberg (1985, 1997). Gardner's theory of multiple intelligences includes dimensions such as interpersonal and intrapersonal intelligences in addition to traditional psychometric intelligence (Chen, Isberg & Krechevsky, 1998; the established view was discussed in Chapters 7 and 8). One of the difficulties Gardner and his coworkers have faced is the development of adequate measures that tap individual differences in some of the new intelligences he posits. When such tests are available, they will no doubt have a large impact on psychological testing and assessment.

Sternberg (1985) introduced the idea of practical intelligence, partly to explain why traditional academic intelligence is not a sufficient condition for success in many walks of life. More formally, intelligence explains less than half of the variance in any salient outcome measure. It appears that many people survive in modern society by their wits, using what might be called 'street smarts', rather than any kind of analytic problem solving or deep analysis (Wagner & Sternberg, 1991). Sternberg regarded practical intelligence as consisting of knowledge of process and procedures rather than knowledge of content, facts, and figures: 'knowing how' rather than 'knowing that'. Practical intelligence is context-based, pragmatically useful, and acquired more through hard-won experience than through formal instruction. Importantly, from an applied perspective, useful measures of practical intelligence have been developed in the form of tacit knowledge tests (eg, Sternberg, 1997; Sternberg & Horvath, 1999; Sternberg, Wagner, Williams & Horvath, 1995). Methods of assessing practical intelligence include simulations, analysis of critical incidents, and situational judgment tests. Proponents of practical intelligence claim their measures are uncorrelated with traditional measures of intelligence yet are as predictive of important outcomes as more traditional ability tests.

Developments have also occurred in the personality domain. Probably the most influential is the emergence of the Big Five model of personality already discussed in Chapter 8. Another important development within personality theory is the rise of the concept of integrity (Ones, Viswesvaran & Schmidt, 1993); that is, the use of tests to measure concepts like dependability, theft proneness, and counterproductive work behaviours. In the current age of heightened security alert, there will no doubt be a growing interest in ideas around the basic construct of integrity. Another burgeoning new construct is emotional intelligence (EQ) (Matthews, Zeidner & Roberts, 2002). A plethora of instruments have been developed to measure emotional intelligence over the past decade and interest in this construct shows no signs of abating. At this stage theorists are still uncertain about exactly where to locate emotional intelligence within existing theory. Some researchers have dismissed it as an amalgamation of known personality traits (Davies, Stankov & Roberts, 1998), but many EQ theorists emphasise the 'intelligence' part of its name and see it as a new category of ability. Alternatively, the whole area of emotions remains largely untapped by psychological tests so we could be witnessing the emergence of whole new domains of individual differences. New developments in the psychology of emotions will no doubt strongly influence these trends.

TECHNICAL AND METHODOLOGICAL DEVELOPMENTS

Technical and methodological developments refer to new approaches to testing made possible by new technology or new ideas in psychometric theory. The most obvious development here is the use of computers. Most of the tests discussed in previous chapters have been of the traditional pencil-and-paper variety. However, there is no doubt that computerised testing has the potential to revolutionise psychological testing and assessment, if it has not done so already. Being a 'universal machine', a computer is capable of being programmed to present any kind of stimulus and collect any kind of response imaginable, although this may require the development of specialised peripherals. Much can be done using a standard computer screen, mouse, keyboard, and joystick. Any static image that can be printed on paper can be displayed on the screen but the screen can also display animated pictures and graphics and even play video clips. Further, computers can play sounds, including spoken words and sentences. They are even beginning to recognise the spoken word. All of these possibilities continue to fire the imagination of young test developers so it may not be long before simple, dyadic question-and-answer sessions give way to fully immersive, interactive experiences incorporating virtual reality and artificial intelligence. Complexity of scoring and presentation rules are no longer an obstacle once a computer takes over. Computers can also score tests and write reports; all within a few seconds of the test being completed (Wise & Plake, 1989). Further, the computer will display the same stimulus in exactly the same way to each examinee. Thus the ideals of standardised administration are perfectly realised.

Oddly enough, the promise of computers to revolutionise psychological testing and assessment has been somewhat slower in its realisation than might be expected, given the statements in the previous paragraphs. It has probably been more of an evolution than a revolution. It has to be said that, even today, most computerised tests use the computer as little more than an automatic page turner to present a series of questions that could just as easily be printed on paper (Drasgow & Olson-Buchanan, 1999).

Three main periods can be identified in the application of computers to psychological testing and assessment (Bunderson, Inouye & Olsen, 1989). The first period began in the 1950s when computers first became available. At this time the potential of applying computers to psychological tests was first envisaged. The idea of computerised adaptive, or tailored, testing (CAT) was conceived and new developments in test theory such as item response theory (IRT) seemed ready to make this a possibility. However the cost and specialised skills required to program large, expensive mainframes kept this technology out of the mainstream of test development for most of this time. The second period began in the 1980s with the widespread proliferation of cheap personal microcomputers. Now test developers had ready access to affordable computing power and development of computerised tests began in earnest (Burke & Normand, 1987). Finally, the 1990s saw the explosive growth of the Internet which heralded in the new era of Internet testing (Barak & English, 2002), including distributed delivery of materials and the ability to self-publish and reach millions of potential users.

A key issue with the advent of the personal computer in the 1980s was the difference between computerised and pencil-and-paper tests (Lee, Moreno & Sympson, 1986). Did presentation by computer fundamentally change the construct being measured? Generally the conclusion was favourable (Ward, Hooper & Hannafin, 1989; Wise & Wise, 1987). Meta-analysis of this research reported a cross-mode correlation of 0.97 between computerised and pencil-and-paper forms (Mead & Drasgow, 1993). There is not much difference between ticking a box on a questionnaire with a pencil and checking a box on a computer screen with a mouse. The psychological processes underlying these slightly different responses remained the same.

The only exception to this was speeded tests (Greaud & Green, 1986). Recall that speeded tests are characterised by a very simple task performed repetitively as quickly as possible within a strict time limit, usually only 1 or 2 minutes. Several examples of speeded tests are discussed elsewhere, such as the Digit Symbol and Symbol Search subtests of the WAIS–III in Chapter 7 and the Cancellation subtest of the WISC–IV in Chapter 11. Psychomotor effects proliferate speeded tests and variations in response modality make a big difference (Parks, Bartlett, Wickham & Myors, 2001). The cross-mode correlation reduces to 0.72 (Mead & Drasgow, 1993). Using a pencil is usually a lot easier than using a mouse.

Smart testing

An interesting exercise in speculation about the technological future of testing was provided by Kyllonen's (1997) *smart test*. Kyllonen's test was designed to incorporate 'all current significant technology associated with abilities measurement' (Kyllonen, 1997, p 347), including computer delivery, item-generative technology, multidimensional adaptive technology, time-parameterised testing, and latent factor-centred design. Although Kyllonen emphasised ability testing, some of the methods would readily translate to other domains. The basic idea of computer delivery has already been covered above, but the use of computers opens up a range of other advanced technologies. Understanding these may provide some suggestion of what might be occurring inside a computer presenting a computerised test in the not too distant future.

Computerised and multidimensional adaptive testing

Multidimensional Adaptive Testing (MAT) is the multivariate generalisation of Computerised Adaptive Testing (CAT) (Segall, 1996). In order to understand MAT, first we must understand the basic ideas behind CAT.

The early promise of computerised testing was nowhere more evident than in the concept of computerised adaptive, or tailored, testing. This is the idea that the computer can continuously monitor an examinee's performance and refine the trait or ability estimate after each item is presented. Further, the computer can choose, as the next item to present, the one that will provide the most information about the ability or trait being measured. This amounts to choosing the maximally discriminating item, based on the examinee's performance on the test so far. Basically, if you get an item right, the computer follows it with a harder item but if you got the item wrong, the next item would be easier. In this way the test adapts to your location on the underlying trait, the point at which you would get about half the items right and half the items wrong.

Traditional static, non-adaptive tests need to be composed of items of varying difficulty, spread across the full range of ability. They must contain easy items for low ability examinees as well as hard items suitable for the most able. An average person taking a static test has to waste considerable time answering the easy items at the beginning of the test. Similarly, they may get bogged down on the difficult items at the end. Wouldn't it be good if the test could adapt to each person's ability and not waste time on items that were too difficult or too easy? Adaptive tests 'zero in' to each person's ability level and spend most testing time administering challenging, appropriately graded items. This is the basic idea behind CAT and it was thought that CAT would result in tests that were much shorter than static pencil–and–paper tests. CAT tests are highly efficient because time is not wasted on items far removed from the person's true score.

One interesting feature of CAT is that each test taker gets a slightly different test. On the face of it, this seems unfair because different examinees are apparently assessed according to different criteria. However, the theory is that all the items are unidimensional, ie, they tap the same underlying psychological construct so a test composed of any subset of items from the same set of items ought to be equivalent. Development of CAT requires much work in order to produce a large set of unidimensional items, graded in difficulty, along a single psychological scale. Analysis of the items can also be quite intensive, requiring a sample of a few thousand examinees, in order to accurately estimate each item's characteristics using item response theory (IRT, see Chapter 5). The large pool of items underlying a CAT is known as an item bank.

MAT takes computerised adaptive testing to the next level by applying the basic idea to a whole battery of tests instead of just to a single test. MAT capitalises on the fact that many of the constructs measured by a battery of tests are correlated. This is especially true of cognitive abilities (see the hierarchical structure of abilities discussed in Chapters 7 and 8). Interdependence among the subtests of a battery means that all the items from all subtests in a battery are related. Thus the score of one item from one subtest could conceivably be related to the score on an item from another subtest. MAT takes advantage of this interdependence and feeds performance on every item in the battery into the score for every subtest in the battery. This allows it to adapt simultaneously over all subtests by selecting the next optimal item to present not from the item bank for a particular subtest, but from an item bank of all items in the whole battery. CAT adapts by dynamically estimating the single ability being measured by the test and selecting the next item that optimally improves that measurement; MAT adapts by dynamically estimating all abilities being measured by the battery simultaneously and selecting the next item, from whichever subtest, that optimally improves the measurement of all abilities. CAT is minimising the error variance around a single trait estimate whereas MAT is minimising 'the volume of the credibility ellipsoid' around the cluster of all trait estimates.

One of the main practical advantages of CAT is its potential to reduce testing time without sacrificing accuracy of measurement due to its selection of maximally informative items. MAT takes this idea one step further and selects the item that will be most informative for the whole battery, thus making testing potentially even more efficient.

Limitations of CAT and MAT

One of the main difficulties in developing a CAT is the effort required to develop a sufficiently large item bank. Even after several hundred items are written, the item parameters must be estimated. IRT provides the best methods for estimating item parameters (eg, difficulty and discrimination) but requires data from large samples of examinees which implies extensive testing during development.

In the case of MAT, another potential drawback is the likelihood of frequent chopping and changing between item types, as the system selects items from any subtest in the battery. This could prove disconcerting or even confusing for examinees. Further, examinees would need to retain the instructions for how to complete every subtest in mind during the whole testing session so they would be ready to respond to whichever item was presented.

Item-generative testing

If the biggest obstacle in setting up CAT and MAT lies in developing a larger item bank, item-generative technologies may be the answer. In adaptive tests, often several hundred items were needed, as opposed to the usual twenty or thirty used in traditional tests. One recent development in testing is item generation in which new items are generated automatically by computer according to some underlying rule or algorithm (Irvine & Kyllonen, 2002). The idea is that if the main source of difficulty for the subtest can be captured by a rule or template, the computer can be used to generate an infinite number of actual items of any desired difficulty by randomly initialising a few underlying variables and applying the rule. This has the potential of producing an infinite number of parallel tests. To date item generation techniques have mainly been used to develop figural ability items. Verbal content seems much more difficult to handle. As with all applications of computerised testing, the possibilities of this method of testing are limited only by the imagination and ingenuity of test developers. It is not inconceivable for there to be a highly complex cognitive model of test performance underlying the item generation, although to date most applications have tended to use generic templates rather than full blown theories of test performance.

Time-parameterisation

The aim of time-parameterisation is to solve the fundamental problem of speed-accuracy trade-off which is a basic dimension of strategy for solving any set of difficult tasks. One can work quickly and less carefully, sacrificing accuracy for speed, in the hope of scoring well by doing more items; or one can work slowly and carefully, sacrificing speed for accuracy, in the hope of making every item that is completed count. This distinction can also be thought of in terms of quantity versus quality. Someone emphasising speed is opting for quantity, trying to answer a large number of items; someone emphasising accuracy is aiming more for quality of thought and problem solving. Unfortunately it is impossible to tell from a final test score which strategy, or part thereof, someone has adopted. Yet each represents fundamentally different approaches to problem solving.

Since its inception, computerised testing made it possible to collect response time information. As well as the actual answer, an examinee's time to answer, or even make a partial response, could be recorded. It was always thought that this timing information would ultimately provide the solution to the speed–accuracy trade-off issue. The problem is that psychometricians have not agreed on how best to combine time and accuracy data. Invariably these two pieces of information are analysed separately, but attempts to combine them into a single 'efficiency' type measure, eg, number right divided by time to answer, have never proven completely satisfactory.

Kyllonen suggests that another way of combining timing information with accuracy scores is to treat time as one of the difficulty dimensions. This suggests a test, such as a digit span test (see Chapter 7), in which the rate of presentation of digits is varied instead of the length of the digit string. A more general way of time-parameterising a test would be the introduction of time limits or deadlines to each item. In this way someone preferring an accuracy strategy could be forced to adopt a more speeded one with the hope of achieving a more uniform number of strategies adopted by examinees over the course of the test.

Latent factor-centred design

Kyllonen argues that test developers need to focus more on the constructs that they want to measure, rather than on the particular tests they use to measure them in any particular test battery. He calls this a construct focus rather than a test focus. Being test focused leaves us too wedded to existing ways of doing things. If we can become construct focused, or latent factor-centred, then we will be more open to new testing forms. After all, the particular test being used is mere surface detail; what we should be interested in is the construct or latent factor underlying test performance.

One thing not considered by Kyllonen is Internet testing. Add Internet delivery to all of the above and you have a truly 21st century instrument.

Internet testing

The Internet promises to revolutionise testing, although it has currently had more of an impact on distribution, ie, publication, than on the development of new test forms. Using the Internet, a set of questions can be quickly disseminated to psychologists and other test users all around the world. Moreover, the Internet version of the test can be kept up-to-date with the most recent changes disseminated to all users as soon as they are developed. It is easy to modify the questions presented and even the scoring mechanism involved. The growth of Internet testing was fuelled by the Internet revolution in the second half of the 1990s. By the year 2000 there were enough high-end PCs with cheap Internet access to facilitate widespread Internet testing.

Corresponding to the ease of keeping test users up to date with the most current version of a test, the other significant advantage of Internet testing lies in getting information back to test developers. If a test is presented on the Internet, it is easy to collect data for norming purposes and this speedy turnaround makes rapid test development possible. There is even the possibility of dynamic norming in which test norms are continually updated as new data come in.

An obvious disadvantage of Internet testing is the so-called 'digital divide' (Bartram, 2000), the fact that some people have better access to the Internet than others and those with the best access tend to be the most privileged. There is a strong tradition in testing of trying to avoid forms of discrimination which the digital divide may entrench. Nevertheless, it is generally believed that any gap in access is narrowing as computers become cheaper and more widespread. One area where Internet distribution of tests is likely to alleviate discrimination is in rural areas, where accessing a professional or getting to a testing centre is difficult. Ultimately, perhaps age will be the most important dimension of the digital divide, even in societies with good Internet access. Older people are less familiar and possibly more anxious about using computers. Internet test users should be mindful of these equity problems, even though it is generally believed that they will tend to decline with time (Rosen & Maguire, 1990).

A more subtle problem associated with Internet testing concerns security of information. Given that psychological test results can be highly personal in nature, it is important that any private information be kept confidential and secure. Recent privacy legislation has sought to strengthen individuals' protection in this regard. Corresponding to the need for security of test scores and protection of privacy, there is also security of the test itself to consider. In the past, access to many psychological tests has been restricted in order to maintain the confidentiality of test items: if the items become well known and the correct or most desirable answers become common knowledge, then the test is rendered useless. How can test security be assured when items are passing from computer to computer around an unsecured network like the Internet? Once the correct answers are discovered, the Internet is also well suited to their rapid dissemination. Internet testers concerned about test security can try to do things like disable the printing and screen capture functions on the browser presenting the test or they can even install a 'security agent' prior to test delivery, but they can never stop someone photographing their computer screen with a digital camera!

Bandwidth limitations also pose unique difficulties for Internet testing. Although computers can time events to the fraction of a second, timing of events across the Internet can be difficult because of lag times. For example, it may be difficult to be sure of exactly when the question appeared on the examinee's screen after it left the server. This issue is called 'ping latency' in computer parlance. Similar bandwidth limitations can seriously impact CAT or MAT delivered over the Internet. For these systems to work, an examinee's answers would typically have to be sent back to the server for scoring so the system can adapt. If there are delays on the network, this could slow down the whole test, resulting in a very unsatisfactory testing experience. One way around this would be for the CAT system to reside on the client's computer, but this would involve downloading the entire item bank every time which may exacerbate test security.

Another difficulty concerns the types of test on offer on the Internet. The Internet is replete with tests of dubious quality that certainly do not measure up to the high psychometric standards set by the profession and advocated in this book. Many of these tests are pop-psychological or even para-psychological in nature. A major problem now facing the profession is how to differentiate itself from unscientific instruments available online and how to educate the public into recognising what is reputable and what is not. Further, although the Internet seems suited to the delivery of psychological tests, at this stage it is not suited to full blown psychological assessment. Recall from Chapter 1 that psychological assessment is more extensive than psychological testing and implies the integration of multiple sources of information about someone, including their test scores, personal background information, and information about the circumstances in which they are living and working. In psychological assessment, the emphasis is on answering the referral question rather than simply providing a set of scores (Naglieri et al, 2004). This is especially true of clinical and neuropsychological assessment. It takes an experienced practitioner many years to become skilled at this and it is hard to see how a present-day computer could possibly perform this function.

One area where Internet testing is expanding rapidly is industrial and organisational applications (Leivens & Harris, 2003). This is mainly due to the explosive rise of online recruiting firms and job markets. Many such providers seek to add selection to their portfolio of services in order to add value and attract applicants to their sites. With the entire Internet full of potential readers, online recruitment promises to dramatically reduce the selection ratio, but only if your web site can come to the attention of sufficient numbers of people. A likely scenario is that specialist recruiting sites will emerge, targeting particular industries. There has even been the suggestion of automatic head hunting in which 'web bots' trawl the web for resumés or other information about potential candidates.

With the need for initial sifting of many applications comes the inevitable temptation of delivering psychological tests and assessments straight to the general public without the intervention of a professional psychologist. Such a method of testing has been called unsupervised mode (Bartram, 2000). The idea is that anyone can log on and complete your test, anywhere, any time. This involves a fundamental shift in how psychology, as a profession, views tests. A long tradition in psychology equates good testing practice with control over the situation by an appropriately qualified professional. The temptation to access potentially millions of users via the Internet has led some entrepreneurial psychologists to question this assumption. Is an unsupervised test really compromised by the absence of a proctor or invigilator? On the face of it the answer would seem to be yes. Most people's first experience of testing is a formal exam at school which was invigilated very closely. Concerns about cheating were paramount. Interestingly however, not all tests seem to need this level of close supervision.

Bartram (2000) has analysed the functions of supervision and considered four levels of supervised testing. He suggests that the main functions of a supervisor include:

(i)   authenticating the test taker, ie, making sure they are who they say they are and that someone else hasn't been substituted in their place;
(ii) establishing rapport with the test taker
(iii) ensuring the test is administered according to the manual
(iv) preventing cheating; and,
(v)   ensuring security of the test itself.

Research suggests that tests of typical performance, eg, personality or interest tests, are not adversely affected by lack of formal supervision (Bartram & Brown, 2002). Variations in conditions are unlikely to affect an examinee's reaction to these items.

However, for maximal performance tests, such as aptitude and achievement tests, answers are likely to be affected by the presence or absence of a supervisor. In the absence of a supervisor an examinee could phone a friend, or look up the answer in a book or online encyclopaedia. This is an important issue because validity generalisation research strongly supports the use of maximal performance cognitive tests (Schmidt & Hunter, 1998), so the temptation to offer these tests in unsupervised mode is likely to be very strong indeed.

In an effort to find a place for unsupervised Internet testing, Bartram (2004) considered four levels of supervision. He called these open mode, controlled mode, supervised mode, and management mode. In open mode, anyone can access the test, there is no user identification and no human supervision. This is the most extreme unsupervised mode and only suitable in low-stakes testing situations. Controlled mode involves users being sent a password and logging on to a testing site. Authentication is still minimal because there is no human supervision. The idea is that open or controlled mode could serve as the first step in a selection process to initially identify unsuitable candidates; however, subsequent use of open or controlled mode results would need to be followed up in a second testing session. Supervised mode involves the presence of a human supervisor, but perhaps in a non-secure environment. Finally managed mode is similar to the formal examination conditions discussed above in which access is highly controlled and the test kept secure.

Internet testing also raises a number of familiar ethical issues such as the nature of the relationship between psychologist and client, confidentiality of responses, feedback to the client and how to ensure informed consent (Naglieri et al, 2004). In the first session with any new client, it is good professional practice to spend some time discussing expectations and the nature of the professional relationship. The question is, how will this be handled in the case of Internet testing? Presumably, it will be done by screens full of boilerplate and disclaimers, but such an approach is hardly conducive to building rapport or establishing a therapeutic alliance. Feedback to the client is another important issue. A psychologist providing feedback can take into account the examinee's state of mind and readiness to handle the feedback. A computer printing a canned report has no such insight. Finally, informed consent could be an issue because it may not be known whether the person taking the test is capable of giving their consent. This may be especially true for examinees with a disability. In short, the removal of human contact, as implied by Internet testing, exacerbates many of the concerns raised by ethical issues in the past.

BOX 12.1

Internet testing in the age of globalisation: Whose laws apply?

A job applicant in Auckland logs on to the Internet and completes an English-language test running on a server in Taiwan. The test was developed in the USA but is being offered by an Australian recruiting agency. The position being sought is for a manager in the Hong Kong office of a European multinational based in Switzerland. The test report was interpreted by an out-sourced HR consultancy in India. Who is the test user? Who is the test supplier? Whose assessment standards apply?

CONTEXTUAL CHANGES

In this section we consider developments in the broader social environment, of which psychological testing and assessment forms a part, that may have an impact on how testing progresses in the future. A number of forces are readily apparent. First, counter to the technological wizardry discussed in the previous section, there appears to be an increasing demand for shorter measures, and measures that can be developed quickly (Kamphaus, Petoskey & Rowe, 2000). Such measures often take the form of behaviour checklists and ratings which utilise observer judgment to document a few gross behaviours indicative of a particular disposition rather than an attempt to accurately measure behaviour to a very fine degree.

Further, the rise of managed care in the clinical domain appears to have brought with it a growing reluctance to utilise psychological assessment (Groth-Marnat, 2000). Some authors report a drop of 10 per cent in the thirty years from 1970 to 2000. The main reasons for this appear to be concerns about the cost of testing and the apparent weak link between many forms of assessment and useful therapies. There is little doubt that burgeoning health care costs put pressure on the ability of providers to supply everything that may be deemed desirable. We may be entering an era in which the costs and benefits of all potential services are compared. In this case psychological assessment may have to compete with various physical tests, drugs, and therapeutic interventions. This problem has been addressed in areas of testing other than clinical psychology, such as through the use of utility analysis in industrial and organisational psychology.

Finally, we live in an age of continually rising expectations on the part of the general public. There are increasing demands for accountability and transparency. Probably the best way to meet these demands is through ever more vigilance in terms of ethics and professionalism and increasing scientific research into the validity of tests.

CONCLUDING REMARKS

Whether or not Kyllonen's *smart test* becomes common place remains to be seen. One thing these considerations make clear, though, is that the test professional of the future will not only need to have expertise in the psychological construct that he or she is trying to measure, but in a range of other technical and professional areas as well. While all of the techniques discussed by Kyllonen are feasible using present-day technology, Groth-Marnat (2000) speculated on what tests might look like in fifty years time. His smart test of 2050 was a 'fully integrated assessment instrument using a combination of AI [artificial intelligence], interactive virtual reality (or possibly hologram), physiological measures, massive interlinked Internet norms, validity/predictions based on chaos theory, branching strategies, genetic measures, in session as well as time series measures' (Groth-Marnat, 2000, p 361). There is no doubt that the area of testing and assessment will continue to offer challenges for both theorists and practitioners for many years to come.

On the other hand, our theory is that by 2050 everyone will start learning psychology in kindergarten so that by the end of primary school they will have mastered all the material covered in this book and be able to assess one another with ease.

Questions for consideration

1   What new constructs could emerge to fuel a new generation of tests?
2   How would a smart personality test work?
3   Think of a pencil-and-paper test you are familiar with, perhaps one of those discussed previously in this book, and try to think of a better way of measuring the construct via computer. Try to utilise some of the potential of computerised testing that is not possible on paper.
4   Discuss some of the ethical issues raised by Internet testing.
5   How can psychological testing and assessment be justified from a cost-benefit point of view?

Further reading

Drasgow, F, & Olson-Buchanan, J B (1999). *Innovations in computerized assessment*. Mahwah, NJ: Erlbaum.

Groth-Marnat, G (2000). Visions of clinical assessment: Then, now, and a brief history of the future. *Journal of Clinical Psychology, 56,* 349–85.

Irvine, S H, & Kyllonen, P C (2002). *Item generation for test development*. Mahwah, NJ: Lawrence Erlbaum.

Plake, B S, & Witt, J C (Eds) (1986). *The future of testing*. Hillsdale: L Erlbaum Associates.

References

Ackerman, M J (1999). *Essentials of forensic psychological assessment.* New York: John Wiley & Sons.

Ackerman, M J, & Ackerman, M C (1997). Custody evaluation practices: A survey of experienced professionals (Revisited). *Professional Psychology: Research and Practice, 28,* 137–45.

Ackerman, M J, & Kane, A W (1998). *Psychological experts in divorce actions* (3rd edn). New York: Aspen Law & Business.

Ackerman, M J, & Schoendorf, K (1992). *Ackerman Schoendorf Scales of Parent Evaluation of Custody (ASPECT).* Los Angeles, CA: Western Psychological Services.

Adams, H E, & Luscher, K A (2003). Ethical considerations in psychological assessment. In W T O'Donohue & K E Ferguson (Eds), *Handbook of professional ethics for psychologists: Issues, questions and controversies* (pp 275–83). Thousand Oaks, CA: Sage.

Afifi, A K, & Bergman, R A (1998). *Functional neuroanatomy: Text and atlas.* New York: McGraw Hill.

Allen, M J, & Yen, W M (1979). *Introduction to measurement theory.* Monterey, CA: Brooks/Cole.

American Educational Research Association (AERA), American Psychological Association, & National Council on Measurement in Education (1999). *Standards for educational and psychological testing.* Washington, DC: American Educational Research Association.

American Psychological Association (1994). Guidelines for child custody evaluations in divorce proceedings. *American Psychologist, 49,* 677–80.

American Psychiatric Association (2000). *Diagnostic and statistical manual of mental disorders (DSM – IV – TR)* (4th edn, Rev). Washington, DC: Author.

Anastasi, A (1988). *Psychological testing* (6th edn). New York: Macmillan.

Antony, M M, Bieling, P J, Cox, B J, Enns, M W, & Swinson, R P (1998). Psychometric properties of the 42-item and 21-item versions of the Depression Anxiety Stress Scale in clinical groups and a community sample. *Psychological Assessment, 10,* 176–81.

Atkinson, J W, Bongort, K, & Price, L H (1977). Explorations using computer simulation to comprehend thematic apperceptive measurement of motivation. *Motivation and Emotion, 1,* 1–27.

Australian Broadcasting Corporation (2003). *Immigration and nation building—Institutions* [Online]. Available: <http://www.abc.net.au/cgi-bin/common/printfriendly.pl?/federation/fedstory/ep2/ep2_instit...> Accessed: 28 February 2004.

Australian Council for Educational Research (1962). *ACER Speed and Accuracy Test.* Melbourne, Australia: Author.

Australian Council for Educational Research (1982). *ACER Advanced Tests AL–AQ* (2nd edn) and *BL–BQ.* Melbourne, Australia: Author.

Australian Psychological Society (2000). *APS accreditation guideline.* Melbourne: Author.

Australian Psychological Society (2003). *Code of ethics.* Melbourne: Author.

Bader, L A (1998). *Bader Reading and Language Inventory* (3rd edn). Upper Saddle River, MN: Prentice Hall.

Bagby, R M, Wild, N, & Turner, A (2003). Psychological assessment in adult mental health settings. In J R Graham & J A Naglieri (Eds), *Handbook of psychology: Vol 10. Assessment psychology* (pp 213–34). Hoboken, NJ: Wiley & Sons.

Barak, A, & English, N (2002). Prospects and limitations of psychological testing on the Internet. *Journal of Technology in Human Services, 19,* 65–89.

Bartram, D (2000). Internet recruitment and selection: Kissing frogs to find princes. *International Journal of Selection and Assessment, 8,* 261–74.

Bartram, D (2004). Assessment in organisations. *Applied Psychology: An International Review, 53,* 237–59.

Bartram, D, & Brown, A (2002). *Online testing: Mode of administration and the stability of OPQ 32i scores.* Paper presented at the ITC Conference on Computer-Based Testing and the Internet, Winchester, England.

Bartram, D, & Lindley, P A (1994). *Scaling, norms and standardization. BPS Opening Learning Programme on Psychological Testing.* London: British Psychological Society.

Beaumont, G (1988). *Understanding neuropsychology.* Oxford, England: Basil Blackwell.

Beck, A T, & Steer, R A (1987a). *Manual for the Beck Anxiety Inventory.* San Antonio, TX: The Psychological Corporation.

Beck, A T, & Steer, R A (1987b). *Manual for the revised Beck Depression Inventory.* San Antonio, TX: The Psychological Corporation.

Beck, A T, Steer, R A, & Brown, G K (1996). *Manual for the Beck Depression Inventory – Second Edition (BDI–II).* San Antonio, TX: The Psychological Corporation.

Bigler, E D, Rosa, L, Schultz, F, Hall, S, & Harris, J (1989). Rey Auditory-Verbal Learning and Rey-Osterreith Complex Figure Design Test performance in Alzheimer's disease and closed head injury. *Journal of Clinical Psychology, 45,* 277–80.

Bland, M (2000). *An introduction to medical statistics* (3rd edn). Oxford, England: Oxford University Press.

Bonnie, R (1992). The competence of criminal defendants: A theoretical reformulation. *Behavioural Science and the Law, 10,* 291–316.

Bonnie, R (1993). The competence of criminal defendants: Beyond Dusky and Drope. *Miami Law Review, 47,* 539–601.

Borman, W C, & Motowidlo, S J (1993). Expanding the criterion domain to include elements of contextual performance. In N Schmitt & W Borman (Eds), *Personnel selection in organizations.* San Francisco: Jossey-Bass.

Bowman, M L (1989). Testing individual differences in Ancient China. *American Psychologist, 44,* 576–8.

Boyle, G J (1995). Review of the Personality Assessment Inventory. In J C Conoley & J C Impara (Eds), *The twelfth mental measurements yearbook* (pp 764–6). Lincoln, NE: Buros Institute of Mental Measurements.

Brenner, E (2003). Consumer-focused psychological assessment. *Professional Psychology, 34,* 240–7.

Brody, N (1972). *Personality: Research and theory.* New York: Academic Press.

Brown, T A, Chorpita, B F, Korotitsch, W, & Barlow, D H (1997). Psychometric properties of the Depression Anxiety Stress Scales (DASS) in clinical samples. *Behaviour Research and Therapy, 35,* 79–89.

Bunderson, C V, Inouye, D K, & Olsen, J B (1989). The four generations of computerized educational measurement. In R L Linn (Ed), *Educational measurement* (3rd edn). New York: Macmillan.

Burke, M J, & Normand, J (1987). Computerised psychological testing: Overview and critique. *Professional Psychology: Research and Practice, 18,* 42–51.

Butcher, J N, Dahlstrom, W G, Graham, J R, Tellegen, A, & Kaemmer, B (1989). *Minnesota Multiphasic Personality Inventory – Second Edition (MMPI–2): Manual for administration and scoring.* Minneapolis: University of Minnesota Press.

Camara, W J, Nathan, J S, & Puente, A E (2000). Psychological test usage: Implications in professional psychology. *Professional Psychology: Research and Practice, 31,* 141–54.

Campbell, J P, McCloy, R A, Oppler, S H, & Sager, C E (1993). A theory of performance. In N Schmitt & W Borman (Eds), *Personnel selection in organizations.* San Francisco: Jossey-Bass.

Carpenter, P A, Just, M A, & Shell, P (1990). What one intelligence test measures: A theoretical account of the processing in the Raven Progressive Matrices Test. *Psychological Review, 97,* 404–31.

Carroll, J B (1993). *Human cognitive abilities: A survey of factor-analytic studies.* Cambridge, England: Cambridge University Press.

Carstairs, J R, & Shores, E A (2000). The Macquarie University Neuropsychological Normative Study (MUNNS): Rationale and methodology. *Australian Psychologist, 35,* 36–40.

Cascio, W F, & Aguinis (2005). *Applied psychology in human resource management.* (6th edn). Upper Saddle River, NJ: Pearson Prentice Hall.

Cattell, R B (1957). *Personality and motivation: Structure and measurement.* Yonkers, NY: World Book Company.

Cattell, R B (1971). *Abilities: Their structure, growth and action.* Boston: Houghton Mifflin.

Charles, D C (1976). A historical overview of educational psychology. *Contemporary Educational Psychology, 1,* 76–88.

Charter, R A, Walden, D K, & Padilla, S (2000). Too many simple clerical scoring errors: The Rey Figure as an example. *Journal of Clinical Psychology, 56,* 571–4.

Chen, I Q, Isberg, E, & Krechevsky, M (1998). *Project Spectrum: Early learning activities.* Cambridge: Harvard Project Zero.

Cianciolo, A T, & Sternberg, R J (2004). *Intelligence: A brief history.* Malden, MA: Blackwell.

Clark, B (1988). *Growing up gifted: Developing the potential of children at home and at school* (3rd edn). Columbus, OH: Merrill.

Cliff, N (1992). Abstract measurement theory and the revolution that never happened. *Psychological Science, 3,* 186–90.

Commonwealth of Australia (2000). *Immigration Restriction Act 1901* [Online]. Available: <http://www.foundingdocs.gov.au/places/cth/cth4ii.htm>

Crawford, J R, & Henry, J D (2003). The Depression Anxiety Stress Scales (DASS): Normative data and latent structure in a large non-clinical sample. *The British Journal of Clinical Psychology, 42,* 111–31.

Crocker, L, & Algina, J (1986). *Introduction to classical and modern test theory.* New York: Holt, Rinehart and Winston.

Cronbach, L J (1951). Coefficient alpha and the internal structure of tests. *Psychometrika, 16,* 297–334.

Cronbach, L J (1970). *Essentials of psychological testing* (3rd edn). New York: Harper & Row.

Cronbach, L J (1990). *Essentials of psychological testing* (5th edn). New York: HarperCollins.

Cronbach, L J, & Gleser, G C (1965). *Psychological tests and personnel decisions* (2nd edn). Urbana, IL: University of Chicago Press.

Cronbach, L J, Gleser, G C, Nanda, H, & Rajaratnam, N (1972). *The dependability of behavioral measurements: Theory of generalizability for scores and profiles.* New York: Wiley.

Cronbach, L J, & Meehl, P E (1955). Construct validity in psychological tests. *Psychological Bulletin, 52,* 281–302.

Crowne, D P, & Marlowe, D (1964). *The approval motive: Studies in evaluative dependence.* New York: Wiley.

Cullum, C M (1998). Neuropsychological assessment of adults. In A S Belleck & M Hersen (Eds), *Comprehensive clinical psychology* (pp 304–47). New York: Pergamon.

Dahlstrom, W G (1993). Tests: Small samples, large consequences. *American Psychologist, 48,* 393–9.

Dahlstrom, W G, & Welsh, G S (1960). *An MMPI handbook.* London: Oxford University Press.

Darby, D & Walsh, K (2005). *Walsh's neuropsychology: A clinical approach.* Edinburgh: Elsevier Churchill Livingstone.

Davis, A G (1993). *A survey of adult aphasia* (2nd edn). Englewood Cliffs, NJ: Prentice Hall.

Davies, M, Stankov, L, & Roberts, R D (1998). Emotional intelligence: In search of an elusive construct. *Journal of Personality and Social Psychology, 75,* 989–1015.

de Lemos, M M (1989). *Standard progressive matrices: Australian manual.* Melbourne, Australia: ACER.

Delis, D, Kaplan, E, & Kramer, J (2001). *Delis-Kaplan Executive Function Scale.* San Antonio, TX: Psychological Corporation.

Drasgow, F, & Olson-Buchanan, J B (1999). *Innovations in computerized assessment.* Mahwah, NJ: Erlbaum.

DuBois, P E (1970). *A history of psychological testing.* Boston: Allyn & Bacon.

Ellis, A W, & Young, A W (1996). *Human cognitive neuropsychology: A textbook with readings.* Hove, England: Psychology Press.

Entwisle, D R (1972). To dispel fantasies about fantasy-based measures of achievement motivation. *Psychological Bulletin, 77,* 377–91.

Exner, J E, Jr (1974). *The Rorschach: A comprehensive system.* New York: Wiley.

Faust, D, & Ziskin, J (1988). The expert witness in psychology and psychiatry. *Science, 241,* 31–5.

Faust, D, Ziskin, J, & Hiers, J B (1991). *Brain damage claims: Coping with neuropsychological evidence.* Los Angeles: Law and Psychology Press.

Fiske, D W (1966). Some hypotheses concerning test adequacy. *Educational and Psychological Measurement, 2,* 69–88.

Fiske, D W (1971). *Measuring the concepts of personality.* Chicago, IL: Aldine.

Fowler, R D, & Matarazzo, J D (1988). Psychologists and psychiatrists as expert witnesses. *Science, 241,* 1143.

Francis, R D (1999). *Ethics for psychologists: A handbook.* Melbourne, Australia: ACER Press.

Freckelton, I (1993). *Current legal issues in forensic psychiatry.* Proceedings of Australian Institute of Criminology Conference.

Gardner, H (1983). *Frames of mind: The theory of multiple intelligences.* New York: Basic.

Gatewood, R D, & Field, H S (2001). *Human resource selection* (5th edn). Fort Worth, TX: Harcourt College Publishers.

Gazzaniga, M S, & Heatherton, T F (2003). *Psychological science: Mind, brain, and behavior.* New York: W W Norton.

Geffen, G M, Butterworth, P, & Geffen, L B (1994). Test-retest reliability of a new form of the Auditory Verbal Learning Test (AVLT). *Archives of Clinical Neuropsychology, 9,* 303–16.

Geffen, G M, Moar, K S, O'Hanlon, A P, Clarke, C R, & Geffen, L B (1990). Performance measures of 16 to 86 year old males and females on the Auditory Verbal Learning Test. *The Clinical Neuropsychologist, 4,* 45–63.

Geiger, M A, Boyle, E J, & Pinto, J K (1993). An examination of ipsative and normative versions of Kolb's Revised Learning Style Inventory. *Educational and Psychological Measurement, 53,* 717–26.

Gilliland, S W (1993). The perceived fairness of selection systems: An organizational justice perspective. *Academy of Management Review, 18,* 694–734.

Gilliland, S W (1994). Effects of procedural and distributive justice on reactions to a selection system. *Journal of Applied Psychology, 79,* 691–701.

Giordano, P J (1997). Establishing rapport and developing interview skills. In J R Matthews & C E Walker (Eds), *Basic skills and professional issues in clinical psychology* (pp 59–82). Boston: Allyn & Bacon.

Glennon, J R, Albright, L E, & Owens, W A (1965). *A catalogue of life history items.* NC: Richardson Foundation.

Golden, C J (1978). *Stroop Colour and Word Test.* Chicago: Stoelting Company.

Golden, C J, & Freshwater, S M (2002). *Stroop Colour and Word Test.* Chicago: Stoelting Company.

Golden, C J, Espe-Pfeifer, P, & Wachsler-Felder, J (2000). *Neuropsychological interpretation of objective psychological tests.* New York: Kluwer Academic.

Goldstein, G (1992). Historical perspectives. In A E Puente & R J McCaffrey (Eds), *Handbook of neuropsychological assessment: A biopsychosocial perspective* (pp 1–9). New York: Plenum.

Goldstein, G, & Hersen, M (2000). *Handbook of psychological assessment* (3rd edn). New York: Pergamon.

Goodglass, H, Kaplan, E, & Barresi, B (2000). *Boston Diagnostic Aphasia Examination* (3rd edn). Philadelphia: Lippincott Williams and Wilkins.

Gottfredson, L S (2002). Where and why g matters: Not a mystery. *Human Performance, 15,* 25–46.

Gottfredson, G D, Holland, J L, & Ogawa, D K (1982). *Dictionary of Holland Occupational Codes.* California: Consulting Psychologists Press.

Graham, J R (1993). *MMPI–2: Assessing personality and psychopathology.* New York: Oxford.

Greaud, V A, & Green, B F (1986). Equivalence of conventional and computer presentation of speed tests. *Applied Psychological Measurement, 10,* 23–34.

Greenberg, S, & Shuman, D (1997). Irreconcilable conflict between therapeutic and forensic roles. *Professional Psychology: Research and Practice, 28,* 50–7.

Gregg, N (1989). Review of the Learning Style Inventory. In J C Conoley & J J Kramer (Eds), *The tenth mental measurements yearbook* (pp 441–2). Lincoln, NE: The Buros Institute of Mental Measurements.

Gregory, R J (2000). *Psychological testing: History, principles, and applications.* Needham Heights, MA: Allyn & Bacon.

Groth-Marnat, G (2000). Visions of clinical assessment: Then, now, and a brief history of the future. *Journal of Clinical Psychology, 56,* 349–85.

Groth-Marnat, G (2003). *Handbook of psychological assessment* (4th edn). Hoboken, NJ: John Wiley & Sons.

Gudjonsson, G H, & Haward, L R C (1998). *Forensic psychology: A guide to practice.* London: Routledge.

Guttman, L (1944). A basis for scaling qualitative data. *American Sociological Review, 9,* 139–50.

Handy, C (1994). *The Age of Paradox*. Boston: Harvard Business School Press.

Hanes, K R, Andrewes, D G, Smith, D J, & Pantelis, C (1996). A brief assessment of executive central dysfunction: Discriminant validity and homogeneity of planning, set shift and fluency measures. *Archives of Clinical Neuropsychology, 18,* 185–91.

Hare, R D (1991). *Manual for the Hare Psychopathy Checklist – Revised*. Toronto, Ontario, Canada: Multi-Health Systems.

Hassed, C S (2000). Depression: Dispirited or spiritually deprived. *Medical Journal of Australia, 173,* 545–7.

Hathaway, S R, & McKinley, J C (1951). *The Minnesota Multiphasic Personality Inventory Manual (Revised)*. New York: Psychological Corporation.

Hebben, N, & Milberg, W (2002). *Essentials of neuropsychological assessment*. New York: Wiley.

Heilbrun, K (1992). The role of psychological testing in forensic assessment. *Law and Human Behavior, 16,* 257–72.

Heilbrun, K (2001). *Principles of forensic mental health assessment*. New York: Kluwer Academic.

Heilbrun, K, Bank, S, Follingstad, D, & Frederick, R (2000). *Petition for forensic psychology as an APA specialization*. Presented to the Committee for the Recognition of Specialties and Proficiencies in Professional Psychology. Washington, DC: American Psychological Association.

Heilbrun, K, Roger, R, & Otto, R K (2002). Forensic assessment: Current status and future directions. In J R P Ogloff (Ed), *Psychology and law: Reviewing the discipline* (pp 119–46). New York: Kluwer Academic.

Heilman, K M, & Valenstein, E (2003). *Clinical neuropsychology* (4th edn). New York: Oxford University Press.

Herriot, P (1988). Selection at the cross-roads. *The Psychologist: Bulletin of the British Psychological Society, 10,* 388–92.

Herriot, P (1989). Selection as a social process. In M Smith & I T Robertson (Eds), *Advances in selection and assessment*. New York: Wiley.

Herriot, P (2001). *The employment relationship: A psychological perspective*. Philadelphia: Taylor & Francis.

Herriot, P (2002). Selection and self: Selection as a social process. *European Journal of Work and Organizational Psychology, 11,* 385–402.

Hesketh, B, & Neal, A (1999). Technology and performance. In D R Ilgen & E D Pulakos (Eds), *The changing nature of performance: Implications for staffing, motivation and development.* (pp 21–55). San Francisco: Jossey-Bass.

Hess, A K (2001). Review of the Wechsler Adult Intelligence Scale – Third Edition. In J Impara & B Plake (Eds), *The fourteenth mental measurements yearbook*. Lincoln, NE: Buros Institute of Mental Measurements.

Holdnack, J A, Lissner, D, Bowden, S C, & McCarthy, K A L (2004). Utilising the WAIS-III/WMS-III in clinical practice: Update of research and issues relevant to Australian normative research. *Australian Psychologist, 39,* 220–7.

Holland, J L (1958). A personality inventory employing occupational titles. *Journal of Applied Psychology, 42,* 336–42.

Holland, J L (1992). *Making vocational choices: A theory of vocational personalities and work environments* (2nd edn). Odessa, FL: Psychological Assessment Resources.

Holland, J L, & Rayman, J R (1986). The Self-Directed Search. In W B Walsh & S H Osipow (Eds), *Advances in vocational psychology: The assessment of interests*. Hillsdale, NJ: Erlbaum.

Hooper, H E (1948). A study in the construction and preliminary standardization of a visual organization test for use in the measurement of organic deterioration. Unpublished master's thesis, University of Southern California.

Hooper, H E (1958). *The Hooper Visual Organization Test manual*. Los Angeles: Western Psychological Services.

Hooper, H E (1983). *Hooper Visual Organization Test Manual*. Los Angeles: Western Psychological Services.

Horn, J L, & Hofer, S M (1992). Major abilities and development in the adult period. In R Sternberg & C Berg (Eds), *Intellectual development*. New York: Cambridge.

Horn, J L, & Noll, J (1994). System for understanding cognitive abilities: A theory and the evidence on which it is based In D Detterman (Ed), *Current topics in human intelligence* (Vol 4). New York: Springer-Verlag.

Howe, M A (1975). General Aptitude Test Battery – An Australian empirical study. *Australian Psychologist, 10*, 32–44.

Howell, D C (2002). *Statistical methods for psychology* (5th edn). Pacific Grove, CA: Duxbury.

Hulin, C L, Drasgow, F, & Parsons, C K (1983). *Item response theory*. Homewood, IL: Dow Jones-Irwin.

Hunsley, J, & Meyer, G J (2003). The incremental validity of psychological testing and assessment: Conceptual, methodological, and statistical issues. *Psychological Assessment, 15,* 446–55.

Irvine, S H, & Kyllonen, P C (2002). *Item generation for test development*. Mahwah, NJ: Lawrence Erlbaum.

Jackson, D N (1970). A sequential system of personality scale development. In C Speilberger (Ed), *Current topics in clinical and community psychology* (Vol 2). New York: Academic Press.

Jackson, D N (1971). The dynamics of structured personality tests: 1971. *Psychological Review, 78,* 229–48.

James, W (1899). *Talks to teachers on psychology: And to students on some of life's ideals*. London: Longmans.

Jensen, A R (1980). *Bias in mental testing*. New York: Free Press.

Jensen, P S, & Hoagwood, K (1997). The book of names: DSM-IV in context. *Development and Psychopathology, 9,* 231–49.

Kamphaus, R W, Petoskey, M D, & Rowe, E W (2000). Current trends in psychological testing of children. *Professional Psychology: Research and Practice, 31,* 155–64.

Kanaya, T, Scullin, M H, & Ceci, S J (2003). The Flynn effect and US policies: The impact of rising IQ scores on American society via mental retardation diagnosis. *American Psychologist, 58,* 778–90.

Kaufman, A S, & Lichtenberger, E O (1999). *Essentials of WAIS-III assessment*. New York: Wiley.

Keats, D M, & Keats, J A (1988). Human assessment in Australia. In S H Irvine & J W Berry (Eds), *Human abilities in cultural context*. Cambridge, UK: Cambridge University Press.

Kendall, I, Jenkinson, J, de Lemos, M, & Clancy, D (1997). *Supplement to guidelines for the use of psychological tests*. Melbourne, Australia: Australian Psychological Society.

Kertesz, A (1982). *Western Aphasia Battery*. San Antonio, TX: Psychological Corporation.

Kline, P (1993). *The handbook of psychological testing*. London: Routledge.

Kline, P (1998). *The new psychometrics: Science, psychology, and measurement*. London: Routledge.

Knight, R G, & Godfrey, H P D (1984). Tests recommended by New Zealand hospital psychologists. *New Zealand Journal of Psychology, 13,* 32–6.

Kohlberg, L (1981). *The philosophy of moral development*. New York: Harper & Row.

Kolb, B, & Whishaw, I Q (2001). *An introduction to brain and behavior*. New York: Worth.

Kolb, B, & Whishaw, I Q (2003). *Fundamentals of human neuropsychology* (5th edn). New York: Worth.

Krantz, D H, Luce, R D, Suppes, P, & Tversky, A (1972). *Foundations of Measurement* (Vol 1). New York: Academic Press.

Kubiszyn, T, & Borich, G (2003). *Educational testing and measurement: Classroom application and practice* (7th edn). New York: Wiley.

Kuder, G F, & Richardson, M W (1937). The theory of estimation of test reliability. *Psychometrika, 2,* 151–60.

Kyllonen, P C (1997). Smart Testing. In R F Dillon (Ed), *Handbook on Testing* (pp 341–68). Westport: Greenwood Press.

Landy, F J, & Farr, J L (1980). Performance appraisal. *Psychological Bulletin, 87,* 72–107.

Latham, G, & Wexley, K (1977). Behavioral observation scales. *Journal of Applied Psychology, 30,* 255–68.

Lee, J A, Moreno, K E, & Sympson, J B (1986). The effects of mode of test administration on test performance. *Educational and Psychological Measurement, 46,* 467–74.

Leivens, F, & Harris, M M (2003). Research on internet recruiting and testing: Current status and future directions. In C L Cooper & I T Robinson (Eds), *International review of industrial and organizational psychology* (Vol 18). West Sussex, England: Wiley.

Levin, H S, Mattis, S, Ruff, R M, Eisenberg, H M, Marshall, L F, Tabaddor, K et al (1987). Neurobehavioral outcome following minor head injury: A three center study. *Journal of Neurosurgery, 66,* 234–43.

Lezak, M D (1983). *Neuropsychological assessment*. New York: Oxford University Press.

Lezak, M D (1995). *Neuropsychological assessment* (3rd edn). New York: Oxford University Press.

Lezak, M D, Howieson, D B, & Loring, D W (2004). *Neuropsychological assessment* (4th edn). New York: Oxford University Press.

Likert, R (1932). A technique for the measurement of attitudes. *Archives of Psychology, 140,* 44–53.

Lipsitt, P D, Lelos, D, & McGarry, L (1971). Competency for trial: A screening instrument. *American Journal of Psychiatry, 128,* 104–9.

Loo, R (1999). Confirmatory factor analyses of Kolb's Learning Style Inventory (LSI-1985). *British Journal of Educational Psychology, 69,* 213–19.

Lovibond, S H, & Lovibond, P F (1995a). *Manual for the Depression Anxiety Stress Scales*. Sydney, Australia: Psychology Foundation.

Lovibond, S H, & Lovibond, P F (1995b). The structure of negative emotional states: Comparison of the Depression Anxiety Stress Scales (DASS) with the Beck Depression and Anxiety Inventories. *Behavior Research and Therapy, 33,* 335–43.

Maddox, T (Ed) (1997). *Tests: A comprehensive reference for assessment in psychology, education, and business*. Austin, TX: ProEd.

Maloney, M P, & Ward, M P (1976). *Psychological assessment: A conceptual approach*. New York: Oxford University Press.

Mapou, R L (1995). A cognitive framework for neuropsychological assessment. In R L Mapou & J Spector (Eds), *Clinical neuropsychological assessment: A cognitive approach* (pp 295–337). New York: Plenum.

Martin, M, Allan, A, & Allan, M M (2001). The use of psychological tests by Australian psychologists who do assessments for the courts. *Australian Journal of Psychology, 53,* 77–82.

Matarazzo, J D (1986). Computerized clinical psychological test interpretations: Unvalidated plus all mean and no sigma. *American Psychologist, 41,* 14–24.

Matarazzo, J D (1990). Psychological assessment versus psychological testing: Validation from Binet to the school, clinic and courtroom. *American Psychologist, 45,* 999–1017.

Mathers, C D, Vos, E T, Stevenson, C E, & Begg, S J (2000). The Australian burden of disease study: Measuring the loss of health from diseases, injuries, and risk factors. *Medical Journal of Australia, 172,* 592–6.

Matthews, G, Zeidner, M, & Roberts, R (2002). *Emotional Intelligence: Science and Myth.* Cambridge, MA: MIT Press.

McCarthy, R A, & Warrington, E K (1990). *Cognitive neuropsychology: A clinical introduction.* San Diego, CA: Academic Press.

McKenzie, A (1980). Are ability tests up to standard? *Australian Psychologist, 15,* 335–50.

Mead, A D, & Drasgow, F (1993). Equivalence of computerised and paper-and-pencil cognitive ability tests: A meta-analysis. *Psychological Bulletin, 114,* 449–58.

Meier, M J (1997). The establishment of clinical neuropsychology as a psychological specialty. In M E Maruish & J A Moses, Jr (Eds), *Clinical neuropsychology: Theoretical foundations for practitioners* (pp 1–31). Mahwah, NJ: Lawrence Erlbaum.

Melton, G B, Petrila, J, Poythress, N, & Slobogin, C (1997). *Psychological evaluations for the courts: A handbook for mental health professionals and lawyers* (2nd edn). New York: Guildford.

Michell, J (1990). *An introduction to the logic of psychological measurement.* Mahwah, NJ: Lawrence Erlbaum.

Milner, A D (1998). *Comparative neuropsychology.* New York: Oxford University Press.

Mirsky, A F, Anthony, B J, Duncan, C C, Ahearn, M B, & Kellam, S G (1991). Analysis of the elements of attention: A neuropsychological approach. *Neuropsychology Review, 2,* 109–45.

Mirsky, A F, Fantie, B D, & Tatman, J E (1995). Assessment of attention across the lifespan. In R L Mapou & J Spector (Eds), *Clinical neuropsychological assessment: A cognitive approach. Critical issues in neuropsychology* (pp 17–48). New York: Plenum Press.

Mischel, M (1968). *Personality and assessment.* New York: Wiley.

Mitrushina, M N, Boone, K B, & D'Elia, L F (1999). *Handbook of normative data for neuropsychological assessment.* New York: Oxford University Press.

Money, J (1976). *A Standardized Road-Map Test of Direction Sense: Manual.* San Rafael, CA: Academic Therapy Publications.

Morey, L C (1991). *Personality Assessment Inventory: Professional manual.* Odessa, FL: Psychological Assessment Resources.

Munsterberg, H (1913). *Psychology and industrial efficiency.* New York: Houghton Mifflin.

Murphy, K R & Cleveland, J N (1995). *Understanding performance appraisal: Social, organisational, and goal based perspectives.* Thousand Oaks, CA: Sage Publications.

Murphy, L L, Plake, B S, Impara, J C, & Spies, R A (Eds). (2002). *Tests in Print VI: An index to tests, test reviews, & the literature on specific tests.* Lincoln, NE: Buros Institute of Mental Measurements.

Naglieri, J A, Drasgow, F, Schmitt, M, Handler, L, Prifitera, A, Margolis, A, & Valasquez, R (2004). Psychological testing on the internet: New problems, old issues. *American Psychologist, 59,* 150–62.

Nathan, P E, & Langenbucher, J (2003). Diagnosis and classification. In G Stricker & T A Widiger (Eds), *Handbook of Psychology: Vol 8: Clinical psychology.* New York: Wiley.

Nauta, W J H, & Feirtag, M (1986). *Fundamental neuroanatomy.* New York: W H Freeman.

Neal, A, & Griffin, M A (1999). Developing a model of individual performance for human resource management. *Asia Pacific Journal of Human Resources, 37,* 44–59.

Nelson, H E, & Willison, J (1991). *The National Adult Reading Test (NART): Test manual* (2nd edn). Windsor, UK: NFER, Nelson.

Nitko, A J (2004). *Educational assessment of students* (4th edn). Upper Saddle River, NJ: Merrill.

Nunnally, J C (1967). *Psychometric theory.* New York: McGraw Hill.

Nunnally, J, & Bernstein, I H (1994). *Psychometric theory* (3rd edn). New York: McGraw Hill.

Ogloff, J R, & Douglas, K S (2003). Psychological assessment in forensic settings. In J R Graham & J A Naglieri (Eds), *Handbook of psychology* (pp 345–63). New York: John Wiley & Sons.

Oliveira-Souza, R, Moll, J, & Eslinger, P J (2004). Neuropsychological assessment. In M Rizzo & P J Eslinger (Eds), *Principles and practice of behavioural neurology and neuropsychology* (pp 47–64). Philadelphia: W B Saunders.

O'Neil, W M (1987). *A century of psychology in Australia.* Sydney, Australia: Sydney University Press.

Ones, D S, Viswesvaran, C, & Schmidt, E L (1993). Comprehensive meta-analysis of integrity test validities: Findings and implications for personnel selection and theories of job performance. *Journal of Applied Psychology Monograph, 78,* 679–703.

Ord, I G (1977). Australian psychology and Australia's neighbours. In M Nixon & R Taft (Eds), *Psychology in Australia: Achievements and prospects.* Sydney, Australia: Pergamon.

Osipow, S H, & Fitzgerald, L F (1996). *Theories of career development* (4th edn). Boston: Allyn & Bacon.

Otto, R K, & Heilbrun, K (2002). The practice of forensic psychology. *American Psychologist, 57,* 5–18.

Overton, T (2000). *Assessment in special education: An applied approach* (3rd edn). Upper Saddle River, NJ: Merrill.

Ownby, R L (1997). *Psychological reports: A guide to report writing in professional psychology* (3rd edn). New York: Wiley.

Ozer, D J (1985). Correlation and the coefficient of determination. *Psychological Bulletin, 97,* 307–15.

Pardo, J V, Pardo, P J, Janer, K W, & Raichle, M E (1990). The anterior cingulated cortex mediates processing selection in the Stroop attentional conflict paradigm. *Proceedings of the National Academy of Sciences, 87,* 256–9.

Parks, S, Barlett, A, Wickham, A, & Myors, B (2001). Developing a computerized test of perceptual/clerical speed. *Computers in Human Behaviour, 17,* 111–24.

Pedhazur, E J, & Schmelkin, L (1991). *Measurement, design, and analysis: An integrated approach.* Hillsdale, NJ: Lawrence Erlbaum.

Penrose, L S, & Raven, J C (1936). A new series of perceptual tests: Preliminary communication. *British Journal of Medical Psychology, 16,* 97–104.

Plake, B S, & Witt, J C (Eds) (1986). *The future of testing.* Hillsdale, NJ: Erlbaum.

Posner, M I, & Petersen, S E (1990). The attention system of the human brain. *Annual Review of Neuroscience, 13,* 25–42.

Powell, M, & Lancaster, S (2003). Guidelines for interviewing children during child custody evaluations. *Australian Psychologist, 38,* 46–54.

Poythress, N, Monahan, J, Bonnie, R, & Hoge, S K (1999). *MacArthur Competence Assessment Tool – Criminal Adjudication.* Odessa, FL: Psychological Assessment Resources.

Prediger, D J (1976). A world-of-work map for career exploration. *Vocational Guidance Quarterly, 24,* 198–208.

Prediger, D J, & Vansickle, T R (1992). Locating occupations on Holland's hexagon: Beyond RIASEC. *Journal of Vocational Behavior, 40,* 111–28.

Prifitera, A, & Saklofske, D H (1998). *WISC–III clinical use and interpretation: Scientist-practitioner perspectives.* San Diego, CA: Academic Press.

Psychological Corporation, The (2001). *Wechsler Individual Achievement Test – Second Edition – Abbreviated.* San Antonio, TX: Author.

Psychological Corporation, The (2002). *Wechsler Individual Achievement Test – Second Edition (WIAT–II).* San Antonio, TX: Author.

Purdue Research Foundation (1948). *Purdue Pegboard Test.* Lafayette, IN: Lafayette Instrument Company.

Ramsden, P (2003). Review of the Delis–Kaplan Executive Function System. In J Impara & B Plake (Eds), *The fifteenth mental measurements yearbook* (pp 284–6). Lincoln, NE: Buros Institute of Mental Measurement.

Randolph, J J, Hicks, T, Mason, D, & Cuneo, D J (1982). The competency screening test: A validation study in Cook County, Illinois. *Criminal Justice and Behavior, 9,* 495–500.

Raven, J C (1938). *Progressive matrices: A perceptual test of intelligence.* London: H K Lewis.

Reitan, R M, & Wolfson, D (1993). *The Halstead-Reitan Neuropsychological Test Battery: Theory and clinical interpretation* (2nd edn). Tucson, AZ: Neuropsychology Press.

Rey, A (1964). *L'examen clinique en psychologie.* Paris: Presses Universitaires de France.

Reynolds, C R, & Kamphaus, R W (Eds)(2003). *Handbook of psychological and educational assessment of children: Intelligence, aptitude, and achievement.* New York: Guildford.

Richardson, J T E (2003). Howard Andrew Knox and the origins of performance testing on Ellis Island, 1911–1916. *History of Psychology, 6,* 143–70.

Rogers, R (Ed) (1997). *Clinical assessment of malingering and deception* (2nd edn). New York: Guildford.

Rogers, R, Bagby, R M, & Dickens, S E (1992). *Structured Interview of Reported Symptoms (SIRS) and professional manual.* Odessa, FL: Psychological Assessment Resources.

Rogers, R, Sewell, K W, Grandjean, N R, & Vitacco, M J (2002). The detection of feigned mental disorders on specified competency measures. *Psychological Assessment, 14,* 177–83.

Roid, G (2003). *Stanford-Binet Intelligence Scale – Fifth Edition.* Itasca, IL: Riverside Publishing.

Rorschach, H (1921). *Psychodiagnostik.* Berne, Switzerland: Birchen.

Rosen, L D, & Maguire, P (1990). Myths and realities of computer phobia: A meta-analysis. *Anxiety Research, 3,* 175–91.

Rounds, J B, Davidson, M L, & Dawis, R V (1979). The fit between Strong-Campbell Interest Inventory General Occupational Themes and Holland's hexagonal model. *Journal of Vocational Behavior, 15,* 303–15.

Russell, M, & Karol, D (1994). *16PF fifth edition: Administrator's manual.* Champaign, IL: IPAT.

Rust, J, & Golombok, S (1999). *Modern psychometrics: The science of psychological assessment* (2nd edn). London: Routledge.

Ryan, J J, Dai, X Y, & Zheng, L (1994). Psychological test usage in the People's Republic of China. *Journal of Psychoeducational Assessment, 12,* 324–30.

Schmidt, F L, & Hunter, J E (1998). The validity and utility of selection methods in personnel psychology: Practical and theoretical implications of 85 years of research findings. *Psychological Bulletin, 124,* 262–74.

Schmidt, F L, Hunter, J E, McKenzie, R C, & Muldrow, T W (1979). Impact of valid selection procedures on work-force productivity. *Journal of Applied Psychology, 64,* 609–26.

Scott, W D (1908). *The psychology of advertising.* New York: Arno.

Scriven, M (1967). The methodology of evaluation. In R W Tyler & R M Gagne (Eds), *Perspectives of curriculum evaluation.* Chicago: Rand-McNally.

Segall, D O (1996). Multidimensional adaptive testing. *Psychometrika, 61,* 331–54.

Sharpley, C F, & Pain, M D (1988). Psychological test usage in Australia. *Australian Psychologist, 23,* 361–9.

Shears, M, & Harvey-Beavis, A (2001). *Self Directed Search, Australian Manual, Second Australian Edition*. Melbourne, Australia: ACER.

Shellenberger, S (1982). Presentation and interpretation of psychological data in educational settings. In C R Reynolds & T B Gutkin (Eds), *The handbook of school psychology* (pp 51–81). New York: Wiley.

Shum, D (2003). Review of the Learning Style Inventory (Version 3). In J Impara & B Plake (Eds), *The fifteenth mental measurements yearbook* (pp 514–15). Lincoln, NE: Buros Institute of Mental Measurements.

Shum, D, & O'Gorman, J (2001). A test of remote memory for use in Australia. *Australian Journal of Psychology, 53,* 36–45.

Shum, D, McFarland, K, & Bain, J (1990). The construct validity of eight tests of attention. *The Clinical Neuropsychologist, 4,* 151–62.

Shum, D, O'Gorman, J, & Alpar, A (2004). Effects of incentive and preparation time on performance and classification accuracy of standard and malingering-specific memory tests. *Archives of Clinical Neuropsychology, 19,* 817–23.

Shum, D, Sweeper, S, & Murray, R (1996). Performance on verbal implicit and explicit memory tasks following traumatic brain injury. *Journal of Head Trauma Rehabilitation, 11,* 43–53.

Simons, R, Goddard, R, & Patton, W (2002). Hand-scoring error rates in psychological testing. *Assessment, 9,* 292–300.

Slattery, J P (1989a). *Report of the Royal Commission into Deep Sleep Therapy.* (Vol 1). *Introduction.* Sydney, Australia: NSW Government Printing Office.

Slattery, J P (1989b). *Report of the Royal Commission into Deep Sleep Therapy.* (Vol 4). *The Deaths.* Sydney, Australia: NSW Government Printing Office.

Slattery, J P (1989c). *Report of the Royal Commission into Deep Sleep Therapy.* (Vol 8). *The Departments.* Sydney, Australia: NSW Government Printing Office.

Slattery, J P (1989d). *Report of the Royal Commission into Deep Sleep Therapy.* (Vol 9). *Psychometric Testing Appendices.* Sydney, Australia: NSW Government Printing Office.

Smith, A (1982). *Symbol Digit Modality Test (SDMT): Manual (Revised).* Los Angeles: Western Psychological Services.

Snyder, P J, & Nussbaum, P D (Eds) (1998). *Clinical neuropsychology: A pocket handbook for assessment.* Washington, DC: American Psychological Association.

Spreen, O, & Strauss, E (1998). *A compendium of neuropsychological tests: Administration, norms, and commentary* (2nd edn). New York: Oxford University Press.

Squire, L. R (1987). *Memory and brain.* New York: Oxford University Press.

Squire, L R (1992). Declarative and non-declarative memory: Multiple brain systems supporting learning and memory. *Journal of Cognitive Neuroscience, 4,* 232–43.

Sternberg, R J (1985). *Beyond IQ: A triarchic theory of human intelligence.* New York: Macmillan.

Sternberg, R J (1997). *Successful intelligence.* New York: Plume.

Sternberg, R J, & Horvath, J A (Eds) (1999). *Tacit knowledge in professional practice.* Mahwah, NJ: Erlbaum.

Sternberg, R J, Wagner, R K, Williams, W M, & Horvath, J A (1995). Testing common sense. *American Psychologist, 50,* 912–27.

Stevens, S S (1951). Mathematics, measurement, and psychophysics. In S S Stevens (Ed), *Handbook of experimental psychology* (pp 1–49). New York: Wiley.

Strong, E K, Jr (1927). *Vocational Interest Blank.* Stanford, CA: Stanford University Press.

Stroop, J R (1935). Studies of interference in serial verbal reactions. *Journal of Experimental Psychology, 18,* 643–62.

Sundberg, N D (1977). *Assessment of persons.* Englewood Cliffs, NJ: Prentice Hall.

Tallent, N (1993). *Psychological report writing* (4th edn). Englewood Cliffs, NJ: Prentice Hall.

Taylor, H C, & Russell, J T (1939). The relationship of validity coefficients to the practical effectiveness of tests in selection. *Journal of Applied Psychology, 23,* 565–78.

Taylor, P, Keelty, Y, & McDonnell, B (2002). Evolving personnel selection practices in New Zealand organizations and recruitment firms. *New Zealand Journal of Psychology, 31,* 8–18.

Thorndike, R L (1982). *Applied psychometrics.* Boston: Houghton Mifflin.

Thurstone, L L (1929). Theory of attitude measurement. *Psychological Review, 36,* 221–41.

Tinsley, H E A (1992). Introduction: Special issue on Holland's theory. *Journal of Vocational Behavior, 40,* 109–10.

Tombaugh, T N (1996). *Test of Memory Malingering.* Los Angeles: Multi-Health Systems.

Tracey, T J, & Rounds, J (1995). The arbitrary nature of Holland's RIASEC types: A concentric circles structure. *Journal of Counselling Psychology, 42,* 431–40.

Tulving, E (1972). Episodic and semantic memory. In E Tulving & W Donaldson (Eds), *Organization of memory* (pp 382–403). New York: Pergamon Press.

Uttl, B, & Graf, P (1997). Color Word Stroop test performance across the adult life span. *Journal of Clinical and Experimental Neuropsychology, 19,* 405–20.

van Dorsten, B (2002). *Forensic psychology: From classroom to courtroom.* New York: Kluwer Academic.

Vandecreek, L, & Knapp, S (1997). Record keeping. In J R Matthews & C E Walker (Eds), *Basic skills and professional issues in clinical psychology* (pp 155–72). Boston: Allyn & Bacon.

Veres, J G, Sims, R R, & Locklear, T S (1991). Improving the reliability of Kolb's Learning Style Inventory. *Educational and Psychological Measurement, 51,* 143–50.

Vernon, P E (1979). *Intelligence: Heredity and environment.* San Francisco: W H Freeman.

Vitelli, R (2001). Review of the Test of Memory Malingering. In B S Plake & J C Impara (Eds), *The fourteenth mental measurements yearbook* (pp 1258–9). Lincoln, NE: The Buros Institute of Mental Measurements.

Wagner, R K, & Sternberg, R J (1991). *Tacit knowledge for managers.* San Antonio: The Psychological Corporation.

Ward, T J, Hooper, S R, & Hannafin, K M (1989). The effect of computerized tests on the performance and attitudes of college students. *Journal of Educational and Computing Research, 5,* 327–33.

Wasserman, J D, & Bracken, B A (2003). Psychometric characteristics of assessment procedures. In J R Graham & J A Naglieri (Eds), *Handbook of Psychology: Vol 10. Assessment Psychology* (pp 43–66). Hoboken, NJ: John Wiley & Sons.

Watkins, C E, Jr, Campbell, V L, Nieberding, R, & Hallmark, R (1995). Comtemporary practice of psychological assessment by clinical psychologists. *Professional Psychology: Research and Practice, 26,* 54–60.

Wechsler, D (1939). *The measurement of adult intelligence.* Baltimore: Williams & Wilkins.

Wechsler, D (1949). *Wechsler Intelligence Scale for Children.* New York: The Psychological Corporation.

Wechsler, D (1955). *Manual for the Wechsler Adult Intelligence Scale.* New York: The Psychological Corporation.

Wechsler, D (1974). *Manual for the Wechsler Intelligence Scale for Children – Revised (WISC–R).* San Antonio, TX: The Psychological Corporation.

Wechsler, D (1981). *Manual for the Wechsler Adult Intelligence Scale – Revised.* San Antonio, TX: The Psychological Corporation.

Wechsler, D (1987). *Manual for the Wechsler Memory Scale – Revised.* San Antonio, TX: The Psychological Corporation.

Wechsler, D (1991). *Wechsler Intelligence Scale for Children – Third Edition (WISC–III)*. San Antonio, TX: The Psychological Corporation.

Wechsler, D (1997a). *Manual for the Wechsler Adult Intelligence Scale – Third Edition (WAIS–III)*. San Antonio, TX: The Psychological Corporation.

Wechsler, D (1997b). *Manual for the Wechsler Memory Scale – Third Edition (WMS–III)*. San Antonio, TX: The Psychological Corporation.

Wechsler, D (2003). *Manual for the Wechsler Intelligence Scale for Children – Fourth Edition (WISC–IV)*. San Antonio, TX: The Psychological Corporation.

Weiner, I B (2003). Assessment psychology. In D K Freedheim (Ed), *Handbook of psychology: Vol 1. History of psychology* (pp 279–302). Hoboken, NJ: John Wiley & Sons.

Weinstein, C E, & Way, P J (2003). Educational psychology. In D K Freedheim (Ed), *Handbook of Psychology* (Vol 1). New York: Wiley.

Weiss, D J (Ed) (1983) *New horizons in testing: Latent trait theory and computerised adaptive testing*. New York: Academic Press.

Wiggins, J S (1973). *Personality and prediction: Principles of personality assessment*. Reading, MA: Addison Wesley.

Winter, D G, & Stewart, A J (1977). Power motive reliability as a function of retest instructions. *Journal of Consulting and Clinical Psychology, 45,* 436–40.

Wise, P S (1989). *The use of assessment techniques by applied psychologists*. Belmont, CA: Wadsworth.

Wise, S L, & Plake, B S (1989). Research on the effects of administering tests via computers. *Educational Measurement: Issues and Practices, Fall,* 5–10.

Wise, S L, & Wise, L A (1987). Comparison of computer administered and paper administered achievement tests with elementary school children. *Computers in Human Behavior, 3,* 15–20.

Wonderlic Personnel Test Inc (1992). *Wonderlic Personnel Test*. Libertyville, IL: Author.

Wood, J, Garb, H N, Lilienfeld, M, & Nezworski, T (2002). Clinical assessment. *Annual Review of Psychology, 53,* 519–43.

World Health Organization (1992–94). *International statistical classification of diseases and related health problems*. Geneva, Switzerland: Author.

Zimbardo, P G (2004). Does psychology make a significant difference in our lives? *American Psychologist, 59,* 339–51.

Ziskin, J, & Faust, D (1988). *Coping with psychiatric and psychological testimony*. Marina del Rey, CA: Law and Psychology Press.

Answers to Exercises

CHAPTER 3

1. Mean of scores = 60, SD of scores = 5.2

Scores	z scores	Transformed scores with a mean of 100 and SD of 15
52	−1.54	77
54	−1.15	83
56	−0.77	89
58	−0.38	94
60	0.00	100
61	0.19	103
61	0.19	103
63	0.58	109
67	1.34	120
68	1.54	123

2 **a.** percentage correct scores

	David	John	Brett
Geography	61.3%	96.0%	80.0%
Spelling	73.3%	66.7%	64.5%
Mathematics	75.0%	82.5%	92.5%

b. z scores

	David	John	Brett
Geography	−1.40	1.20	0.00
Spelling	0.50	0.00	−0.15
Mathematics	1.00	1.60	2.40

c. percentiles

	David	John	Brett
Geography	8th	88th	50th
Spelling	69th	50th	44th
Mathematics	84th	95th	99th

d. T scores and average T scores

	David	John	Brett
Geography	36	62	50
Spelling	55	50	48.5
Mathematics	60	66	74
Average T score	50.3	59.3	57.5

3 **a.**

scores	*z scores*
16	−2
18	−1
19	−0.5
20	0
21	0.5
22	1
24	2

b. Percentage of scores that fall between:
18 and 22 = 68.26%
19 and 21 = 38.30%
16 and 24 = 95.44%

4.
The percentile of a score with a z score of 1.0 is 84
The z score of a score at the 98th percentile is 2.05
The T score for a score with a z score of 2.0 is 70

5.   For a test with a mean of 30 and an SD of 10

Raw score	*z score*	*Percentile*
40	1	84
35	**0.5**	69
36.7	0.67	**75**

CHAPTER 4

1. Mean for test = 2.0, SD = 1.91
Variance for test = 1.91^2 = 3.65

Mean for item	SD for item	Variance for item
0.13	0.33	0.11
0.11	0.32	0.10
0.11	0.37	0.14
0.06	0.24	0.06
0.21	0.41	0.17
0.08	0.28	0.08
0.08	0.27	0.07
0.19	0.39	0.15
0.11	0.31	0.10
0.23	0.42	0.18
0.01	0.12	0.01
0.10	0.30	0.09
0.15	0.36	0.13
0.01	0.13	0.02
0.11	0.31	0.10
0.01	0.09	0.01

$$\alpha = \left(\frac{k}{k-1} \right)\left(1 - \frac{\Sigma \sigma i^2}{\sigma t^2} \right) = \left(\frac{16}{16-1} \right)\left(1 - \frac{1.50}{3.65} \right) = 1.07 \times 0.59 = 0.63$$

2 **a.** Answer provided by student

b.

Test	Reliability Coefficient	SD	SEM
A	0.85	15	5.81
B	0.85	5	1.94
C	0.55	15	10.06
D	0.55	5	3.35

Tests A and B and Tests C and D have the same reliabilities and hence the scores within each pair of tests are of the same accuracy. The SEM is expressed in the raw score metric of the test and it so happens that scores for Tests A and C have a wider range than those for Tests B and D. This does not mean they are less accurate. Put another way, you wouldn't say that scores on the subtests of the WAIS are more accurate than Full Scale IQ, even though the SEMs are smaller for the subtests.

c. The SE_{diff} should be larger than the SEM of the two subtests.

3. Reliability of ASAT = 0.90, SD of ASAT = 15

a. The reliability of the ASAT can be considered high

b. Despite its high reliability, it should be noted that a score obtained by an individual may not be 100 per cent accurate. SEM of ASAT = $SD \sqrt{1 - r} = 15 \sqrt{1 - .90} = 4.74$. That is, the true score could be higher than 115. We would, however, argue that the cut-off of 115 should stand and the student not be admitted as to do otherwise is to shift the cut-off to 112 and then raise the same set of issues for someone with a score of 111. Scores have errors but we have to make decisions oftentimes on what we have got.

CHAPTER 5

1 **a.** If a cut-off score of 31 is used, the new test will have perfect discrimination, that is all 10 members of the prison population are correctly classified. It is not necessary to calculate the validity coefficient. If it is calculated, with a split like that, you obtain a phi coefficient of 1.0. That is, the correlation between test score and classification is 1.0, the test has perfect predictive validity.

b. The valid positive rate = 30% (percentage of psychopaths correctly classified)

c. Although the test seems to have perfect discrimination using a cut-off score of 31, more information (viz, base rate and selection ratio) is needed to properly evaluate the utility of the test in a prison sample. The problem becomes greater if we try to use it in a non-prison or community sample where the base rate is likely to be considerably lower than 30%. Although it looks like a great test, it may lead to a number of misclassifications.

2.

False Negative = 0.10	**Valid Positive = 0.20**	**Base Rate = 0.30**
Valid Negative = 0.60	False Positive = 0.10	1 – Base Rate = 0.70
1 – Selection Ratio = 0.70	**Selection Ratio = 0.30**	

3.

		Test		Rating	
		EQ	IQ	EQ	IQ
Test	EQ	0.75			
	IQ	**0.6**	0.92		
Rating	EQ	**0.8**	**0.5**	0.45	
	IQ	**0.5**	**0.8**	**0.4**	0.45

There is no one correct answer to this question. Students are expected to show their understanding of the principles of the multitrait-multimethod matrix (eg, criteria for convergent and discriminant validity) by making up values for the rest of the table. The values (in bold) included above are examples that point to the validity of the new test.

CHAPTER 6

1   **a.** In analysing the items, students can consider (a) the variances of the items (by squaring the standard deviations provided in Chapter 4), and (b) item-total correlations. 'Good' items are those that have large variances and large item-total correlations.

b. Spearman-Brown formula:

$$k = \frac{r_{yy}(1 - r_{xx})}{r_{xx}(1 - r_{yy})} = \frac{0.90(1 - 0.63)}{0.63(1 - 0.90)} = 5.29$$

No. of items required for a desired reliability of .90 = 5.29 × 16 = 84.6.
No. of extra items needed = 85–16 = 69

2.   Students can check their own answers in the text

3   **a.** No, 50/50 chance of correct

b. No, question may confuse individuals with language problem

c. No, double/triple negative

d. No, too easy

Index